YOU BREW GOOD ALE

YOU BREW GOOD ALE

A History of Small-scale Brewing

IAN P. PEATY

SUTTON PUBLISHING

First published in 1997 by
Sutton Publishing Limited · Phoenix Mill
Thrupp · Stroud · Gloucestershire · GL5 2BU

British Library Cataloguing in Publication Data
A catalogue record for this book is available from the British Library

ISBN 0 7509 1592 7

ALAN SUTTON™ and SUTTON™ are the trade marks of Sutton Publishing Limited

Typeset in 11/13pt Perpetua.
Typesetting and origination by
Sutton Publishing Limited.
Printed in Great Britain by
Ebenezer Baylis, Worcester.

CONTENTS

ACKNOWLEDGEMENTS   vii

INTRODUCTION   ix

A QUART IN A PINT-POT   1

THE ABBOT'S ALE   14

SEATS OF LEARNING   44

'A NOGGIN OF STRONG ALE, M'LORD?'   69

'A PINT OF YOUR BEST, LANDLORD'   122

'BLESSINGS OF YOUR HEART, YOU BREW GOOD ALE'   186

GLOSSARY   208

BIBLIOGRAPHY   210

INDEX   211

ACKNOWLEDGEMENTS

Because of the very nature of the broad area of research for the subject matter of this text, it has been necessary to consult many publications and to draw upon the researches of many people.

To my fellow members of the Brewery History Society I wish to express my appreciation to them for generously allowing me to draw from their own researches. Many have also kindly loaned photographs and other illustrations. I would like to thank: Andrew Davison, Ian Stratford, Ken Smith, Jeff Sechiari, Paul Travis, Mike Tighe, Amber Patrick, David Parry, Peter Moynihan, the late Ken Goodley, John V. Richards, Chris Marchbanks, Michael Jones, Philip Eley, Ken Page, Pam Moore, Robert J. Flood, Tony Diebel, Adrian Phipps-Hunt, Nick Redman, Colin West, Peter Roberts, David Fletcher and Brian Glover.

The following officials of the National Trust have unstintingly answered my numerous enquiries and I am most appreciative of the information so freely given: Gary Marshall, Richard Ellis, A.J. Youel, J. Alwyn-Jones, Warren Davis, J.P. Haworth, Dip, Arch, RIBA, D.R. Brown and H. Beamish.

My thanks are also warmly extended to Chris Copp and Adrienne Whitehouse, formerly of the Staffordshire Museum Service, for information and the permission to use a report on the Shugborough brewhouse, and to John Oliver for his assistance on Chatsworth House. Also, Paul Pollack, archivist of Kings' School, Canterbury; John Kaye, Keeper of the Archives of Queen's College, Oxford; Mrs Elizabeth Boardman, archivist at Brasenose College, Oxford; Mrs P. Hatfield, archivist at Eton College, Windsor; Roger Custance, archivist at Winchester College; Mr B. Holloway, Proctor's Office, Oxford University; Mrs Hodgson, archivist at Canterbury Cathedral; George Chesterton, Malvernian Society Ltd; Kemble, Solicitors, Milton Keynes; John Stratford, MA; Kimbolton School and English Heritage.

Both Mike Ripley and Fiona Wood of the Brewers' and Licensed Retailers Association have been of immense help in both answering my numerous questions and permitting me to consult their library and archives. The Essex Record Office and the Hertfordshire Record Office have given me much assistance as has the Winchester Museum Service and the Calderdale Museum Officer, R.J. Westwood; Mary White, from the Shrewsbury Museum Service and Dr Elfyn Scourfield of the National Museum of Wales.

Many of the micro-breweries mentioned in this book have either been visited or consulted and my thanks to them all is acknowledged. Keith Hardman (All Nations); Dominic Wood (Three Tuns); Alec Pennycook (Stanway); Richard Jenkinson (Chiltern Valley); Farmers Arms (Apperley); Mrs Diana Lay (Bass Museum); Traquair House; J.W. Dorsey (Bugthorpe); Charles Eld (Morrells); Tony Colleya (Lansdowne Hotel); T.E.

The Arms of the Worshipful Company of Brewers.

Benham (Hardys & Hansons plc); John Hughes and Lee Cox (Sarah Hughes, Beacon Brewery) and Ushers Brewery, (Trowbridge).

Numerous individuals have provided me with much information and photographs, not least among these has been Mr James W. Buckley, who most generously allowed me to fully use his records, and those of the late Clarence Hellewell, and loaned me his photographs of Hickleton Hall. Mr Keith Osborne has kindly loaned me copies from his extensive collection of beer labels, and he was instrumental in pointing me in the right direction for several areas of my research. At CAMRA headquarters, Jo Barnes has been of great assistance; my thanks also to Gwen Jones and H.L. Wood. The following were kind enough to permit me to examine and photograph their old brewery premises: Mr and Mrs J. Lanfear; Mr and Mrs John Perkins; Mr and Mrs J. Horsnell; Mr and Mrs H. Lilley; Mr H.L. Wood and Brian Fleming.

INTRODUCTION

In these hectic times we often ignore daily practices and take for granted many old buildings that are 'just there'. These commonplace facts of life applied to many occupations for hundreds of years, simply because they were everyday jobs. Such was the case in the preparation of food and drink. It is not until there is a sudden change of circumstances, such as a building being demolished or a mundane occupation no longer existing, that we become aware of its demise. This was just the case with the publican brewer and the landed gentry's estate brewing. The cataclysmic effect of the outbreak of the First World War in 1914 changed the patterns of life for everyone. Social barriers began to break down with everyone working towards the war effort. No longer would the large houses have numerous servants and staff, nor would there be cheap and plentiful labour on the land.

With the further growth of industrialization and urbanization, the inevitable development of the larger common brewers and their tied houses swallowed up innumerable home-brew pubs and small local breweries. These were once to be seen in every town and many villages. Soon, keg beers, including lager, became more and more noticeable in our pubs, until they accounted for 50 per cent of all beer production. Those home-brew pubs, that had once been taken for granted, had all but disappeared by the 1960s. Only four remained. But, just as all was nearly lost, interest was suddenly revived and the Campaign for Real Ale was born. Several new home-brew pubs were started in the early 1970s and, during the 1980s and into the mid-1990s, the small groundswell of revival has turned into a stronger tide, there now being over 200 commercial home-brewing operations.

In this history of home-brewed ales we can trace the early beginnings of our public houses and the beers brewed in monasteries, colleges, cottages, farms and on the landed gentry's estates. Numerous detailed histories, many selected for their individuality, illustrate the rise and fall of so many of them and the multiplicity of reasons for their demise. The common brewers of today, many now international companies, are also examined and how they have evolved from the most humble of origins. There is no clear-cut definition of a common brewer, but it is generally accepted that it was one who brewed more than 1,000 barrels (36,000 gallons) a year, and who wholesaled his beer to publicans. He may also have owned more than five or six of his own public houses. Within the current trend of new smaller breweries, several have already developed into the common brewer status, bringing the wheel around full circle. An example of this is the Wychwood Brewery at Witney, Oxfordshire, who have a chain of forty Hobgoblin pubs associated with them. The former Clinch & Co. maltings off the market-place in Witney, now serve as offices and the brewery where, in 1983, the Glenny Brewery was founded.

Because brewing was considered a 'mystery and an art', the secret preserve of the brewer, many of the old recipes have been lost for all time. However, some were duly recorded and have come to light, as have the many varied ingredients used in ale and beer in the past. All these aspects, including some of the tools and machinery used, have been encompassed within this review of the small-scale brewer.

A turn-of-the-century West Midlands beerhouse, with a variant on Shakespeare's quotation painted on the wall.

A QUART IN A PINT-POT

Today there are more than 200 licensed home-brewing firms but, only thirty years ago, there were but four. In contrast, 300 years ago, there were 47,500 publican brewers and only 780 common brewers. The fall and gradual rise of these home-brewers is the story that will be told here.

Firstly, the several different sizes of brewing operations need to be defined and how they fitted into the commercial scene of the day. The most basic brewing was that done on a domestic level, ranging from only a few gallons of beer produced by the housewife in her cottage to the aristocratic gentry with their brewhouses. These operations were entirely for personal consumption and that of employees. Higher up the scale, in terms of quantity at least, were the retail brewers and the publican brewers, or brewing victuallers. In the case of the retail brewers, these were firms that had no public houses of their own and supplied chiefly to middle-class families, farms and smaller estates without their own brewing facilities. Often the retail brewer combined other trades with that of his brewing. This would have given them an advantage because, on their regular deliveries of other business products to households, it would have been most convenient to add a beer delivery also. Publican brewers had the other advantage of a guarantee (so long as their beer was good), of selling it in their own alehouse. In nearly all cases the brewhouses were situated behind the pub and today many are still standing, having been put to other uses, such as garages, storerooms or residential. In both the retail and publican brewers' businesses, there would have been the brewer, usually the owner, and perhaps only one or two assistants. These helpers would have been either casual labour or staff who had other jobs to perform. As will be seen in more detail, many of the brewers on farms and larger estates also had other jobs to do. In many cases, itinerant brewers would call during March and October, to brew large quantities for the households in country areas, and also for some public houses.

Publican brewers were by far the largest group, and it is from them that nearly all the present-day major brewing concerns can trace their ancestry. There are still quite a number of small common brewers owning around twenty or so public houses today. All of these had their origins as publican brewers, brewing behind their original first retail outlet. These include such firms as the Hook Norton Brewery, Oxfordshire; Bateman's of Lincolnshire; Adnam's of Southwold; Arkell's of Swindon; J.C. & R.H. Palmer of Bridport, Dorset; T. Hoskins Ltd of Leicester and Daniel Batham & Son Ltd, Brierley Hill. Many of these common brewers can trace their earliest efforts back to farming and malting; a medium-sized brewer such as the Home Brewery, Daybrook, Notts is a good example. John

Robinson's family had been farming at Home Farm and running the family business of malting in Cross Street prior to 1875. That was the year in which it became a limited company carrying out both malting and brewing. At the time of its acquisition in July 1986, it had grown to become a large company owning 447 public houses, which were then transferred under the auspices of Scottish & Newcastle Breweries. In the course of just over a hundred years, the business had expanded immensely.

The international giant, Allied Domecq, started in the smallest possible way as a publican brewer. Mr George Cardon founded his small brewhouse in 1708 behind his Star Inn in South Street, Romford, Essex. Situated close by the River Rom, he soon found that his beers were being well received, particularly by the traders in the ancient market-place. Other publicans approached him and soon he had to purchase a horse and trap to deliver his beers. Some ninety years later the Star Inn & Brewery were purchased by Mr Edward Ind and his partner Mr J. Grosvenor. In 1845, Mr C.E. Coope joined the firm and the business then became known as Ind, Coope and Company. By the early 1850s railway sidings had been laid into the brewery which then covered twenty-five acres. In 1856 the company purchased a partially built brewery adjacent to Samuel Allsopp and Sons brewery, in Burton-on-Trent. In 1934 these two companies amalgamated and, through further acquisitions of numerous smaller breweries, it went from strength to strength. In the early 1960s, Ind Coope, Tetley's of Leeds and Ansell's of Birmingham, came together and welded into a formidable brewing company covering the entire country. More recently the business has grown even more with foreign acquisitions in the drinks industry, changing its name from Allied Breweries, Carlsberg/Tetley to Allied Domecq. It is now one of the world's major drinks combines. From tiny acorns do great oak trees grow.

These are but two examples of how today's major companies have grown; there are many others with very similar brewing histories, not least of these is Bass, at Burton-on-Trent. This company can trace its roots in the trade back to being a carrier in the town, which was sold to Pickfords when the Bass family took up brewing. Partnerships with Mr Ratcliff and Mr Gretton set William Bass on the road to success, from his founding in 1777. Merging with another Burton brewer, Worthington & Co. in 1926, Mitchells & Butlers Ltd of Birmingham in 1961, and the London brewers, Charrington & Co Ltd of Mile End in 1967, the firm became the largest brewers in this country.

The growth from retail brewer to common brewer was much easier to achieve in a growing urban market than in the rural areas. The major factors which assisted in this growth were the expanding populations and the development of transport. Also the economy of scale in brewing gave a more consistent quality product and the price of beer production became more competitive. Many brewers had their own maltings and some even their own hop farms, such as Shepherd Neame in Faversham, Kent. A greater control over the raw materials not only improved the quality, but also reduced basic costs. As breweries grew in size, specialization of jobs came in with professional and full-time brewers, laboratory technicians, maltsters and coopers. The publican brewer, by necessity, however, was all things to all men. Not only did he brew his own beer, he also had to buy the materials in his local town, run his public house and arrange any necessary staff. It is no wonder that many a home-brewer found that he could not compete against the growing tide of common brewers.

The highest number of brewing victuallers was in 1750, when there were 48,421. In that year they brewed 2,227 barrels of strong beer, and about half that amount in small beer. By 1790 this figure of publican brewers had fallen to 27,000, while the increase of common brewers nearly doubled to 1,300. A hundred years later, there were another thousand common brewers, and publican brewers had been reduced to only 6,350. The proportion of small beer to strong beer was that small was about a quarter of that to strong beer produced. Consumption per head in the 1850s was 23 gallons, rising in 1874 to 33 gallons, dropping in 1982 to the same level as in the mid-nineteenth century. These figures have remained much the same, with a low of 18.4 gallons per head in 1959, rising to 26.9 gallons in 1979, and settling back, in the early 1990s, to 23 gallons per head per annum. Currently there has been a decline of around 2 per cent per annum for the last five years in brewery production. In 1981, there were between 25 and 30 publican brewers who had been established for three or four years. At the same period there were 80 common brewery companies who were operating 138 breweries. In 1991, the number of home-brewers had increased to about 90, with a reduction to 65 brewery companies operating 99 breweries.

Probably the most crucial year to the brewing industry, if not to the whole nation, was the year of the outbreak of the First World War. In 1914 there were 880 retail brewers, 1,477 publican brewers, and 1,335 common brewers. There were 88,445 public houses in England and Wales, but the number had fallen by over 24,000 in the course of only thirty years. This was the last year in which statistics were officially kept of brewing victuallers producing under 1,000 barrels a year. In this year the declared volume of barrels brewed by 'Brewers not for sale, liable to duty', was 5,198. The excise duty from 1909 to early 1914 was 7s 9d per standard barrel but this was increased later in 1914 to 23s a barrel by Chancellor Lloyd George. Sweeping changes to limit production and the sale and transport of beer were introduced in May 1915. Opening hours, which varied between 16 and 19½ hours, were reduced to 5½ hours a day or less, with all pubs closing at 9 p.m. Such was the drastic effect of the war. In 1915 there were threats to nationalize the brewing industry, which fortunately did not happen, with one isolated case. This was in the Carlisle area of Cumbria where, as a result of several munitions factories, all the breweries and public houses were brought under state control in 1916. The company formed was the Carlisle & District State Management Scheme, which was sold to private enterprise in 1971 – including some 206 public houses. The Defence of the Realm Act gave licensing justices the authority to close public houses in the First World War, without compensation. The effect of all this legislation on many hundreds of businesses throughout the land, including many family-owned home-brew pubs, was catastrophic.

A survey carried out in the 1830s showed that one in three victuallers brewed their own beer, but in Yorkshire the figure was as much as 60 per cent. Thirty years later, one John Fielden noted that, out of over 9,800 families visited in the Halifax to Leeds and Bradford areas, some 7,500 brewed their own beer. Leeds was a stronghold where the home-brewer held on to his rights to brew, as the quantities of malt used in brewing showed that only 12 per cent of malt used in 1825 was by common brewers. This figure had only risen to 64 per cent by 1892. Generally speaking, the heyday of the publican brewer was in the mid-nineteenth century. With the growth of the common brewers who were acquiring as many public houses as possible in order to give them a guaranteed retail outlet, competition became fierce. So the tied house system evolved, many originating from tied financial loans to assist the privately-owned publican's houses. In order to fund this scramble for pub acquisitions, the Companies Act in the 1880s enabled previous sole proprietorships or partnerships to become limited liability companies. Shares were issued and the minnows of the brewing world were swallowed up by the sharks; home-brew pubs and numerous retail brewers disappeared for ever almost overnight. With this high level of competition, there was little incentive for the publican brewers to remain in business.

Notices started to appear in local newspapers and the trade journals, advertising breweries for sale. '*Brewer's Journal*, Act 1868: To be Sold. Worle Brewery, near Weston-super-Mare, 2 Qtr plant and a 60 Qtr Maltings. The brewery has been established 50 years and carries on with great success by May & Castle, the late companies predecessors in the business.' 'July 1873. For Sale at Paignton Steam Brewery, and Malthouse with 4 Qtr; plant plus 12 Cottages and Ship Inn, situated near the Quay at Brixham, Devon.' Was it in desperation that John Parkyn, a brewer at the Bassett Arms Hotel, Camborne, Cornwall tried to 'cook his books'? He was summoned for not making a correct entry of malt in his brewing books, and was fined £25 in August 1872. On Sunday 7 March 1897, police searched a house at Cwindegwell Street, Dognells, occupied by Elizabeth Thomas and her daughter, after seeing several people entering and leaving the premises with beer. In the back room they found two 9-gallon casks of beer on tap, in the backyard a complete brewing plant was discovered and in another room about a hundredweight of hops. Beer measures and other indications of an extensive trade were also found. Subsequently, at the Kemes Petty Sessions held at Eglwyswrw before 'a full bench of Magistrates', both women were charged with selling beer without a licence. A previous conviction having been proved, on which occasion the brewing utensils had been confiscated, the defendants were then fined £25 with costs.

Very few brewhouses or breweries were let, the owners preferring to realize their capital and discharge all interests in a business. However, as early as 8 June 1768, an advertisement appeared in the *Kentish Gazette*: 'To be sold or let at Michealmus next. And also to be let, the King's Arms Alehouse at Milton, near Sittingbourne, with two brewing coppers and other utensils; one copper contains about 200 gallons and has a cock at the bottom, the other about 70 gallons. For particulars enquire of Mr James Tongue, Sittingbourne.'

A mysterious epidemic broke out in 1900, firstly in Lancashire then throughout the country, but chiefly in the areas of Manchester and Salford. Investigations soon revealed that of the 70 deaths and some 6,000 sick people, all were beer drinkers. Closer detailed examination revealed that several were employees of a Salford brewer. Scientists discovered that arsenic could be found in the glucose used in the brewing process. The supplying firm of the brewing glucose was traced and the problem eradicated but not before considerable disquiet had spread throughout the country. Many brewery companies took out advertisements to assure their customers that all was well, and their establishments were approved by the local health inspectors.

Some of the earliest drinking vessels and carrying jugs were made of leather, being the most readily available material and, of course, one of the cheapest. In the Middle East today, as in Biblical times, the hides of cattle, sheep and goats are used for carrying liquids. Many references are made to leather bottles, blackjacks and bombards which were made of this material. Being unbreakable and light they were ideal for their purpose. The leather bottles were usually barrel-shaped, made of one hide and stitched along the top, with an opening which was sealed with a wood peg. The rounded ends were stitched in and usually a leather thong was provided for carrying over the shoulder or attached to the belt. The blackjack was a large pitcher which was waisted towards the mouth with a lip for pouring. As with the bottle, one skin sufficed, being stitched up one side with a circular base sewn in. A large handle built up of several layers of skin provided a stout carrying loop. To make these leather containers the hide was softened in water and when supple, stretched over a wooden block. When dry, the leather containers were sometimes sealed internally with pitch. Later, designs provided for aristocratic families were often mounted with silver on the rims and a coat of arms emblazoned on the side. Sometimes a date and initials were painted on. There is one still kept in the buttery of Queen's College, Oxford, and having examined it, it is most surprising to find how light it is. The term 'jackboots', referring to the long knee-length boots worn by horseriders, is derived from the re-use of these leather bottles, eloquently described by Thomas Tusser, the Essex farmer, in 1560:

'TANKARD AND JACK'

A Leather Bottel he know is good,
Far better than glasses or cans of wood,
For when a Man is at work in the Field,
Your Glasses and Pots no comfort will yield,
Then a good Leather Bottel standing him by,
He may drink always when he is dry.

When this Bottel doth grow old,
And will good Liquor no longer hold.

Out of the side, you may take a clout,
Will mend your shoes when there worn out,
Else take it and hang it upon a pin,
It will serve to put odd trifles in,
As hinges, awls and candle ends,
For young Beginners must have such thinges.

Then I wish in Heaven his soul may dwell,
That first devised the Leather Bottel!

A bombard was a very large leather jack, so called because of its similarity to a very early type of cannon: these were short and stumpy. Also made of leather were mugs, cups and cans in smaller sizes for drinking from. 'Cans' were also made of wood, as in Tusser's first verse.

Two earthenware pitchers, now kept in the parish church at Hornchurch, Essex, were made for the bell-ringers' use. They were filled with home-brewed ale from Hornchurch Hall. Formerly in the church belfry there was a set of rules:

> *If you ring with Spur or Hat,**
> *Three pints of beer you pay for that;*
> *If you swear or give the Lye,*
> *A pot you pay Immediately;*
> *If a bell you overthrow,*
> *A pint you pay before you go.*

T S 1798

*This meant a man who was of a better social position than an ordinary ringer i.e., one wearing a hat and spurs.

In later years the pitchers were used for supplying refreshment to the tenants of the hall, when they came to pay their tithes (audit time). However, it is evident that both the pitchers were intended to belong to the church, but in more recent times (the 1920s) they had been

The eighteenth-century bell-ringers' ale jugs from Hornchurch, Essex.

kept at the King's Head Inn. This was the taphouse opposite the previous Old Hornchurch Brewery. After the death of Colonel and Mrs Holmes, the brewery owners, the family bought back the two pitchers at an auction sale at their house and presented them to the church. The smaller of the two has a brownish-coloured earthenware glaze, with two large open handles on the shoulders and neck, which has a 'thumb print' indent around the neck. It measures 13½ inches high and 40 inches in girth. Inscribed in a cursive hand is the date 1731 and the names of six ringers and two churchwardens. The larger pitcher is of a very dark, burnt umber-coloured earthenware, very thickly and highly glazed. It measures 20½ inches high and 50 inches in girth at the widest part. The heavy handles are on the shoulders and it a pronounced neck with a lip. It too has an inscription with the date, 'May 24th, 1815'. This pitcher was made by Rt. Aungier and also bears the names of ten ringers and two churchwardens. It was the gift of Mr C. Cove who owned the local pottery, and it is believed that the earlier one was also made there, the pottery having been in existence since around 1720.

An interesting account for supplying beer to bell-ringers illustrates the importance of such activities in those times; this example comes from Ely, in Cambridgeshire.

1778. The Gentleman Churchwardens of Ely, St Mary's to E. Olley.

June 4th to one Ringing boy	6.8
John Athin, Lowance beer	1.9
To Lawrances Beer	3.9
Aug 12th to one Ringing day	6.8
1779	
Jan 18th to one Ringing day	6.8
To charge for Vestry Easter Monday	10.0

£1.15.6

Received her mark 'X' E. Olley

Elizabeth Olley was the landlady of the White Lion who supplied the beer from Hindes Brewery, on the Waterside, Ely. The two spellings of 'Lowance' and Lawrance Beer refers to the beer allowance permitted for the parishioners at vestry meetings. Evidently Elizabeth was unable to sign her name, giving the customary 'X'. She was the landlady at the White Lion for about fifty years, finally retiring in 1811.

Costrels, or Pilgrim's bottles, were made of earthenware. They measured about 6 inches in height and had two small holes beside the neck, allowing a leather thong to be threaded through and hung around the owner's neck or from the waist. Horn mugs, made from part of a bullock's horn, with a finely carved 'plug' to seal one end, were commonly used by cottagers and farm workers. A smaller version of these horn mugs have been used until quite recently by several brewers as a 'sampler' of beer, to taste each gyle with. Farm workers also made their own wooden cups and bottles, sometimes with a plaited horsehair strap, often with coloured inserts. These containers resembled very small coopered barrels, and it was the custom to incise or brand their initials on the heads. These delightful miniscule barrels

would be taken out to the fields. Examples of these may be seen at the Three Tuns Brewery, Shropshire, and The Fleece, Bretforden (both mentioned in detail in another chapter), and many other old public houses. A survival of the Pilgrim's bottle was the 'Dorset Pill', a glazed earthenware bottle, which was used at harvest time: these were still being made in 1925. Of better quality glazed ware were the toby jugs, introduced in the eighteenth century. These depicted a stout character in period dress, a tricorn hat forming the lip of the jug. The gentleman was invariably depicted holding a foaming tankard of ale and the entire jug was glazed in full colours. Many different personalities of the day were depicted and these jugs are still made. Dating from the same period were the puzzle jugs and whistling jugs which were also decorated and glazed. The puzzle jugs usually had a top section cut out in a decorative design, with a hollow handle connecting the bulbous base to the top rim. This rim was hollow too, with three or four protruding hollow spouts. A rhyme on the base would challenge the drinker to attempt to drink the beer without spilling any.

Here Gentlemen come have a drink,
I'll hold a wager if you think
That you don't drink a single drop
Without you spilling the lot.

The trick was to put one's mouth to one of the spouts, cover the ends of the others and then suck! Even this did not always work as some of the jugs were a little more ingenious. These had another small hole under the top part of the handle which also had to be covered over before successively sucking up the beer! Further similar challenges were presented by the glass 'yard of ale'. These long trumpet-like containers are bulbous at one end and have a bell-mouth at the other; this is put to the mouth. Initially all is well until the air suddenly rushes into the bulbous end, causing the beer to drench the drinker. Drinking can indeed be fun!

Pewter was introduced into this country by the Dutch in 1482; they also brought in hops and the names of the sizes of beer casks. Many different forms of pewter tankard were made, initially only available to the wealthy because of the cost. An early type with a hinged lid was called a 'Tappit-Hen' and others had a glass bottom. The most likely explanation for the glass was so the drinker could see the colour of his beer. A more romantic idea said that it was so the drinker could spot the king's shilling, should one have been dropped in. If he removed it, he was deemed to have signed up for the army! Pewter was beloved by the Victorians and many pubs of the period had large sets of tankards, in quart, pint and half-pint sizes with smaller spirit measures. The measures would usually have a brass rim and were stamped to indicate the quantity. Most of these pewter tankard sets were inscribed with the landlord's name and that of the pub, either on the side or more often on the base. The Pewterers' Company was the sixteenth Guild Company of the city of London.

From the seventeenth century 'peg tankards' came into fashion although these had been in use as early as the twelfth century. One of the earliest records shows that in about 1102, the Archbishop of London, Anselm, instructed his priests not to 'drink to pegs'. The Glastonbury Abbey peg tankard, made of oak, has a handle and cover. It holds two quarts and has eight pegs equally spaced inside. Thus the inside is divided into half pints between each peg. The outside is elaborately carved with ecclesiastical designs on the lid and on the barrel. The first person to drink did so to the first peg, then passed the tankard on to the next fellow and so on. Should anyone drink short of or over a peg marker they then had to drink to the next. Thus it may be seen, liberal quantities of beer were drunk by the monks and priests.

Posset pots, usually made in Staffordshire, were so named because of their pronounced spout, similar to today's invalid's drinking cup. This same type of spout was also to be found on Victorian quart pewter tankards; they were for drinking from, not for pouring. From the seventeenth century, a stoneware pottery jug of an amber glaze was called a Bellar-mine. These were decorated with a caricature of a bearded face which depicted the Jesuit cardinal of that name whom the Dutch of the Reformed Church wished to characterize. In England these jugs were called Greybeards and today are very collectable.

Left to right: Mocca Tankard; 1pt pewter posset; Doulton harvest jug; Toby jug; horn beaker and a quart pewter, 1930s.

Drinking glasses first came into general usage in the late seventeenth century. These were bulbous and thick with a baluster stem supporting a heavy bowl. They were used mainly for wine, although strong ales were supped from them by wealthy families. Decorations to the glass began with the plain designs of the eighteenth century, air-twist and bubble stems coming into fashion in 1735. From the 1750s onwards twisted white or coloured inserts to stems became fashionable and at the end of the century, cut and faceted stems in unlimited designs were popular. Beer glasses of the eighteenth century were made in a variety of shapes and sizes, sometimes engraved with hops and barley stalks. Others bore the name of the owner or a family coat of arms. When the glass-making industry moved into mass production, not only were glass bottles for beer made widely available, so too were drinking glasses. During the 1930s glass tankards had virtually replaced pewter tankards which then became used as bar-room decorations. Silver and pewter tankards have had a revival of popularity during the last twenty years, with many regulars retaining their own personal pewter tankards behind the bar.

Trick glasses were the height of fashion in the nineteenth century and later. These were usually highly decorated with floral or geometric designs, perhaps with an ornate border design near the rim. A minute hole or two would be cut right through the glass, so that when the drinker drank the contents, he found them dribbling down his chin! Another nineteenth-century novelty drinking vessel was known as the Sussex Pig. These were made of pottery at Rye. The pigs' heads were detachable so that the body was used as a cup. The inference here was that the drinker had drained a 'hogshead' of beer! Frog mugs were a popular joke in Victorian times. A toad, painted in realistic colours, was part of the base of a pottery tankard. As the drinker emptied his beer he would suddenly be confronted by the toad. Although quite harmless, many suspected them of being venomous. A 'Mazer' was a wooden drinking vessel originally made of maple. 'Mocka Ware' was a cheap form of decoration applied to late eighteenth-century earthenware. Mugs and bowls were decorated in this particular style. The decoration on each article was never exactly alike as it was carried out when the pottery was wet. This process always varied the effect. The design seen on mugs is best described as like a bare tree in outline against a fawn background. Bands of blue, black and yellow to the top and bottom were also the general style. The correct measured quantity of the pottery tankard was marked near the rim.

At the time of the Civil War, both sides desperately needed funds and King Charles had been attempting to raise money by taxes for several years. On 16 May 1643 a Parliamentary Ordinance was issued, imposing a duty on beer at a rate of 2s a barrel for strong beer and 6d for small beer. Despite the people's considerable dislike of this tax and the understanding that as soon as the war was over it would cease, the beer duty continued throughout the Protectorate. Oliver Cromwell, who had himself been a brewer in Huntingdonshire, declared the excise duty 'to be a most easy and indifferent levy on the people'. With the two opposing armies roaming the countryside, both parties would acquire silverware from more wealthy landowners in exchange for cheaper pewter. Such was the case at The Fleece, Bretfordon, where there is an excellent collection of pewter plates and salvers on display in the bar.

Ever-increasing rates of duty were to continue for another 200 years. The 1643 duty included private brewers, with the result that Revenue Officers often had difficulty gaining entry to people's cottages and farms. In order to overcome the visits, the duty payable by the private brewer was compounded into a reasonable sum for each householder to pay! This too was unsatisfactory and was abandoned in 1653, giving the landed gentry a distinct advantage over the poorer working classes. This subject was to crop up again in the early nineteenth century. *The Brewer's Assistant*, published in 1815, reported in detail a letter written on 16 July 1812 to Lord North and Mr Pitt from a Mr G. Sleigh: 'what I allude to, sir, is an additional duty on malt used by the private brewer, or those that brew their own beer and pay no duty so as to be in proportion to the duty paid by the public or common brewer. I cannot see any reasonable or just grounds why the wealthy and most opulent or those that have the means or advantage of brewing, should be exempt from paying tax which the poorest person in the Kingdom is subject to: for upwards of %oths of the people and those principally of the middle or lower order, or the mechanic and labouring hand not only are obliged to pay the duty on beer but also the brewers and publicans profits, or extra charges: while the nobleman and gentlemen, the farmer and others that have the means of brewing pay nothing, and who it must be admitted are the best able.' He further pointed out that the tax would increase revenue and throw a greater proportion of trade into the brewers' hands, with a decline in home-brewing: 'It is well known, and generally understood, that the common brewer makes a greater quantity of beer from a quarter of malt than either the victualler that brews or the private family.' The Beerhouse Act of 1830 was for 'the better supplying of the public with beer in England'; the effect was 24,000 beerhouse licences opened in six months! Prior to this act drunkenness and great distress was prevalent, due to the increased drinking of spirits, particularly of gin. The effect of the act was an increase in beer consumption of 40 per cent.

Mr Gladstone had repealed the hops duty in 1862 and the malt duty in 1880. These were replaced with what has been referred to as his 'worts duty', still in force today. Stricter restrictions on opening times for licensed houses in 1872 brought about a decline in many beerhouses, they had been required to have a Justices Certificate to obtain an excise licence since 1869. In 1895 the excise duty on a standard barrel of beer was increased from 6s 3d to 6s 9d, in 1901 another 1s was added to pay for the Boer War. The Compensation Act of 1904 allowed for compensation to be paid to owners of licensed houses that were refused licences to trade. With the outbreak of the First World War, the Defence of the Realm Act (DORA) restricted the opening hours of public houses and this continued in force for nearly eighty years. In the same year, excise duty was 7s 9d a barrel but by the end of the war, after four years, it had risen to 50s a barrel; the price of a pint then was 5d. In 1920 the duty was £5.00 a barrel. With the nine-day General Strike in 1926 which heralded the start of the great depression, trade began to slump and many publican brewers ceased to trade. The Labour government of 1931 raised the duty on a barrel to 114s, giving a further increase of a penny on a pint of beer. Trade continued to decline with the onslaught of the Second World War, and limitations on production and opening hours were introduced. At the end of the war duty was £17.15s 0d per barrel, having increased three times in the twelve months from the beginning of 1940. Materials were still in short supply up until 1950 when the chancellor adjusted the duty so that the strength of beers was increased by 3 per cent, without a price increase to the public. On 3 April 1963 Reginald Maudling, then Chancellor of the Exchequer, abolished the excise duty on brewing beer at home. This immediately gave an impetus to the home-brewer and several companies produced home-brew kits and equipment: a new hobby was born. From 1 April 1973 as a member of the EEC, beer became liable to VAT at 10 per cent, in addition to the beer duty. The most recent legislation to encourage the micro-brewers was issued on 1 May 1990, enabling a 'guest beer' to be sold in brewery tied houses. The first few years of this policy have not been as successful as was at first hoped, although with the major brewing groups selling off hundreds of pubs, many of these pubs have since become 'free houses'.

A perhaps unexpected venue at which brewing took place was in hospitals. The Radcliffe Infirmary at Oxford was opened in 1770 and continues to this day. When first built there was a brewhouse behind the main building and, as so often was the case, this was the province of the porter who acted as the brewer. Brewing took place once a month with small beer for the patients and 'ale' for the nurses and other staff. The 'ale' referred to may well

ENJOY GOOD HEALTH

COMBE'S
XXX
BEVERAGE

THE FINEST TONIC

have been strong beer, as this term has been used in other parts of the country in this context. Patients received 1 to 1½ pints of beer a day, while nurses were allowed 1 pint as a prevention against illness. Strong beer was used for poultices, the alcohol acting as an anaesthetic. A curious advertisement placed in 1776 said: 'Any strong Beer not fit for drinking will be an agreeable present for the use of surgeons.' Brewing ceased here in 1853. At the General Hospital, Nottingham, on Tuesday 25 June 1782, the governors ordered 'that Mr Hallam be desired to purchase at the Feathers Inn, the following brewing materials for the use of the hospital viz. 12 half Hogsheads, a fathering tub, a square cooler, Thralls, wooden spout, a Vat to mash, Strikes, Buckets, Brewing Sieve, Tubs, a Tun dish, three brass cocks, provided the above articles are such as are good and will suit to a copper that boils 100 gallons'. From this description it would appear that the copper had already been purchased and that the Feathers Inn was giving up its own brewing prior to the General Hospital having its own brewhouse. The beer allowance here was 2½ pints of beer a day for patients and the same amount for staff. In 1819, however, the allowance was reduced to 1½ pints for male patients and 1 pint for females. The staff continued with the previous allowance. By 1833, probably in line with extensions to the hospital and the growing number of patients, authorization was given by the governors to extend the beer cellar and to obtain a further six beer barrels. The General Hospital accounts for the year 1870 show an expenditure of

£37 19s 0d on malt and £5 15s 6d on hops. Previous years had shown a joint expenditure of £130 on malt and hops and as these items are no longer shown in the accounts after 1870, it is reasonable to assume that this was the last year of brewing. In 1871, when there were 130 patients, the hospital purchased 3,300 gallons of beer at a cost of £172 19s 0d. By 1906 only 5 gallons of beer was purchased.

Stouts were seen as a medicinal aid, with the brewers' advertisements underlining the beneficial qualities of their products. In the 1930s the Lion Brewery, Blackburn, promoted their own Lion Oatmeal Stout as 'a splendid pick-me-up'. A doctor writes: 'I have given Lion Oatmeal Stout, and recommended it to many of my patients. In every case they have put on weight and their appetites have greatly benefited.' Not to be outdone, the famous Guinness advertisements told us for years that 'Guinness is good for you'. Even up until recent times Guinness have supplied a special bottling of Foreign Extra Stout from their Liverpool bottlers. The black bordered label has a broad, pale orange band encircling the familiar Guinness label. At the centre, on each side of the band, is printed 'Not for Sale' in red letters. At the top it reads 'To assist your recovery', and above that, 'for hospitals and similar use only'. On the lower half is written: 'With compliments of your medical adviser and the house of Guinness'. Good health and good drinking!

THE ABBOT'S ALE

The monastic community naturally focused their religious life around their church. To support themselves they required many varying types of buildings to ensure their economic survival. These buildings were grouped around courtyards or precincts, often with covered cloisters linking kitchens, refectories, dormitories and toilet blocks. There were usually inner and outer courtyards, with the buildings most closely associated with the daily life of the monks built nearest the church. The outer courtyard was associated with guest-houses for visitors – both pilgrims and lay visitors – and a place where the poor could receive alms. Stables, often several barns to store grain and also breweries and bakehouses, were grouped around the outer courtyard. Access from the outside was obtained via a gatehouse with the doors being locked each night at sundown. At the larger monasteries it was also necessary to have outhouses for the several building trades. Plumbers for working lead to roofs and water systems, tilers and stone masons, all required their own workshops. Outside the monastic precincts there were often water mills for grinding corn or fulling wool. Gardens for growing vegetables and especially herbs, fruit orchards and a few vineyards and grass meadows all came within the 'home farm' enclosure. Where herds of cattle were kept there were slaughterhouses and tanneries. Dovecotes and fish ponds were also essential requirements; the dovecotes provided meat all year round while the fish ponds, often large and numerous, provided the necessary meal for Fridays.

These monasteries were carefully sited as it was essential they were closely situated by an abundant water supply. With monasteries having as many as 100 people to cater for, the volume of water needed for both drinking water and that required to flush the latrines meant that all had to be well planned. The nearby rivers were either diverted to suit the local needs or a small 'leat' was constructed, which was controlled by sluice gates. Water was then directed to the various buildings, gardens and latrines as required. Finally, when the water had been used for its various purposes, the effluent was discharged downstream from the community. The earliest recorded map of the watercourses supplying an English monastery is the one made by Prior Wilbert in the mid-twelfth century at the Christ Church Priory, Canterbury. The Saxon monastery suffered a fire in 1067 and was rebuilt by Archbishop Laufranc, housing some 200 monks. Abutting the nave of the cathedral was the great cloister, as it remains today, and to the west side of the cloister was the long range of the cellarer's lodging. On the south side of the cloister was the buttery between the refectory and the cellarer's lodging. Further south of the refectory was a kitchen court and the kitchens, with cellarer's court and hall to the west. On the east side of the cloister is the chapter house, still extant, and the dormitory linked with the refectory. Further east was a smaller dormitory and a long building called the 'necessarium' (toilet block). Between the smaller or secondary dormitory and the church nave was a rectangular courtyard, referred to as the infirmary cloister (the infirmary being situated to the east). Here is sited the great laver, the baptistry or conduit house. An abundant and pure water supply was essential to the monastic community and the Christ Church, founded in the sixth century within the Roman city, relied on wells. Archbishop Theobold, or most likely Canterbury's most famous citizen, Thomas à Becket, granted a source on the north eastern side of the city some three-quarters of a mile away. This water supply, emanating from many springs, was piped via five settling tanks outside the city walls. It passed into the precincts in the vicinity of the existing Forren's Gate and along the eastern side of Green Court; thence it went via the infirmary into the infirmary cloister. Here, in about 1160, was built the baptistry, laver, conduit or 'Great Lavatory Tower' as it is referred to in *Archaeologia Cantiana, c.* 1868. Within this cloister was also the herb garden. From this great conduit the main water supply passed under the great dormitory into the great

Canterbury Cathedral's twelfth-century laver or conduit house.

cloister where it discharged into a second conduit on the north side. From this conduit flowed two branches. One returned parallel to the main supply from the east, via several secondary branches, to the southern conduit which supplied the extreme eastern piscina and infirmary. The second supply from the great cloister ran due north, passing under the refectory, the kitchen, and finally to the brewhouse, adjacent to the bakehouse and New or North Hall (beside the extant court gate). This description of the water supply is based on the detailed drawings from the priorate of Wybert, *c.* 1530–67. The return flow of all this water was fed into a decorative fish pond and thence to flush the two latrine blocks. It then flowed across the outer court via a vaulted drain which was discharged well away from the priory buildings into the town ditch. It is not known whether the pipes were made of lead, wood or pottery.

The brewhouse and adjacent bakehouse are shown to be situated on the north side of Green Court with two tap outlets in the brewhouse and one in the bakehouse. On this drawing the bakehouse is shown to be smaller than the brewhouse and to the east of it, adjacent to Forren's Gate and on the far side of the gateway, was the granary. Forren's Gate led through to the stables. To the west of the brewhouse, facing the southerly Green Court, is Hodgson's Hall and dining hall, once the clothes-making area, built in 1659. A 'tank building', or conduit, stood next to the granary for centuries, 'wherein a cistern supplying almost the whole precinct, supplied by springs a mile away'. The waterhouse was parted from the dean's brewhouse many years ago. At this time the conduit was a square building,

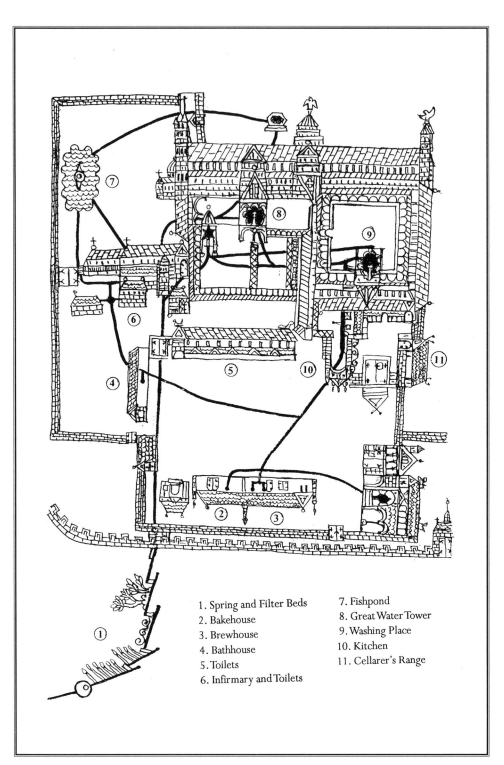

1. Spring and Filter Beds
2. Bakehouse
3. Brewhouse
4. Bathhouse
5. Toilets
6. Infirmary and Toilets
7. Fishpond
8. Great Water Tower
9. Washing Place
10. Kitchen
11. Cellarer's Range

Wibert's twelfth-century water system for Christ Church Priory, Canterbury.

like a country pigeon house, and stood so near the prebendal house that it was an inconvenience, as well as a disgrace to the whole court besides due to its poor condition. The building still called the brewhouse has long since ceased to be used as such. In about 1750 a 'vast leaden tank with 60,000 gallons', was placed in the upper part of the brewery and bakery, this being removed in about 1948. It is most likely that the conduit house beside the granary was demolished at the time when the water tank was installed. 'The good "Saxon Ale" which the prebends of old were wont to use; and which contributed to gladden many a cheerless heart, when Christmas and its merry train arrived has been abandoned; the good old times are sunk into oblivion and the poor into a state of comparative vassalage', so wrote William Gostling in 1825 in his book, *A Walk in and about Canterbury*.

The cellarer was one of the four great officers of the monastery, the 'Cellarer's Office regarded the Cibum Monachorum, the provision of food for the Monks, and the ordering thereof to which end he had the Pistrinum and the Bracinum [bakehouse and the brewhouse] under his charge'. The cellarer had an assistant, the sub-cellarius, 'to assist him and share with him in the managing of this burthensome office, and weighty province'. The cellarer was allotted a large principal house which bore his name and coat of arms and rebus or name device. One famous cellarer was Richard Dering, the monk. He conspired against Henry VIII and was hanged at Tyburn for his sins. The king subsequently reserved the cellarer's lodgings for his own use and it was then passed on to the see.

In Chillenden's list is an entry for 1301, translated from the Latin, which indicates that a new stable for the treasurer with an upper chamber and a small granary was being built. In 1303 there is an entry describing a 'New Granary in the Brewhouse or Malthouse'. Somewhat confusingly the entry for 1317 reads: 'For the new Brewhouse and Granary, with chimney etc'. It may have been that the position of the brewhouse was moved, hence the observation of 1317 referring to the 'new' building, the earliest having been shown in 1150. Repairs to the brewhouse, new tailor's shop, new granary, new stable for the prior and new barn for the prior's hay were all recorded between 1390 and 1411.

The almonry would have served a large number of the poor people of Canterbury on a daily basis. Judging by its apparent size, this could have catered for up to one hundred people. The almonry was situated adjacent to the court gate on its northern side and was supplied with water from the conduit in front of the brewhouse. As there were various allowances of beer for the different grades within the monastery, one can roughly calculate the volumes of beer produced. Small beer, for the daily use of the monks and given as alms to the poor, would have been in the region of 250 gallons a day, with a very much smaller quantity of strong beer for the senior clerics and for celebrating the numerous religious feast days. This could have amounted to about 50 gallons or more a week, making a total brewing of 15,000 gallons in a year. This would explain the large size of the brewhouse, equal in size to the extant chapter house. However, as there have been references to a malthouse in connection with the brewhouse, it is possible that the monks also did their own malting. The brewhouse, or Bracinum as indicated on the earliest plans, is built mainly in the Decorated style, but has had Perpendicular insertions, such as two square windows. There are four buttresses and a projecting arched porch, which is attributed to DeEstria's style. Today the entrance porch has double doors which give access to stairs leading to six classrooms on the first floor, where the large lead water tank was once housed.

Christ Church Priory, Canterbury. The brewhouse is to the left of the front chimney.

Thomas à Becket, then Lord Chancellor and afterwards Archbishop of Canterbury, was sent to France in 1158 to secure the hand of Princess Margaret, daughter of Louis VII, for Henry, the eldest son of Henry II. Becket led a glittering cavalcade including two wagonloads which 'bore nothing but beer, made by a decoction of water from strong corn and carried in iron-hooped barrels, to be given to the French (King Louis) who admire liquor of this sort, for it is certainly a wholesome drink, clear of the colour of wine and of a superior flavour'. It was further described as 'so pure, sparkling and delicious as to fill the French with envy'. This would appear to describe a strong ale with a 'maltiness', and could well have been brewed in the Christ Church Priory brewhouse. It was commonplace at that time to use hogshead-sized casks, with two being carried on a single-horse tumbril. Based on this assumption, the quantity sent to France would have been about 288 gallons, a very early example of English beer being exported. The entourage of the chancellor included 8 great wagons (of which two were the beer drays), 28 packhorses and 200 men. Thomas à Becket took with him sufficient clothes for each day of the twenty-four day trip, and these were left for the French king's use. He returned from his mission having obtained his agreement that the baby Princess would marry the three-year-old Henry.

At the dissolution of the monasteries by Henry VIII, the first effect was the re-establishment of selected Benedictine cathedral priories. Among these were Canterbury, Carlisle, Durham, Ely, Norwich, Rochester, Winchester and Worcester. The previous prior became the dean and the monks became a chapter of canons and so the transition from the Papal Church to the Church of England was made. It is for this reason that several of these magnificent cathedrals still retain many of their original monastic buildings; Canterbury is one of the foremost. Despite this comparatively easy change, many parts of the monasteries were demolished, particularly buildings which were primarily for the use of the closed community and therefore no longer required. After the Reformation Henry VIII established the class of King's Scholars in 1541, which was administered by the Dean and Chapter.

In the fifth and sixth years of the reign of Queen Elizabeth I, accounts for 1562–3 show in detail the dietary menu for the forty-eight commoners, of whom twelve were scholars. From the latter no payment was received, but the rest paid sums varying from a halfpenny to three halfpence per week for their commons. About half a pound of beef and mutton per head was supplied for the first five days of the week only. Bread, butter and milk were provided but no cheese. There was no lack of beer; no less than 6 kilderkins (108 gallons) were charged to the account for the Christmas week. On Christmas Day forty-eight people were treated to plum pudding, the cost for this one week was £3 11s 1½d. In Lent, however, the same number of people could be fed for less than half that amount at Christmas time. Of the 6 kilderkins of beer (bere, not ale) accounted for, two were unused in this Christmas week. From the fact that only twelve of the scholars were commoners we may infer that the Common Table was patronized only by those who were boarders, and that the majority who were day boys, dined and supped at home. It is apparent from these accounts that the Common Table was not well supported and that from about 1600, the King's Scholars were fed and supplied with their small beer through private arrangements made by the headmaster.

An interesting reference in *Monumenta Franciscana* in the mid-thirteenth century concerns the arrival of nine Franciscan monks in Canterbury during September 1224. Five others lodged in the 'Priests Hospital . . . where a tiny room was granted to them under the School house; there they sat day-after-day, almost in unbroken confinement. But when the Scholars went home in the evening, they entered the room where they had been in session and there made a fire for themselves and sat near it; and after when the time came for them to keep the Collation [this was the custom in monasteries, to read from the book of this name, with some light refreshment] they placed on the fire a small pot which held the dregs of their beer (cum Faecibus Cerevisiae), put a ladle in the pot and drank, each in his turn, adding some word of edification.' Evidently this drink was sometimes so thick that water had to be added before it could be heated up. This evidence is translated from the Latin and there is some ambiguity in this wording. The word 'discus' for ladle can also be translated to mean a measure of salt or corn. It is therefore conceivable that either salt or corn was added to the libation, as both were in common use as beer adjuncts at this time. The reference to the Franciscan monks staying in the school house relates to an unidentified location, although records indicate that a school was founded in about 1597 and that a Mr Twine, headmaster at this school, was the first headmaster of Henry VIII's reformed King's Scholars' school.

There were at least two guest-houses within the monastic confines of the walls, one beside the secondary 'Porta Curie' or gatehouse. This was called the Aula Nova and still retains many original Norman architectural features. Underneath it was a prison, and adjacent to the gatehouse was the almonry for dispensing victuals to the poor. At the east end of the Cathedral Church is a large, two-storey flint and clunch stone building with five dormer windows. This was called Meister Omers and was the superior guest-house for the most wealthy pilgrims. In 1335 Archbishop Stratford instructed the cellarer to reduce his staff, and it may be that one of the two porters at the Aula Nova was dispensed with along with several others. However, in 1400, it was noted that there were twice as many servants as monks, there being some 200 servants. There were twenty-five obedientiaries or officials who lived in their own neighbouring houses. Among these officials was the granger, whose responsibility was the granary. The bartoner supervised the home farm, situated north of Canterbury, where there was a mill for grinding corn and a malthouse. Under the granger was the garnerer who, besides also looking after the granary, was the baker. The beadle was the rent collector, ensuring that the essential tithe rents were paid. In 1304, and again in 1319, the Chapter issued ordinances on lawful measures for both corn and beer; a list of precautions for keeping malt was also drawn up. At the dissolution there were only fifty-three monks of whom twenty-eight joined the new Collegiate establishment; the remainder left with handsome pensions.

Of much less importance than Canterbury was the more rural Hulme Abbey, located on the River Bure, near Ludham, Norfolk. This site was founded in the ninth century and because of the low-lying terrain of the Broads, fishponds were in great evidence. Alongside the river to the south was the brewery, bakery, steward's office and barn. At Furness the large precinct was enclosed with a chapel beside the northern gatehouse. The outer court lay to the north of the claustral buildings with fishponds to the south. The water supply came from the north via elaborate leats, feeding the monks' and lay brothers' accommodation as well as the abbot's house and the guest-house. The stone sluices are still in excellent condition.

Besides the superbly preserved conduit house at Canterbury, other examples exist. At Alnwick Abbey the stone built pyramidal conduit survives, as does that at Mount Grace Priory, North Yorkshire. Set in the western folds of the Cleveland Hills, Mount Grace Priory is less well known than its neighbours Byland Abbey, Newburgh Priory and Rievaulx Abbey, a few miles further south. Founded in 1400 as a Carthusian order for sixteen monks, a sacrist and a prior, a further six monks took up residence twenty years later following an endowment which permitted the building of their cells and a large barn with attached stables. Each monk had a two-storey cell measuring 27 feet square, and each unit had its own walled garden and pentice. The later six were built around the south and east side of the church, while the earlier ones were built around the northern cloister, which measured 272 feet by 231 feet. In the centre of the cloister was a conduit and around its inner edge were a cloister alley and pentice allowing the monks covered access to their cells. On the western side of the outer court were two large guest-houses, divided by a gatehouse and the porter's lodge. Where the northern section of the guest-houses abutted the cloisters with the church, chapter house and prior's cell, the kitchen, bakehouse and brewhouse were situated, all part of the original construction carried out in about 1400. The brewhouse was 'L' shaped, measuring 32 feet by 13 feet, with the stone-built circular copper housing situated on the external wall of a small courtyard. There were few windows but a doorway led into the adjacent bakehouse and another into a storeroom. Forming the infill to the 'L' shape of the brewhouse is an old malthouse kiln, still with its pyramidal stone roof and embattled chimney-stack. In the corner of the cloisters there were two 14-feet square cellars with lofts over them. To the north-east of the great cloister is a stone reservoir and a conduit head known as St John's Well, a circular tank with a pyramidal stone roof a short distance to the south-east of the priory buildings. It fed an octagonal conduit in the centre of the great cloister and lead pipes carried the water supply to each of the monks' cells and other buildings, including the brewhouse, bakehouse and kitchen. In 1450 a few further additions adjacent to the southern stables were made, forming another court between the brewhouse area and the church. After the dissolution the partly demolished buildings and lands came into the ownership of Thomas Lascelles, who transformed the western range of the two guest-houses into a manor-house in 1654. Final additions were made to the northern guest-house by Sir Lowthian Bell in 1901–2. Half a mile away up a steep bank is the Lady chapel which became a place of pilgrimage after the Dissolution. There is evidence of Calvary crosses marked on both the inside and outside walls. The malthouse measured 35 feet by 20 feet wide, but was divided into two rooms by Thomas Lascelles with a wall and two fireplaces, back to back. The entrance door was to the perimeter, and part of the malthouse growing floor area became a part of the residential house. The drainage system and water supply are in an excellent state of preservation at Mount Grace; there is also a mill which was situated in the outer court.

Monks of the Carthusian order lived the most austere of lives, centered around their individual cells. Silence was the order of the day, with food and drink being brought to a small hatch in each cell by a lay brother. On the second floor of each cell there was a workroom, in which each monk carried out varied crafts and trades. The comparatively small church was used less than in other religious orders, the Carthusian monks performing nine acts of prayer in their cells, and attending church three times during the day. Reference has already been made to the guest-house as this was an important feature of all monastic sites. Travellers, especially pilgrims, had often travelled great distances and required accommodation overnight. The more wealthy gentry stayed at the many large estate houses and so the guest-house was there primarily for the common man. Free board and lodging were provided and alms were given to the priory by those able to do so. Endowments came from local landowners and other benefactors, while visits from the wealthy provided a fund from which to pay the poor. Both the brewhouse and bakehouse, often built beside each other, provided for the needs of the visitors.

Mount Grace Priory, Yorkshire; all that remains of the brewhouse chimney.

Farm produce, either from the monasteries' own home farm or given by the local community, eked out the monks' meagre diet and that provided in the guest-house. The guest-house was the forerunner of today's public house.

The classic design of a medieval double courtyard layout may be seen at the St Cross Hospital, Winchester. This was the last remaining location where a horn of beer and a piece of bread was given to travellers, just as all monasteries had done for hundreds of years before. Bishop Henry de Blois, the grandson of William the Conqueror, was born in 1101 and at the early age of twenty-eight, was created Bishop of Winchester; this see he held for forty-two years. He founded St Cross Hospital in 1136, for thirty-five brothers and three nurses, later to be increased to seventy brothers in 1446 by Cardinal Beaufort. The brothers were of 'noble poverty'. In 1350 the master was paid £8 a year and the four priests 13s 4d each, the seven choristers living on the leavings of the master and brethren. The brethren have been dressed since that time in black gowns, bearing the silver cross of St Cross on their chest. A hundred years ago the brethren were inclined to wear an assortment of hats but nowadays, they have returned to wearing their Tudor-style hats. The Hundred-Hall poor were allowed to take home what they did not consume at dinner which consisted of three quarts of small beer, a loaf of bread and two messes. For the brethren, the allowance was four 'Lagenae' of better beer, served in leather jacks. These are still displayed today in a glass cabinet in the Meunes Hall or Brethren's Hall, a large reformatory built in 1336. The hall measures 36 feet by 24 feet and has a raised dais at the east end for the table of officers, those for the brethren are ranged along the sides below four fourteenth-century windows. A fifteenth-century staircase leads to a minstrel's gallery, and at the other end is a window through which the master could observe those in the hall below. Black leather jacks, candlestick holders, salt cellars and pewter dishes, with a bell which was rung to call the Brethren to meals, are all stored in the Hall. Below is a groined cellar in which the beer was stored. Passing through the small outer gatehouse one enters the small outer court, to the left is a clunch stone building, 40 feet long; this is the brewhouse. To the right is the hall and kitchens.

St Cross Hospital, Winchester. The brewhouse seen in relation to the outer courtyard.

Immediately in front, across the cobbled yard and forming the northern side of the outer courtyard, is the imposing Beaufort's Tower built of flint and clunch stone in 1404–47. Beneath it is an arch with a richly groined vault with the Founder's Chamber and muniment room above. The tower leads into the large inner courtyard. On the left-hand side (east) is a low cloister from the sixteenth century, built of brick with a fine oriel window. This ambulatory leads to and connects with the Norman church of St Cross. Facing the ambulatory on the west side are the brethren's houses, with their quaint, tall stone chimneys, one to each house. On the north side (to the right of Beaufort's Tower) is the stepped entrance to the hall and the master's house. Within the archway of Beaufort's Tower is the porter's lodge,

Dole being given to a wayfarer at St Cross Hospital.

from which a daily 'dole' was offered to travellers. This was the last remaining monastic custom of offering free beer and bread to all who called; the usual allocation was two gallons of beer and two loaves a day. This was divided into thirty-two portions, giving a horn of beer and a slice of bread to each wayfarer. A visitor in the late 1890s described her visit thus: 'From an urn shaped vessel [actually a wood firkin cask with six polished hoops] placed in a niche in the wall, the Portress filled two drinking cups – horn, bound with silver – with pale amber coloured beer, and presented them to us with bits of bread about two inches square. "The poor get a whole slice," she said consolingly. The beer was not so bad as to flavour that day, but it was certainly amazingly weak.' This custom has now been carried out for 700 years. It is not known precisely when brewing ceased at St Cross but it was likely to have been around the outbreak of the First World War. The beer for the dole was subsequently supplied by one of the several Winchester breweries and more recently by Marston Thompson and Evershed Ltd who acquired the Winchester Brewery Co. Ltd, at Hyde Street (near the old abbey), in 1923.

St Cross Hospital (a hospice) is situated in the water-meadows of the River Itchen, on the Southampton side of the city. The streams which irrigate the meadows divide into two; one called the Lock Burn leads down behind the brethren's houses, then turns south under the outer court and reconnects with the Itchen. The other stream passes, via sluice gates, behind the brewhouse, from whence liquor was supplied. It then passes on behind the porter's lodge and the ambulatory into the master's garden. Here the stream feeds the old carp fish pond, and then it too joins the River Itchen.

In 1840 there were fifteen recorded maltsters in the city of Winchester and hops were also being grown locally at that time. The production of beer at St Cross Hospital was about twenty barrels per week, and this would have been divided between the first gyle brewing of a stronger beer and the weaker second mashing. Each of the fifteen brethren (the numbers fluctuated) had three quarts of beer per day, and a loaf of bread weighing 1½ lbs. On the 'Gawdy' or 'Extraordinary Days', such as special religious feast days, the brethren had an extra dinner provided of about 45 lbs of roast beef with mince pies and plum broth, a jack of beer (containing 4 gallons), besides 4s among them to buy more beer. The accounts for 1835, when there were only thirteen Brethren, indicate that malt and hops cost £133 5s 0d and brewing cost £8 0s 0d; beer on Gaudy Days cost £1 0s 0d. Coals, which would have been used in the kitchen and as a small allowance given to each brethren for heating, amounted to £15 16s 0d. Income to pay for all the running expenses was derived from numerous tithe rents, largely from neighbouring villages such as Hurstbourn, Whitchurch and Owlesbury with St Faith's Parish in Winchester a major contributor. Even licences for the excellent trout fishing on the River Itchen brought in a small revenue.

Reporting in 1836 the Charity Commissioners observed that the 'Hundred Hall should consist of forty poor men and women, who received soup and a peck of wheat of the home-made bread'. This was made into forty small loaves. They were also to have a barrel of beer every time they brewed for the house, and that women should have one pint of beer. Much earlier, in 1696, the custom was 'that there should be three bushels of malt toll free for every hogshead of beer; and that the Porter was to receive every day from the Butler a cast of bread and three quarts of beer to relieve at the gate such poor persons as come and craved relief there'. This was the 'dole'.

From the foundation of St Cross to about 1350, the staff included the master, thirteen brethren, the steward, thirteen 'clerici', seven choristers, two servants, three bakers, three brewers, one cook and ten other persons. In addition there were eight horses and three carts which suggests that the 'ten other persons', were engaged in farming around the meadows. Certainly within the author's younger days, there was a small dairy herd which grazed the meadows surrounding St Cross and the small ancient farmhouse backed onto the brethren's rear gardens.

A lengthy enquiry commencing in 1372 ensured that the muniments of St Cross Hospital were handed over to the bishop, William of Wykeham, after he had rescued the premises from becoming denegrated. In an ancient portrait of Wykeham, his beloved cathedral is depicted in the left-hand corner and the St Cross Hospital is on the right. It is from Bishop Wykeham that Winchester College boys are known as Wykehamists, in honour of their founder. In 1557, some two hundred years later, the master, Dr Robert Raynolds, contrived to lease away the outer courtyard area consisting of the bakehouse and brewhouse, also the orchards, gardens and closes adjoining, rents of wheat and malt, and a small manor called Ashton. However, John Watson, clerk, later himself to become master, was able to defeat this move. Fortunately for us today he was successful, as otherwise the complete and unspoilt community of brethren would almost certainly have been lost for ever.

On the five Festival days in the year, special food and additional beer was provided, including a pint of stronger (extraordinary) beer to each brethren. On Good Friday, at dinner, a cast (piece) of sliced bread and three pounds of honey were added to their pot of beer and boiled altogether. This they called 'honey sop'. At Christmas every brother had a new gown made for him. On the death of a brother, his silver cross was placed on a cushion at his funeral and afterwards handed by the master to a new entrant. The brothers had their own cemetery. In addition to the Brothers of St Cross who wore black gowns were eight Brothers of the Noble Poverty Foundation who wore a similar style of gown and cap but in a claret colour with a circular silver badge. The brethren's houses, like those of the Carthusians, had two rooms, a pantry and a garden to the rear, where they grew both vegetables and flowers. The tall chimneys are attributed to Cardinal Beaufort (1420) and face the greensward in front of the church. A similar style of hospital accommodation is that of St John's Hospital, Lichfield, with its eight, brick-built chimney-breasts. These date from the Smyths re-foundation in 1495, although a tablet over a doorway is dated 1720.

At Kirkstall Abbey, Yorkshire, the thirteenth-century guest-house had an aisled hall with an open central hearth. A service wing was at the south end, where the detached kitchen had piped water. A drain ran north and then turned west. The service wing was rebuilt in the late thirteenth century as a cross-wing and the brewhouse and bakery were extended. An additional hall was built on the west side for the 'commoner' visitors. During the fifteenth century the guest-house complex was once again improved, with the main hall being rebuilt in stone and the secondary 'commoners' hall converted into a stable and smithy.

The Magna Carta, signed at Runnymede in 1215 beside the River Thames, provided a standard measure for ale besides numerous other statutes. In 1267 Henry III introduced the 'Assize of Bread and Ale' which fixed prices of malt in each town. In London in 1276, small beer was priced at ¼d per gallon with strong ale at 1d per gallon. The assize said: 'no brewster henceforth sell except by true measure, viz. the gallon, the potel and the quart'. There were numerous cases of bending the law as, 'Edith Katys and five others were amerced in the sum of 3d for breaking the assize, also for using cups and other false measures', at the law courts of Hokke Term, Dorset, on 15 May 1397. In Gloucestershire regulations issued in 1520 stated: 'The bruers to sylle XIII gallons of ale for the dozen standing measure, with a cowle sealed by the Meyre. The typlar or sellar of ale shall lett sett at there howses a stone upright, levelled so that the bruar's men shall always sett there cowles sealed to trye truly there measures.' In 1522 the same authority decreed: 'No comon bruear was to tappe non ale within ther owne houses. No typler shall alter any ale which he or they shall receive and by of any brewer, with barns, worte or any wyse.'

Wiltshire's mayor of Wilton made a determined effort to limit the number of brewers and to confine their brewing to certain days of the week. In 1469 he ordained that no one, except common brewers of the Wilton borough, was to brew without a licence. A penalty of 20s could be incurred and had to be paid to the common box. In 1474 Mondays were assigned for brewing to five brewers as were Wednesdays, with Fridays given to alternate groups of two brewers. In 1572 Dorset authorities dictated that brewers were 'to brew with fuel, not with hard or faggot wood, on pain of 5/-'. This would seem to suggest that not only were cottagers clearing wood from local sources for free, but that many home-brewers were doing the same. No doubt this was denuding the countryside of spare wood, the instruction presumably made to ensure that anyone in business had to pay for their requirements. From the same county came a rather strange edict in 1612 which said that no one was to tipple for more than one hour in one house. Perhaps an early incentive for a pub crawl?

An ordinance regarding prices issued at Bristol in the fourteenth century said that: 'beer was to be sold at ½d a gallon when the price of grain was 3/- to 3/4 a quarter for wheat, 1/8 to 2/-

for barley, 1/4 for oats'. Apparently the prices outside the city were slightly lower. In London the Ministry of Brewers cooperated with the mayor, as evidenced by the city Letter Books for 1419: 'Whereas it had been formerly established that no brewer, hosteler, huckster cook, or pyebaker should sell a gallon best beer within their houses for more than 2 pence by marked measure, and outside their houses for more than 1½d, many brewers etc., sell a gallon best beer for 3d, 4d and 5d and by "hanaps", and not by the gallon, potel or quart duly sealed'. Those found guilty were made to forfeit their beer and brewing vessels and be committed to prison.

In the city of Coventry in 1421, John Leeders proclaimed that 'new ale is fixed at 1¼d per gallon; stale ale at 1½d a gallon'. Further enactments regarded the sealing of measures and the setting out of the ale sign, a bunch of ivy or garland on a pole, put out to show that a brewing had been completed. This was known as the 'ale-stake' and would summon the Ale-Conner, or taster. He was appointed by the bailiff and received a gallon of best ale on the detection of any fault in the brewing. Tradition has it that he wore leather breeches and would place a few drops of beer on his wooden bench; he would then sit on it. After quaffing his ale should his breeches stick to the beer-sodden bench on rising, then he knew that sugar had been added, but if there was no sugar in the liquor, then he would not stick to the seat. It was stated before a Parliamentary Committee in 1833 that the position of the Ale-Conner was a 'mere farce'. Despite this, at Northleach in Gloucestershire, Mr John William Sly, town constable, assisted by Mr Harry Barrett, ale taster, were reappointed to their ancient posts by the 'Manorial Court Leet'. This meets once a year to appoint its traditional officials, and in the 1960s the two gentlemen were in their eightieth and seventieth years of age respectively. Harry Barrett commented then that he 'ought to be able to tell a good glass of beer, I can bring fifty-eight years beer-drinking experience to the job!'

One of the earliest inventories that exists for a brewhouse combined with a bakehouse is for the one which was at Prittlewell Priory, Essex. The inventory was made on 8 June 1527 between Sir John Seyntclere, Knight; Humfrey Browne, Francis Jobson and Thomas Myldenoye, Commissioners to the King on the one part, and Thomas Norwiche, pryor.

IN THE BRUEHOUSSE AND BACHHOUSSE

Furste a horsse mylle praysed a		XXs	
Item, a cesterne of leade to watter barley at		XXs	
Item, a yellynge fatte at			VIIId
Item, a messhinge fatte at			VId
Item XIIII helers at		IIIIs	VIId
Item a brynge lead a		VIs	VIIId
Item brasse panne			XXd
Item one bultynge tubbe a knedynge trogh and other vessel at		VIs	VIIId
Item XXII seams matte at VIs VIIId the sealme	VIII	XIIIs	IIIId
Summa IXII		XVIIs	VId
also cartehorsse at XIIIs IIIId a pece			VIIII
Item a horsse at		VIs	VIIId
Item in the Graunge, item IX seame barley at VIs the sealm		IIIIIs	

Monastic life evidently had its attractions to those who lived outside its strict way of life. In the thirteenth century a mason bound himself to serve the Abbey of Winchcome for life, in return for the livelihood of a chief servant. 'When well he feeds at the abbey table, when sick he is entitled to have two monks loaves of 3 lbs each, two noggins of ale, and two dishes from the abbot's kitchen, also a robe like the stewards, two wax candles every night, and four tallow candles a week'.

The office of cellarer was held in high esteem, only second to the abbot. His duties were as the administrator of all the daily needs of the monastic community. He ensured that the farms produced the desired crops and purchased any additional items of food. He maintained the buildings and ensured that all servants employed were duly paid. His prime considerations were the running of the brewhouse and bakehouse and in the smaller communities, he would carry out the work himself. In the priory of St Swithin at Winchester, special prayers were offered up for the cellarer.

Three different qualities of beer were normally brewed. Bona Cervisia, the best beer, was given to important guests in the refectory. Mediocris Cervisia, probably a mild ale and Debilis Cervisia were for the lower grades and servants; this was later defined in the eighteenth and nineteenth centuries as small beer. A fourth grade, known as Skegman, was given to the cook and poor almsmen. Like the 'trencho bread', it was of the poorest quality. Each different official and servant was entitled to varying allowances of beer. In 1240 the cellarer at Worcester was deemed to be entitled to one measure of prime and one of second. 'In the brewhouse four measures of the prime are to be distributed, and two measures on the day on which the ale is to be moved. The servant of the church is to have the holy-water bucket full of "mixta", i.e. part prime and part second, or, it may be, mixture of all three first qualities.' This 'mixta' seems to be the forerunner of the nineteenth-century 'half-and-half' and 'three threads', popular in the north. At Ely Monastery in the time of Henry VI, the priory cook and tailor were allowed a weekly ration of seven measures of Skegman. The carter had seven measures of Mediocris and the keeper of the High Bridge claimed one measure of 'Bona' (the best), whenever the bridge was raised. The washerwoman, it seems, was more highly thought of than the cook, as she had three measures of Mediocris. A bell-ringer, whose job it was to go around the city ringing his bell on solemn anniversaries, received one measure of 'the best'. Bishop Balsham gave his own brewhouse to the monks, somewhere near Queen's Hall, to ease the pressure on the priory's own brewhouse.

Not all brewings were a success. At Dunstable in the year 1262, it was ruefully reported that 'in this year, about the Feast of John the Baptist our ale failed'. Again, twelve years later, the records indicated 'At the Feast of Pentecost our malt failed'. This time the holy fathers were equal to the occasion as they drank five casks of wine, 'and it did us much good'. Plaintive complaints were made in 1515 by the brethren of the monastery at Ely saying 'that by the fault of the monastic brewer, the ordinary ale was so weak that the pigs would not drink of it, and much of what was served was refused'. The brewer had evidently withdrawn the beer which they usually had in the cloister after dinner. He was ordered by the abbot to restore it so that the monks did not slip out into town for beer from alehouses – that was no doubt his greatest worry. In contrast, John of Brokehampton who became abbot of Evesham in 1282, had once filled the office of cellarer, so it was not surprising that during his term of office as abbot, he built both a bakehouse and brewhouse. They were 'not only strongly but sumptuously' built.

Battle Abbey, Sussex, had some thirty Benedictine monks in the late fourteenth century, while during the period from 1500 to 1531, the number had dropped to an average of twenty-four. The cellarer was responsible for providing all the food and drink for the monks, maintaining all the kitchen equipment and drinking utensils. He looked after all the revenues and rents from their own lands (demesne) and oversaw all the staff and servants. St Benedict had suggested an allowance of 1 gallon of wine a day for each monk, imported via the old port of Winchelsea. One of the strange customs of the time was to 'bleed' the monks and nuns for their good health, so it was believed. On these occasions they were provided with extra food and drink. Battle Abbey was predominantly a wine-drinking community, although it had its own brewhouse and cider mill. They also owned their own apple orchards. One of the early accounts of Brother Nicholas, the cellarer at Battle in 1278–9, was 'for binding tankards, 3d. For mending sieves for the bakehouse and brewhouse, 10½d.' Under 'Works' for 1369–70, the cost for scything and gathering the hay was evidently higher than usual, as it was done 'without bread, ale and cheese' and the cost was 65s. In the following year 'For making kindling for the bakehouse and the brewhouse' cost 47s. 'For repairing the brewing mill, 3/4d.' In 1407–8 ale was bought for the haymakers at the cost of 3s 5d. The brewing plant required attention as part of the 'necessary expenses' in 1435–6, when wooden hoops were bought for binding wooden vessels in the brewery, costing 12s 4d and the purchase of one brass ladle cost 1s. Further brewhouse improvements were required in 1512 when John Rycard was paid 3s 8d for 'splitting timber for the great cask in the brewery'.

Abingdon Monastery's cellarer, who was also the brewer, had his 'Oblatam Cervisiae' – a jugful of ale. He was assigned 383 quarters of malt 'to brew for the convent'. In 1440 ale was defined in *Promptorium Parvulorum* as 'cervisia' while beer (bere) is 'cervisia huminulina', that is hopped. Hops are 'sede for beyre'. At Ludlow Parish Church the beautiful dark oak choir pews date from the fourteenth century. One depicts a cellarer with his casks of ale,

One of several misericord seats in Ludlow Parish Church

another shows tuns of wine, a fitting tribute to the medieval brewer. These carvings are on the misericord choir seats. There are a few other churches where similar carvings of the cellarer and his art are to be found. At the parish church of Fairford, Gloucestershire, there are fourteen misericord seats which are believed to have come from the neighbouring Cirencester Abbey at the time of the dissolution in 1540. They were made during the reign of Edward I (1272–1307). One depicts two men either side of a wheatsheaf, one holding a mug of ale in one hand. Another shows a man filling his cup from a barrel while he urges a woman to partake in his beer!

Alewives began to take a more active part in domestic brewing from the early fourteenth century. For example we find that, in 1327 in the Kent town of Faversham, of the 252 tradespeople who paid taxes, 84 were alewives. In Warwick, Alys Brooks, an alewife, was presented at court for selling a gallon of ale 'too little by half a pint'. Bodily punishment was frequently inflicted on offending alewives, as in the case of Mary Somers who was whipped at Lyme in 1653, for selling ale without a licence. The village ducking-stool, a long pole pivotted near the middle with a seat at one end, was where the culprit was tied then dipped into the water of the pond. Stocks were to be found in most villages, but no reports have come to light in which defaulting brewers were locked up in stocks.

The languid River Avon winds its way through the parkland of Lacock Abbey, Wiltshire, which boasts a mixture of architectural building styles, ranging from the medieval, renaissance and eighteenth-century Gothick. Lacock Abbey is probably most famous as the home of William Henry Fox Talbot, one of the pioneers of photography, born in 1800. The early history of the house dates back to its founding in 1291 by Ela, Countess of Salisbury, who endowed two religious houses — one at Hinton Charterhouse for men, and one for women at Lacock some sixteen miles distant — on the death of her beloved husband, William. The abbey was built of local stone quarried near Box and the all-important water supply came from a spring on Bowden Hill: this supply still remains to this day, as does the sixteenth-century conduit. A prioress and fifteen nuns were joined later by Ela, who became the first abbess. She died at the age of seventy-five in 1261. In 1535 the King's Commissioners visited the abbey and found everything in order, it being one of the last to be suppressed in 1539. As with most other religious houses which were dissolved, the nuns were given a

Lacock Priory stable courtyard with the two entrance doors leading into the sixteenth-century brewhouse.

Rear view of the Lacock Priory brewhouse and bakehouse chimney stacks.

The copper and staging of the Lacock brewhouse.

pension and the property sold off, in the case of Lacock to William Sherington for the sum of £783. William had no children and so his brother Henry succeeded him, being knighted by Queen Elizabeth after her visit to Lacock. Henry's youngest daughter Olive married John Talbot of Worcestershire and thus the ownership came down the line of the Talbots with Matilda Theresa, who assumed the name of Talbot in 1918, bequeathing Lacock Abbey to the National Trust in 1944: she died in 1958. William Sherington had artistic talents and was responsible for the retention of many of the monastic buildings still evident today. He also made additions including the stable court, built in about 1540–53. The stable court is to the north of the house which has its frontage facing east, with the old destroyed monastic church and Lady chapel to the south. On the northern wing of the courtyard, beside the clock tower, is situated the complete sixteenth-century brewhouse built of lovely warm-coloured stone in two storeys, with a horizontal string course and drip over the brewhouse doorway. The roof is clad in graduated stone tiles. Set into the roof are three dormer windows with exposed timbers and colour-washed like the top section of the clock tower with its small cupola. Massive stone chimney-breasts are surmounted by tall hexagonal stone chimney-stacks to the outer walls, two of which serve the brewhouse and the adjacent bakehouse. Windows are stone mullioned with diamond-leaded, glazed panes, there are no louvred windows to the brewhouse. The entrance door from the stable court is of heavy timber and nail studded, and opens inward onto a stone flagstone and pebbled floor on two levels. Immediately facing the door is the stone-built

The large valve which discharges the wort from the copper to the cooling tray via a wood channel.

platform with a flight of six stone steps. Built into the corner atop this platform is the circular, rendered stone structure around the copper. To the left of the stone platform a further three steps up give access to the top of the copper, this second staging is of heavy timber. A brass cock near the base of the copper discharges into a wooden channel which in turn allows the wort to precipitate into the shallow cooler. This is built of timber planks on close-set rafters, the sides of the trough supported by tapered wooden pegs set into the ends of the joists. The inside of the cooler is lined with lead. Level with the top of the lead cooler is a window to the rear wall and it is possible that in the past this would have been made of wood louvres to allow the heat and steam to dissipate. Set immediately below the cooler, which is on wood stilts, is a coopered fermenting vat, set on stone blocks in a recessed floor area. This allows for any overspill of yeast and for washing down after cleaning, allowing the discharge to run into a grilled drain in the outside rear garden. This grill is in the corner beside the stone-built platform to the copper. The fermenting tun has a brass cock which also discharges into the lower floor level. To the left of the copper an internal doorway leads to another room, situated beneath the clock tower, and it is most likely that this was the malt and hop storeroom. Brewing probably took place here until at least the eighteenth century and possibly later. The first floor above the brewhouse was originally hay lofts and it is lucky that no fires spread from the brewhouse furnaces below, probably good testimony to the excellent craftsmanship put into the building of this range of outbuildings some 450 years ago.

A lead-lined cooling tray rests above the coopered fermenting vat.

Corn produced on the demesne, or accrued to the convent by way of rent or tithe, was in the charge of the granger who was responsible for distributing it to the baker, brewer and largerer, to be made into bread, ale and pottage. The convent owned fishing rights on the River Avon and also had a fish pond at Heddington, but dried and salt-water fish were bought in bulk from Bristol, Salisbury and Southampton (large quantities required at Lent). In 1476 the nuns owned 2,000 sheep at Chiltern, and they also had 300 hogs. Wool was a major source of revenue and there were fulling mills at Bishopstrow and Hatherop.

The bridge at Southwark was the lowest crossing point on the River Thames in London and consequently there were many inns in the vicinity. Among these was the Tabard, made famous by Chaucer in his *Canterbury Tales*. A William Kyng and his wife Cassandra, with Thomas Wente, 'being jointly seized of a brewhouse in the Borough, sold it together with another messuage and certain goods in the same to one Thomas Warham for £68 13/4d'. An inn called the Peacock and also the Moon in the parish of St George were leased for forty years from Easter 1436 to John Stanley, a citizen and brewer of London, the rent being £3 6s 8d per annum. Stanley being thus seized of the tenement 'with certyn ledus and brewyng vessell in the same', sublet from Easter 1440 to Thomas Muddle of Southwark, brewer, and Felicia his wife, rent this time was £5 16s 8d. In the same borough of Southwark, a Henry Leake owned the Dolphin and the Bear, with their attached brewhouses, in 1554. In his will made in 1560, he stipulated that he should be buried in St Olave's with money going to a free school. His son, also named Henry, employed eighteen aliens when he was permitted to employ only four. A list of Sussex aliens made in 1465 mentioned the Flemish brewer Dirik Berebrewer. Southwark and the south coast were logical areas for Flemish brewers to live. They not only brought with them the names of cask sizes, still used today, but also the use of hops. John Brabon had a brewhouse in Hastings called The Rosares, where he produced an excellent and much appreciated beer, so much so, that when the bailiffs of the Cinque Ports visited Yarmouth, they took a supply of his beer with them. Not all brewers' efforts were so appreciated, however, for in Yarmouth, John Brett, who had recently erected a brewhouse and malthouse in 1609, received complaints. It was said that his buildings were a fire risk, but more importantly that 'the liquor out of the Bourne below the Courthouse wher with he breweth and yeateth his malt in them, is very corrupt and unwholesome for mans' body. It is ordered therefore that henceforth he shall not sett up any pull gally to take up water there but the same shall be taken downe. And he is further injoyned not to use

The main entrance door to the brewery beneath the viewing gallery, and the interconnecting door to the store and the furnace room.

in brewing or yeating any of the Bourne water between the south corner of the George and the sea, upon paine of 100*s*.' Not a very auspicious start for a new brewery.

Somerset Justices of the Peace called all tipplers in 1613 and instructed them to sell according to the Winchester standard measures. These dated from Henry VII and Elizabeth I and are now kept in the Westgate Museum at Winchester. In 1615, at the General Sessions held at Taunton on 11–14 July, the court ordered that 'our innkeeper or ale house keeper should brew any beer or ale to sell again, but that they take the same from the common brewers, viz. Robert Hill, John Thompson, Tristram Gardner and Michael Smalls, who were to make good wholesome beer at 3*d* per gallon – the barrels to be marked on their heads how much they contain'. This edict seems to suggest that the publican brewers were all having trouble with the quality of their brews. It may also have been a reflection on the actual quantities that they were racking. In Berkshire the Justices issued instructions in 1579 which indicated that a heavy fine of 10*s* would be imposed: 'for every pot of liquor was ordered to be levied on all innkeepers, vintners and victuallers who should brue in his howse any Beere or Ale to be sold, offered or drunke in his Howse, either by the pinte potte, quarte potell, or gallon potte'. The increase of incorrect measures for selling beer was a constant problem. It is clear that many innkeepers and brewhouse keepers attempted to get away with defrauding their customers. John Dorkynge of Harting, Sussex, was fined in 1402 for 'selling ale by the bowl, or dish, instead of in official stamped measure'. Henry

Cobeliay, also of Sussex, was one of several hikkesters, or beer-sellers as opposed to brewers, who kept 'cappelboothes'. He was sent to court for using false measures and 'commonly selling food' and drink: he was evidently a travelling beer-seller, visiting such places as fairgrounds.

Taxes have loomed throughout the last five hundred years, especially within the licensed trade. Nicholas Michell, mayor of Coventry, levied a tax of 4d on a quarter of malt, to pay for the building of the city wall in 1367. The taxing on malt was the matter of collecting tax from all sources of brewing for a long period of time. Again, at Rye, Sussex, in 1456: 'That every ale brewer of the town of Rye shall answer gader and pay the "Maltode" [tax] off all such ale as thei shall brewe and delyver to the hikkester to the said maltster during the said yere upon payne and lesynge of the said brethyrne he that doth the contrarie. Also the beer brewer which bryngyn bere to the said town of Rye shall pay for maltode off every hole bune bere 2d.' At Dover it was decided that the best way to pay for the building of the harbour in 1557 was to levy a local tax. Since 1657, Revenue Officers have been empowered to enter, search and gauge all brewing vessels. Even to this day, a brass plate fitted to the top rim of vessels permits accurate assessments of quantities brewed. All brewing vessels are required to be initialled according to their function. Hops were imported to Poole from Holland in the sixth year of the reign of King Edward IV (1467) by Adryan Cornelis, who imported six 'pokis' of hops valued at £1 for which he paid 1s in subsidy and 3d in customs duty. The export of beer in the reigns of Elizabeth and James received a levy of 1d per kilderkin.

The king granted the Carmelite friars the right to found a priory at Hitchin, Hertfordshire, in 1317. The convent was dedicated to the Blessed Mary until its dissolution in 1539. The mansion house was repaired but the remainder of the buildings, including the church, were in a poor state of repair with the bells, glass and lead all removed. The estate was granted to Sir Edward Watson after the dissolution and seven years later it passed to Ralph Radcliffe who died in 1559, leaving it all to his heir, his eldest son Ralph. It then passed via three Edwards until 1727, then via two John Radcliffes, the last one dying in 1783. On his death the priory passed to his eldest sister, Penelope, the wife of Sir Charles Farnby of Kent, who assumed the name of Radcliffe. Penelope died without issue so her heir, her niece Anne Millicent, inherited and married Emilius Henry Delme who also assumed the name of Radcliffe. His eldest son, Henry Delme Radcliffe, predeceased him so the priory devolved at his death in 1832 to his second son, Frederick H. Peter Radcliffe.

The house stands to the south of the lovely ancient town of Hitchin and part of the premises incorporates White Friars, built of original flint rubble and clunch stone with the church on the south side. The house as it exists today was built mainly in about 1770–1 by John Radcliffe around a courtyard which has on the north and west wings many of the original cloister arches. Under the north wing there are cellars and incised in shields set into the spandrels of an open arcade are the initials RRS and the date 1679. The north elevation of the house was of the popular eighteenth-century Palladian style. In the south chapel of the parish church there is a large monument to Ralph Radcliffe, 1559, with another Ralph dated 1621, Sir Edward Radcliffe, 1631, and Edward, 1660. There are also other members of the family buried in the vault.

A family record book records 'The Stock of Beer in the Sellers at the Priory April ye 24, 1773': Ale 23 pipes, Small Beer 18 pipes.

Another handwritten book records the days of brewing between the years 1771 and 1780, and the quantity of malt and hops used to produce 2 pipes of ale and 2 pipes of small beer. It is apparent that 40 bushels of malt were used in each brewing, but that the quantities of hops used were consistently an average of 28 lbs for the years 1771 to 1776, while from 1777 onwards the hops were increased to 37 lbs per brewing. The records were signed by one William Knight, almost certainly the brewer, and it is interesting to note the near one-third increase in hops, denoting a marked preference for a stronger bitter-flavoured beer.

High Down, Pirton, also within the old Hitchin Hundred, was later owned by Mr F.A. Delme Radcliffe. The old manor-house stands on high ground and was built in about 1504, this date and the arms of Docwra appear on the north-east gable. Thomas Docwra Miles was the prior of the Order of St John of Jerusalem. A further coat of arms of Thomas Docwra and the date 1599 is on the south side of the house, also on the entrance gateway to the stables is the date 1613. The house is of two storeys, built of rendered flint and clunch stone, with a gabled porch and a courtyard with outbuildings forming the north and western boundary. The entire northern range of outbuildings are devoted to stables with an archway midway between, and the coach-house backing onto the larger stable block. Linking the stables at right angles was the western range consisting of a large brewhouse, which also abutted the house beside the ground floor morning-room. The size of the brewhouse suggests that it produced beer for a large number of servants and farmworkers, and the household, and it may well be that other farms were also supplied. The high standing of the Delme Radcliffe family was maintained when Mr Henry Eliot Delme Radcliffe was elected exhibitioner on 19 June 1851 and scholar of Queen's College, Oxford, on 22 November 1855.

Saint Francis of Assisi sent a mission to England in 1224 consisting of a band of nine Grey friars, as they were popularly known, who landed at Dover in that year. The friars were unable to hold any personal wealth and lived in the poorest part of towns. King Henry III ordered the payment of 40s towards the fabric of the church which suggests that the Friars were still building their church dedicated to St Francis. The friary was founded just outside the Bridgnorth town boundary, close to the River Severn and the bridge which had St Sythes Chapel upon it. By 1272 the friars were evidently in trouble with the town borough council for depositing rubbish into the river. This was to reclaim land for their own use, probably to be used as vegetable gardens. Ten years later the friary received the gift of six oak trees, suggesting that construction was still under way. By this time there were now some fifteen friars who, by 1303, had constructed the town's water supply of a conduit of spring water which terminated at the friary.

On the dissolution of the monasteries, King Henry VIII's commissioner for 'Visitation and Suppression of Friaries' visited Bridgnorth in the August of 1538 and reported that: 'he had taken into the King's hands the Grey Friers of Bridgnorth, which is the poorest house he has seen, and not worth 10 shillings a year, and all the houses are falling down'. In the certificate of surrender signed by Thomas Hall and Randolph Rodes, the inventory included details of the brewhouse which had a fixed furnace, a mash-tub and a brass pan or cooler. In 1540 the contents were sold and a lease of the remaining buildings was granted to Nicholas Holt. On

18 July 1544 the house was granted in fee to John Beaumont. Until 1795 the property had continued to become dilapidated and then changed hands once more, becoming an alehouse called the Malthouse. There is some evidence that the old refectory of the friary had also been used as a malthouse, as medieval floor tiles and perforated malting tiles were discovered. During the 1860s several of the ancient buildings were demolished for the Carpet Manufacturing Company. In the early nineteenth century an appropriately named inn known as The Old Friars opened a few yards away from the friary site. It would appear from an inscription which was posted outside the door, that this alehouse brewed its own beer.

> *I am a friar of orders Grey,*
> *Who lived in the Friary over the way,*
> *Tho' my Friary's gone I still have a cheer,*
> *Come in and taste our Bridgnorth Beer,*
> *And still keep temperate with the same,*
> *Nor bring this house to evil fame.*

Also in the lovely county of Shropshire one of Shrewsbury town's grandest medieval houses was once a brewhouse. William Rowley was born in 1572 and during his lifetime he became one of Shrewsbury's eminent tradesmen, being made a burgess in 1594, thus one of the town's

Rowley's brewhouse and wool store, Shrewsbury.

governing elite. Taxation records from 1297 indicate that Shrewsbury had many brewers and maltsters, with seven out of the twenty-two named brewers in 1306 being women. The population at this time was between 2,500 and 4,000 and the production of ale amounted to 13,000 gallons a year. In the 1630s Rowley rented a large three-storeyed gabled building, now known as Rowley's House, from the Drapers' Company, of which he was master. This magnificent timber-framed building was used as a wool warehouse and brewery, and as his brother had a malting business at Worfield, some twenty miles downstream on the River Severn, it is more than likely that William Rowley purchased his malt from him. The malt would be brought up river in the Severn Trows and carted to William's brewhouse. The River Severn had been used as a major transport artery since Roman times. The only description of Rowley's brewhouse to have survived said that it was 'a very vast, great brewhouse, the brewing vessels wherein are capable of 100 measures'. William Rowley died in 1645, but the house to which he gave his name was opened as a museum in 1931, following the clearance of many nearby dilapidated buildings under the supervision of the Borough Surveyor, Mr Arthur W. Ward.

The early forms of power which brewers harnessed were, of course, horses. To raise water from deep wells was one of their primary jobs and for this purpose 'horse-gins' were constructed. These took a number of forms, either the horse walking around a circular track of about 15 feet in diameter, or else walking inside a large vertical drum. The open horse-gin required the horse to be harnessed to a pole which turned a central cog wheel and drum, thus winding up a water bucket. The winding-up system was also used for lifting sacks of malt and hops to upper storage floors. With some refinements, this power could also grind the malt to form grist. An example of this type of horizontal horse-gin was to be seen at the Linden Tree, Lichfield, Sussex. Only the track remains, with some of the brewery buildings. The second horse powered system of walking inside a large drum wheel, exists at Berden Priory, a private farmhouse in Essex.

Berden Priory is an Augustinian timber-framed house built in the late sixteenth century on the site of a twelfth century priory of the Austin canons, with a seventeenth-century weatherboarded malthouse with a timber frame. Standing some 50 feet from the main house is a black bitumen painted timber well-house built in the seventeenth century. The roof is of handmade red clay tiles and has two pitches, the highest, some 7 feet wide, houses a treadmill. There are four windows, two to each side, with either vertical or horizontal wooden mullions; a door is at the opposite end to the treadmill. This is 15 feet in diameter and constructed of oak. The heavy central spindle is continued to a supporting curved cross-beam with an open slatted drum above the well itself, on which a rope would be wound to draw up a bucket. Nearest the entrance door there is a lead-lined trough measuring 3 feet wide by 7 feet 6 inches long and 10 inches deep and supported on brick piers, at a height of 1 metre. From the brick well with its wooden covers, a dished shute discharges water into the shallow tank. The depth of the well varies. Recent readings record that in June 1991 it was 108 feet deep, in October 1992, 115 feet deep, in June 1993, 103 feet 6 inches and on 24 March 1994 it was 96 feet 5 inches deep. The floor is constructed of small Tudor red bricks, the treadmill and walls are all of oak. Judging by the width of the wheel and the limited access to it, it would appear to have been powered by a donkey. The overall measurements of the building are 20 feet wide by 22 feet 5 inches long and the entire structure remains in a very good condition. A donkey treadmill was also to be seen at the Fox & Hounds, Beauworth, Hants.

A horizontal horse-gin previously at the Linden Tree home-brew pub.

In addition to horsepower was the use of water power. This too has been in use until recent times by several small breweries. Still in situ, and in working order, are water-wheels at J.C. & R.H. Palmers' Old Brewery, Bridport, Dorset. This family firm was founded in 1794 and remains independent today, running sixty-eight tied houses. It is the only brewery in the UK today that can boast that it still uses a bottling hall with a thatched roof. The Donnington Brewery at Stow-on-the-Wold, Gloucestershire, another staunchly independent firm, has its delightful old brewery buildings, some dating to the thirteenth century, beside the mill pond. This lake supplies the power to the water-wheel and, with the mellow Cotswold stone buildings set in a small valley, this is surely the loveliest little brewery in the country. The brewery serves seventeen public houses, now one of the very few small common brewers left, with ties going back centuries.

Burton-on-Trent, in Staffordshire, is this country's capital of brewing. It can trace its brewing links back to the founding of the Benedictine monastery in AD 1002. Saint Modwen is credited with its foundation in the seventh century, an Irish abbess who had her abbey sacked by the Danes in 870. The new monastery was on a new site on the west bank of the River Trent, the founder, Wulfric Spot, a descendant of King Alfred. The first abbot and a few monks came from St Swithin's Priory, Winchester, which also has strong connections with King Alfred. The Burton abbot was a secular lord who collected the taxes in the diocese. In 1295, Matilda, daughter of Nicholas de Shobenhale (a district of present-day Burton is named Shobnell, renowned for over a hundred years for its vast malthouses), released to the abbot and convent certain tenements and interests within and without the

The vertical horse-gin wheelhouse at Berden Priory Farm, Essex.

town. Matilda had the hereditary keepership of the abbey gate and, in lieu of her surrendering this, 'she was granted daily for life, two white loaves from the monastery, two gallons of the convent beer, and one penny, besides seven gallons of beer for the men'.

The cellarer was suspended for a year in 1498 for failing to keep satisfactory records. In the same year the bishop forbade visits to 'taverns and other suspect places in Burton'. Forty-three years previously Abbot Henley resigned, no doubt with suitable pressure from the bishop, for gaming, drunkenness and absence from the monastery services – it couldn't have got much worse. Following these misdemeanours, the abbot had to ensure that the gates were locked to prevent women visiting. St Cross Hospital continues the practice of closing its gates every evening, perpetuating similar ancient customs. The staff at Burton Abbey consisted of the abbot, prior, sub-prior, precentor, sacrist, cellarer, kitchener, chamberlain, infirmerer, hospitaller, almoner, pittancer and martyrologer. By the fifteenth century a third prior, the precentor, sacrist and cellarer each had a deputy. Abbot Wallingford made new grants to the cellarer for 300 loaves and 200 gallons of ale, 600 herrings from the kitchen for alms on the anniversary of founder Wulfric Spot. In the early thirteenth century Abbot Lawrence had a 'house of stone next to the church for the reception of the poor', the almonry.

At the dissolution of the monasteries brewing was carried out in the alehouses of the town of Burton. Possibly the cellarer and his helpers found financial benefits from their brewing skills. From these early brewing experiences eventually grew the fine traditions which Burton upholds today. Benjamin Wilson is credited with the founding of his small business in

1742 in the High Street. His early plans for brewing 1,000 barrels a year soon exceeded this as, with the help of the Trent Navigation Act, the canal was able to transport beer to the eastern port of Hull. From here the beer was shipped to London and also to the Baltic countries of Russia, Poland, Sweden, Norway and Germany. By 1774, Wilson's orders to St Petersburg alone had exceeded 600 hogsheads in a year. William Bass, who was a local carrier, soon spotted a way to make his fortune and in 1777 he changed his profession to brewing. The *Derby Mercury* records that on 10 May 1765, William Bass advertised his house for letting. Samuel Allsopp, another of the great Burton brewers, inherited the Wilson's brewery through the marriage of his father to Benjamin Wilson's daughter. This was typical of the way that brewing families intermarried and also built up the great brewing empires – the forerunners of the large common brewers. Today Bass and Carlsberg/Tetley (in Burton the old Ind Coope who acquired Allsopps) are now international brewing companies. With their success in mind, a last word from St Benedict as to the way the cellarer should be. 'One who is wise, mature in character, sober not given to too much eating . . . not prodigal. . . . All the utensils of the monastery and all its substance, he shall look upon as though they were the sacred vessels of the altar.'

Brewing did not cease at all monasteries during the dissolution. At Ely Cathedral the verger, William Sotherby, brewed Dean & Chapter Ale. His brewhouse was in the lower part of the Ely Porta (gatehouse) in the mid-nineteenth century. Special brews were made for dinners given by the Dean and Chapter at two great annual gatherings at the time of audit. This cathedral brewing was abolished in 1858 by Dean Harvey when it was decided to hand the Ely Porta gatehouse over to the King's School. From then onwards the Dean and Chapter

A GOOD JUDGE.

THE MONKS' RETREAT.
A Unique Bar (part of a 12th Century Benedictine Monastery).
The Most Curious Bar in England.

FLEECE HOTEL,
GLOUCESTER.

took their beer supplies from Burton brewers. King Henry VIII instructed his commissioners at the time of the dissolution to make surveys, plans and inventories of all the monastic sites that he took over. At Wilberfoss in the Vale of York, the Benedictine nunnery had mostly timber buildings to the inner court, where a combined brewhouse and bakehouse measured 22 feet long by 16 feet wide. Also in Yorkshire at Rievaulx Abbey the plan drawn up in 1538–9 shows a detached brewhouse to the north of the cloister, with a kiln house between it and the access road. Further north was the corn mill and a guest-house, with a well-house and the stables to the north-east. To the west of the cloister was a tannery and on the south west a fulling mill. The brewhouse was large, measuring approximately 75 feet long by 30 feet wide.

There were at least eleven breweries that were named Abbey Brewery, and a few more that took ecclesiastic names. Such was the case of the Hyde Abbey Brewery at Winchester, built just opposite the old Hyde Abbey. Adjacent to the abbey was the Winchester Brewery company, now the local depot of Burton brewers Marstons. Two other small brewers, one Mrs Sarah Smoker, a retail brewer, were situated in Hyde Street. There are still several large remains of this once royal abbey.

Ireland's oldest brewery was Joseph Watkins & Co, Dublin, erected on the site of what was formerly the brewhouse of the Monastery of St Thomas. Mention of this was made in the year of the Magna Carta, 1215, when grants of land were made to the abbots of this order down to the period of the dissolution of the religious houses. The abbey at this time was granted to Sir William Brabazon, Knt. who was Vice-Treasurer and General Receiver of Ireland up to his death in 1552. The family gave a permanent lease of the brewery site to certain persons whose interest was thence invested in the firm of Joseph Watkins & Co. The monks of St Thomas are known to have brewed their own beer. In the 'Pot and Close Roll Chancery, Ireland, 1583 (16 Henry VIII)' there is the record of an award in which the mayor and alderman of the city sued the abbot for the duty on his home-brewed beer. In the lease from the Meath family, dated about 1627, part of the premises demised consisted of 'brewhouse, malthouse and mill'. Towards the close of the nineteenth century the brewery was owned by Messrs Taylor and Trevor and then in the early part of the twentieth century it came into the hands of Richard and Joseph Watkins, who came over to Ireland from England. The old crypt of the monastery was used as storage cellars by the brewery and consisted of several vaulted areas which could store up to 5,000 casks.

> *Jolly friars tippled here,*
> *Ere these abbey walls had crumbled:*
> *Still, the cellars boast good beer,*
> *Still, the ruins boast good cheer,*
> *Tho', long ago the cloister tumbled,*
> *The monks are gone, well well,*
> *But that's all one, let's ring their knell:*
> *Ding Dong! Ding Dong! to the jolly old monk*
> *He set the example, we'll follow the sample.*

In 1904, Joseph Watkins & Co merged with Jameson, Pinn & Co., North Anne Street Brewery, also in Dublin, who were founded in about 1715. This amalgamation formed the firm of Watkins, Jameson Pinn & Co Ltd who closed the oldest brewing site in Ireland in 1937.

A portion of the present Abbey Brewery of William Younger, Edinburgh, dates back to 1600 when it was owned by John Blair, a brewer to the nearby Holyrood Palace in the time of Prince Charlie. These, with other buildings, were acquired by the founders of the firm of Wm. Younger & Co. and altered to present-day brewing requirements and named as the Abbey Brewery. The monks of the old abbey of Holyrood were famed for their nut-brown ale.

This review on medieval brewing was begun by looking at Canterbury Cathedral in some detail. We now return to Canterbury for a last look where a unique 'modern' brewery was situated in monastic buildings. Appropriately named Alfred Beer & Company's Original Brewery, this company's origins dated from the 1770s. A Mr Hill converted parts of the St Augustine's Monastery gatehouse into a brewhouse. A local writer in 1794 complained that: 'so little veneration is paid at this time to the remains of this once sacred habitation that the principal apartments adjoining the gateway are converted into an alehouse, the gateway itself into a brewhouse, the steam of which has defaced the beautiful paintings over it; the great yard is turned into a bowling green; the chapel and aisle of the church on the north side into a fives court and the great room over the gate into a cock-pit'.

Two years later the son of the founder, John Hill, was the brewer, who early in the nineteenth century went into partnership with John Saunders Bennett. Soon afterwards Hill was replaced by William Beer, who at that time was a grocer in Canterbury. On 16 December 1826 this later partnership was dissolved and William Beer took full ownership of Saint Augustine's Brewery. As a common brewery it owned some eighteen public houses, but

St Augustine's Priory gatehouse, formerly used as a brewery.

under the energetic ownership of William Beer, trade increased. However, all was not well, for in a religious newspaper in 1843 mounting opposition was voiced about the siting of the brewery. Following this moralistic rhetoric, it was sold a year later to Mr A. J. Beresford-Hope, MP, who returned the premises to its original religious purposes. In the last few years the entire site has been occupied by Canterbury King's School as an extension to their premises in the Cathedral Close.

A malthouse was in operation in 1290, adjacent to the gatehouse, which was completed in 1309. The gatehouse measures 63 feet high, 35 feet wide, with a depth of 40 feet. To the right-hand side was a small prison and adjacent to it was a chapel. To the south of the gatehouse was the Pilgrim's guest-house, kitchen and offices built in the later thirteenth to early fourteenth centuries. The almshouse or hospital outside the precincts near the gateway was where the daily dole of bread and ale was handed out. The earliest record of the monastic brewhouse at St Augustine's is in 1267, when Kyngesnorth gave endowments for altering the brewery and bakehouse and for building a new bathhouse. All three buildings were mentioned again in 1432 when the brewer was paid £1 13s 4d a year, and the baker and bathhouse keeper were paid £1 6s 8d each. Clearly the brewer had the best job. A grace cup, fashioned from a coconut on a round pedestal and mounted in silver, dates from 1505. Inscribed on the silver rim are these prophetic words: 'Velcom ye be, dring [drink] for Charite.' During the installing of Abbot Fyndon (1283–1309) a great banquet was held at which six thousand guests attended. There were 58 casks of beer valued at £17 10s 0 d and 11 tuns of wine, costing £24 0s 0d; the total cost of the banquet was £287 7s 0d. At the dissolution there were only thirty monks left and these mostly became local officials. Today the two monastic sites in Canterbury are both used by the King's School scholars, continuing to uphold a part of the ancient traditions of this fine city.

SEATS OF LEARNING

Oxford University proudly proclaims the earliest founding of a college, this being University College in 1249. The Assize of Ale in 1251 regulated the price of beer – in towns it was to be 1*d* for 2 gallons and in the country districts about half this price. Throughout many succeeding centuries following this decree, edicts are made by the chancellors of the university to control malt and beer prices. Oxford Castle, situated beside the river, had its own brewhouse, as recorded by Wood in his *City of Oxford* in 1267. This area was the later site of several small breweries.

In 1254 a minor tiff between a scholar and a taverner over a quart of wine turned into a fisticuffs and the lengthy divide between 'Town and Gown' was established. The outcome of the affray was that the chancellor of the university was granted complete authority by the king for the supervision of the assize of bread, ale and wine and all victuals to the exclusion of any interference from the mayor. It is fascinating to note that one hundred years after the assize of 1251, the price of beer remained the same.

On 22 February 1513 the university vice-chancellor held a court meeting at the Brewers' Corporation master's house to impose certain regulations upon the city brewers. Evidently these rules were insufficient as twelve years later he ordained that there should only be sixteen brewers in the city. Thus the Brewers' Guild was imposing a monopoly and keeping out newcomers, much to the dissatisfaction of the university authorities. A complaint had it thus: 'that Mychaell Hethe and other of the brewers of Oxford, will let no-man entre into the crafte'. An enactment 'Made that at a court holden in the house of Robert Donham, master of the craft or occupation of brewers in Oxford the 22 of February in the 4th yere of the reigne of King Henry the Eight it was enacted, established and statuted for everymore hereafter, that if any bruer of Oxford which hath refused or else hereafter doe refuse to brue, and give over his house by the space of a hole yere and afterward will take a brue house and a bryw againe within the towne of Oxford, and the surburbes of the same, or else if that bruer in time of derth of malte doe refuse and will not brew, and afterwards in time of good cheap of malt will take uppon him to bryw againe that then the person or persons so taking upon them to bryw shall first make such fyne to the occupation of bruers aforesaide as the hole body of the said occupation or the more part of them shall putt to him, of forfetor and losse XL's for every borden or brywinge made to the contrary, halff thereof to be applied to my Lord Chancellor of the Universite or his commissary for the tyme beinge, and X's parcell of the other halfe to the use and profytt of the sayd occupation of bruers and X's the residue thereof to be applied into the use of the master and wardens of ye saide occupation for the time being.

In witness whereof etc.'

Another annoying restriction for the brewers of Oxford came in 1568 when they were required to have their malt ground at the old Castle Mill and not at their own malthouses. Seventeen articles were implemented on 4 February 1571 for the Company of Brewers, of which the most important was that, 'No customer, typler or hucster may lend, sell, brake, or cutt any brewers vessell or put therein any other ale or beere then of ye owners, of the same vessell, under the payne of 3*s* 4*d* to the fellowship of the brewers'. Another said that: 'None but freemen may brewe ale or bere under payne of forfeyture of their drinke to the Baylives and 40's to the company.' The Brewers' Corporation was confirmed by a seal on 16 February 1571 with the town clerk appointed as the solicitor in the following year. Despite this edict the Oxford brewers still remained under the authority of the university, for example in 1574, the chancellor, who was the Earl of Leicester, ordered that ale was to be sold for 3*d* a gallon. The formation of the Brewers' Corporation was not a success as there was mistrust of it from all sides, and it ceased in May 1575. It was seen as 'newly devysed to the disturbance of the liberties of the University, is and hath bin one of the chief and original causes of the variance and strife betwixt the Universite and citie'. With the dissolution of the Brewers' Guild, the university authorities continued to set the price of ale. In May 1579 the vice-chancellor instructed that the best strong ale should be sold at 3*s* 4*d* a kilderkin, best double beer at 3*s*, best single at 1*s* 6*d*. The retail price per gallon was to be 4*d*. Continued commands came from the university regarding prices, but perhaps more galling was the restriction that brewing was to be done only on certain days. One brewer, Thomas Smith, was imprisoned in the castle for disobeying this instruction.

Once again the price of beer was altered, this time in 1615 by Dr Goodwin the vice-chancellor, who ordered that a barrel of double beer was to cost 10*s*, while a quarter of ale was priced at 5*s* 4*d*. Sixty years later Vice-Chancellor Bathurst issued a notice on 22 June 1676 noting that unwholesome beer and ale was due to the lack of sufficient boiling of the wort, giving a 'mixture of crude and sweet with bitter wort, both become less wholsome for men's body'. His instruction was that all brewers, as from 24 June, 'they and every of them well and sufficiently boyle or cause to have boyled all their several worts for the making of Double Beer, Middle Beer and Ale'. Licences to sell ale were also issued by the university. They were frequently granted to bedells and college servants, also booksellers, in order to increase the profits of their trades. The holders were required to give sureties that they would not allow gambling, nor permit the eating of meat on fasting days. Numerous occasions occurred following the granting of licences by the mayor when the university chancellor directed that innkeepers and wine sellers were to cease trading. William Potter at 'the sign of the Bear', was instructed by the bedell on 16 September 1619 to take down his sign. On 21 September 1620 the vice-chancellor issued a prohibition to the mayor (Oliver Smith) restraining him from granting a licence to the above named William Potter. He subsequently surrendered his licence to the registrar of the vice-chancellor's court. Among the university employees granted tavern licences were Edward Wainwright, cook at Magdalen College, and Richard Cornyshe, cook at Queen's College on 30 January 1567. In the same year Thomas Crane, a servant of Dr Barber of All Souls received his tavern licence. In 1596, the University stationer, Henry Miller, was granted a tavern licence.

The university exercised extensive rights over many trades in the city of Oxford including carriers, carpenters, booksellers and bookbinders, parchment sellers, leather sellers, bakers, innkeepers and vintners and of course brewers of ale and beer. In the last category were included brewers' clerks and some workmen. Thus in 1585 it is found that William Longe was admitted as a brewer's clerk to Giles Swete, bailiff of St John's College. In 1617, both William Prichett and Robert Carpenter were admitted 'workman-foreman-brewer'. A William Carpenter was admitted 'ale-brewer's clerk' in 1622, as was John Cumber on 25 January in the same year.

Prices featured again in November 1701 when Roger Mander, the vice-chancellor, issued his orders 'that no public Ale Brewers nor Beer Brewers within the precincts of this University, presume to sell their Double Beer or Ale for more than ten shillings the Barrel (besides the duty of Excise) and so proportionately for any other vessel'. So here is noted again a period of nearly one hundred years without any price increases.

Many of the brewers of Oxford have been recorded over the years, the earliest known was Ralph in 1240. In 1380 there were no less than thirty brewers; twenty years later we know that John Sprant brewed in Shoe Lane. He was fined for throwing rubbish into the street, despite him being a wealthy brewer owning property in two parishes. In the mid-fifteenth century there was Alice Bedale and Alice Everarde, both brewsters. Another brewster was Agnes Treders, but there were several men such as John Clif, John Keele, Robert Wode, John Wilmott, John Walker, Henry Ffelipe, William Hans, Richard Coore, John Belymasone, John Shymere and Henry Barwicke. A number of these had violated the assize by making weak or unwholesome beer and had been recorded for posterity. In 1460 Robert Heath was known as one of the chief brewers of the city and in Henry VIII's time, the best known was George Havile whose brewhouse was in Broad Street. Robert Heth's brewhouse was called Trill Mill Hall and was mentioned in 1504 and 1525. Several of these brewers became eminent citizens of Oxford, no less than fourteen were mayor between 1603 and 1650, with others becoming bailiffs. A number of Oxford maltsters also held both posts during the seventeenth century, clearly the brewing and malting trades were well in favour. A small brewery situated near the castle on an island called the Swan's Nest – where the city probably kept a flock of swans bred for the table – was in existence in 1718 according to deeds held by Hall's Brewery who acquired the Swan's Nest Brewery. Hall's in their turn were taken over by Samuel Allsopp & Sons, Burton, in 1926. The brewery was demolished in the last ten years. This same Swan's Nest Brewery had been in the ownership of Sir John Treacher who was also appointed an alderman and mayor. In 1793 there was a meeting of the bursars of the colleges to discuss taking into consideration the advance of 2s per barrel-load on beer by the Oxford brewers. Among these brewers were Sir John Treacher, John Archer, Edward Tawney, Thomas Sutton Hood and brewster, Anne Turner.

Alfred Barnard, the author of *Noted Breweries of Great Britain and Ireland*, visited the City Brewery, Oxford, in 1890 where he related that 'All Colleges had a brewhouse'. 'In the last few years several have been abolished, among them Brasenose and Magdalen', the utensils and plant being purchased by Mr Henley of the City Brewery. Wadham College was founded in 1612 by Dorothy, the daughter of Sir William Petre, of Ingatestone Hall, Essex. She married Nicholas Wadham who died in 1609 at the age of seventy-seven. She bought the site which was once a monastic college of Augustinians and lived to the age of eighty-four, seeing her foundation for a warden and fifteen fellows and scholars, two chaplains and two bible clerks. Wadham College has three quadrangles, the back quadrangle with Holywell Street and Parks Road had its former brewhouse and a warehouse situated on the corner between these two streets, dating from about 1693.

University College, the earliest to be founded, has records that confirm that a brewhouse was in existence from 1733. On 3 June 1809 the minutes record that £100 a year was to be paid to the brewhouse account, probably for the purchase of hops and malt and the wages of the butler. The entry for 5 June 1810 records that brewhouse charges were to be kept in a separate account book. On 31 March 1864: 'It was agreed that for the two ensuing terms no Table Beer be brewed in College, but that a light Table Beer be got in from some Brewery.' A final entry on 21 April 1883: 'Agreed that the Brewhouse Fund be abolished and the balance transferred to the Servants Fund in General Accounts for the three-quarter year ending 31st December 1882'.

Balliol, the second oldest of Oxford's colleges founded in about 1262, had a brewhouse in 1695, as shown on a plan of that date. Curiously there are no references to be found in the accounts for the period, so it is possible that there was some connection with St Catherine's Inn. Also from a similar date, in 1692, there are accounts relating to the brewhouse at Oriel College, and in the period 1841–73 the accounts relate to expenditure on malt and hops specifically for beer for the provost. Exeter College has the rector's accounts for 1569 and 1583–4 in which mention is made of a payment to Thomas Cogan as brewer (pandaxator). In 1603 the mending of a basket for the brewhouse (promptuario) is recorded and for other expenses in 1621. Earlier in 1565 there is reference to a lease for a brewhouse in St Giles to Thomas Cogan and later in 1620 to Henry Cogan. An Edmund Cogan was admitted to brew on 21 June 1588 and Thomas Cogan on 3 April 1611. Rector Prideaux's survey of Exeter College buildings made in 1631 makes no mention of a brewhouse, despite the mentioning of cock lofts, ball courts, privies and so forth.

Corpus Christi College brewhouse was demolished in the summer of 1927. It was situated in the small kitchen quadrangle which had access onto Merton Street, and backed onto the gardens of Merton Grove. The brewhouse was in existence in the eighteenth century. Brasenose College has had three brewhouses in its history, one was built between 1695 and 1697 at a cost of £300: the site of this brewhouse is unknown. Another set of bills for building a brewhouse in 1826 in what is now the New Quadrangle was for over £750. This was demolished in 1889 to make way for the erection of new buildings. It is probable that a brewhouse had been built sometime before 1692 as in that year the junior bursar had brewing account books and since the college was founded in 1509, it may be that the first brewhouse was built shortly after that date. An unusual custom is still retained, despite the closure of the brewhouse, that of the Ale Verses which was revived on Shrove Tuesday 1909, the college's 400th anniversary year. On the morning of Ascension Day each year, the door between Brasenose and Lincoln Colleges is opened and

University College
Oxford
◆
Audit Ale

BOTTLED BY
BASS, RATCLIFF & GRETTON LTD
FOR MITCHELLS & BUTLERS LTD
MINIMUM CONTENTS
9²/₃ FL. OZ.

any Brasenose members wishing to do so can visit Lincoln to be entertained with free beer. The origin of this custom is obscure, but the most plausible explanation is that centuries ago a Brasenose man, being pursued by a mob from the town, found himself at the gates of Lincoln College. Lincoln refused to open their gates and the Brasenose student was killed. The ivy beer is Lincoln's permanent penance, the ivy added to ensure that the Brasenose visitors do not drink too much today. In the past, ivy was a normal item for the flavouring of beer, not so much to the tastes of present day imbibers! 'Brasenose Ale' is presented in a bowl to the assembled college in hall on Shrove Tuesday by the butler, while verses written by undergraduates are recited. These would be in praise of the ale and would mention topical subjects and people of interest to the college. For his troubles, the butler would receive money. According to *Oxford Nightcaps* published in 1827, the Brasenose Ale custom has prevailed from its foundation (1509), it being 'introduced into the refectory on Shrove Tuesday, immediately after dinner'. The 1827 recipe was: 'Three quarts of ale, sweetened with refined sugar finely pulverised, and served up in a bowl with six roasted apples floating in it.' A much later recipe stated: 'Warm Beer. Half a pound of sugar to one gallon, sprinkle with nutmeg and spice, add baked apples when cool, drink when milk warm.' Typical of the older stanzas, mentioning 'in' people, is the following from 1827:

> *Shall all our singing now be o'er,*
> *Since Christmas carols fail?*
> *No! let us shout one stanza more*
> *In praise of Brasenose Ale!*

> *A fig for Horace and his juice,*
> *Falermian and Massic;*
> *Far better drink can we produce,*
> *Though 'tis not quite so Classic.*

> *Not all the liquors Rome e'er had*
> *Can beat our matchless Beer;*
> *Apicius self had gone stark mad,*
> *To taste such noble cheer.*

Henry Chichele, Archbishop of Canterbury, founded All Souls in 1437. As early as 1466 the college had leased a brewery to Richard and John Frier, in the parish of St Mary, on 1 September. All Souls evidently had a second location for a brewery. On 23 November 1535 the college sold brewing implements to Thomas Munday, previously a butcher by trade, from their brewhouse situated in the parish of St Peter le Bailey. It is evident that the College retained the brewhouse, as they leased the premises to Christopher Arundell thirty-five years later. It may be that the brewing equipment in 1533, by then nearly a hundred years old, required complete replacement. Doubtless, after other replacements of the plant, the brewery was still active in the college in 1890. In that year, a Mr Strudwick, the butler, carried out the brewing, producing a small beer and an old ale. A brief inventory of this time included a 'step ladder to the gallery, malt mill the size of a grocer's coffee mill, next a wooden mash-tub 5 ft in diameter and a small copper holding 180 gallons. Below there were two coolers, a hopback and wood square and hand pump; three fermenting tubs with a pipe through to the cellar below where the beer was racked.' When All Souls ceased brewing around the turn of the century beer was supplied both by Mitchells & Butlers, Cape Hill Brewery, Birmingham, and Bass, Ratcliff & Gretton of Burton-on-Trent. One of these beers was an 'Old Ale' produced by the Birmingham brewery.

In 1340 the founder of Queen's College, Oxford, was Robert de Eglesfield, king's clerk and chaplain to Queen Philippa, wife of Edward III, who gave instructions in the college statutes that baking and brewing were to be done on the premises. The college was founded for forty fellows, thirteen chaplains and seventy-two poor boys, some of whom acted as choristers. Expenditure on beer was 1s 6d for Fellows and 8d each for the boys; they had two meals a day consisting of two courses. Loaves and pea soup were provided at the gate for the poor. The staff consisted of a butler or steward, cook, kitchen boy, baker, brewer and a miller boy to grind the corn for flour and malt for the brewer. The strong emphasis on chaplains highlights the original intention of the college as a training school of theology. A barber also acted as the porter and there was a gardener and watchman. The washerwoman was not allowed to enter any dwelling room. In the statutes, instructions were given that baking and brewing were to be done by the college's own servants acting under the supervision of the steward and of the treasurer's clerk. Before it was baked every loaf was to be weighed and whatever the market price of corn, or whatever type of bread baked, everything had to be strictly controlled. There was a horse mill belonging to the fellows for grinding their wheat, barley and other corn within the college. The purpose of their own grinding was to save the excessive tolls and payments to millers. Accounts of the daily expenses of the provost and the remainder of the college, so far as eating and drinking was concerned, were kept by a presbyter who was called treasurer's clerk. He was assisted by purveyors and dispensers and the accounts for the week were written out in the presence of the steward of the hall in the evening of each day. Among the duties of the clerk to the treasurer was the attendance to all the necessary expenses in the college and to the collection of rents and tithes. George Fothergill wrote in 1722: 'To give you a notion of what we Servitors do, – we are seven of us and we wait upon the Batchelors, Gentlemen Commoners and Commoners at meals. We carry in their commons out of the kitchen into the Hall, and their bread and beer out of the Buttery.'

Accounting was essential and was carried out with due care. All decisions taken by the provost and fellows were duly recorded. 'Agreed at a meeting in pursuance of a Register made June 13th last [1846] that the allowances to the Taberdars be increased to sixpence a day in the Buttery and one shilling a day in the Kitchen.' Earlier, on 16 August 1803, 'The Bursar is no longer to receive profits on the sale of wine, but to be paid in addition to what he now receives in the Larder and Brewhouse accounts'. Brewing accounts for 30 May 1691 show that 24 barrels of strong and 2 barrels of middle beer were brewed, with surplus barm being sold for 7d, and the spent grains selling for 10s 10d. Materials and costings for this brew were:

10 qtrs of Malt @ 20/8	=	£10 - 06 - 08
Coles, 15 @ 42/-	=	£00 - 18 - 01
Hops 23 1bs @ 7	=	£00 - 13 - 05
Faggots	=	£00 - 00 - 03
Flower [Flour]	=	£00 - 00 - 09
Brewer	=	£01 - 07 - 06
		£13 - 06 - 08

Not included in this account for the May brewing in 1691, but indicated in January, was charcoal at 10d and an excise duty of £7 15s 10d. The average brew at this time was 23 barrels of strong beer and 4 barrels of small beer, giving an annual total of 168 barrels of strong and 40 barrels of small.

From the first two decades of the 1700s the beer produced was referred to as either strong or small, but in the last two decades of that century there are references to Double Beer, Middle and Small Beer. In 1785 24 barrels and 1 kilderkin of Double Beer was sold for £51 9s 0d, 6 barrels of Middle at £3 12s 0d and Small Beer (no quantity given) at £3 14s6d; a total value of £58 15s 10d for the year. The brewer from 1711 until at least 1773 was paid 7s8d but earlier, on 13 September 1703, the brewer's wage was only 7s. In 1758 the brewer was a Mr Grubb and in that year a cooper's bill of £14 9s 7d was paid, so evidently fairly extensive repairs or a renewal of vats took place. Excise duty paid was £4 1s9d in addition to 'Mr Anderson's bill for Ale and Small, £32 5s 9d'. This entry seems to suggest that beer was purchased from an Oxford brewer to supplement the college's own production. A brewing took place on 24 December 1772 when 13 barrels and 1 kilderkin of Double Beer, and 5 barrels of Middle Beer were brewed, valued at £28 7s 0d and £3 0s 0d respectively. The costing for this brew was:

Malt, 72 lbs	=	£15 - 0 - 0
Hops, 29 1bs	=	£ 1 - 16 - 3
Coals, 9 Bush	=	£ 0 - 16 - 6
Faggots, 3 @ 1d	=	£ 0 - 0 - 3
Excise (Duty)	=	£ 6 - 3 - 2½
Brewer	=	£ 0 - 7 - 8
		£24–3–10½

At this time the malt was consistently supplied by a Mr Clark, and the hops by Mr Lawrance. However, in 1710, several different suppliers of malt were tried. Mr Barllet supplied a quarter of malt for £1 14s 0d, as did Mr King in 1711. Both Mr Clin and Mr Trow charged an additional 1s a quarter. Hops cost 10d per pound and coal cost 1s 3d a bushel. In 1710, 136 barrels and 1 kilderkin of strong beer and 38 barrels, 5 kilderkin and 1 firkin of small beer were brewed.

During the nineteenth century, stock levels in the cellar beneath the buttery varied somewhat. The average stock was 150 gallons of Chancellor Ale, 100 gallons of Ale, and 90 gallons of Bitter. Cider is only occasionally mentioned in the account books, with an average

Queen's College, Oxford. The beer cellar with an assortment of wooden coopered casks and buckets.

of only 10 gallons' stockholding. The highest stocks held were in 1867 at 150 gallons of Chancellor Ale, 422 gallons of Ale and 100 gallons of Bitter valued at £20 0s 0d, £56 5s 4d and £13 6s8d respectively. The 'Bitter' description seems to have come into use in about 1860, for it is shown in the accounts alongside both 'Ale' and 'Small'. The valuation given of these three grades of beer at that time were: Bitter at £4 16s 0d a barrel, Ale at £4 4s 0d a barrel, and Small at only 18s a barrel. For the year 1861 there were two brewings in September and March, with one in October, November, December, January, February and April. Total quantities brewed were 55.5 barrels of Ale, 29 barrels of Bitter, 5 barrels of Small and 3 barrels of 'Extra', valued at £6 a barrel: this would almost certainly have been the Chancellor Ale. Fuel for the year amounted to £8 12s 4d (including that for the buttery) and the brewer's bill was £8 7s 6d. In 1862 the accounts show 11 gallons of Stout, valued at 9s 2d, also 22 pints of Stout for the same sum, and 39 pints of Bass costing £1 5s 10d. The unusual reference to Stout possibly suggests a trial brewing or else the more probable explanation was that, as with the Bass, it was purchased from an outside brewery. A visitor to the college in the mid-nineteenth century described the Chancellor Ale as 'like port wine', but that 'the College Ale had a deposit of yeast'. This would not have been unusual. An analysis of the two beers revealed that College Ale was 1068.2.OG and that Chancellor Ale was 1135.3.OG The colour of Chancellor Ale was more than three times greater than College Ale, and was therefore a very deep rich ruby colour.

Mr Louis Gunter (left) with Mr Charles Eld of Morrell's Brewery, Oxford, enjoying the fruits of their labours.

Mr Owen, the butler, was the brewer from 1860 until about 1890, in which time Mr J.F. Hunt gradually took over from about 1870. He retired in 1927, having been involved in Queen's College brewing for fifty-six years. One of the gardeners, George White, assisted in brewings up until 1939, the supervising being done by Louis Gunter, brewer at Morrell's, Lion Brewery, Oxford. Brewing started at 5 a.m. with the raising of hot water which had to be at 168° before the malt was added in the mash-tun. The second mash (for small beer) was raised to 90°. In the two boils, 10 lbs of hops were added to each brew. It is more usual for the second mash to be carried out at a higher temperature than the first, and a further unusual aspect of brewing was that yeast was added at 68°. This is very high. The thermometer was the only modern piece of equipment used in the Queen's brewhouse. Boiling with the hops took three hours. Wort was allowed to remain in the fermenting vessels overnight, consisting of nine barrels. This was then ladled by hand into barrel-sized casks with the bung-hole left open, allowing the yeast to bubble out. This would seem to have been an early forerunner of the Burton Union yeast system. After a week of this fermentation the casks were sealed up. After a further six days the beer was drawn off into 108-gallon-capacity upright tuns where it stayed for two or three weeks before broaching. In 1927, when the above brewing style was carried out, beer was charged in Hall at 4*d* per pint, but shortly afterwards there was a large increase to 1*s* a pint, due to excise duty increases. Chancellor Ale was stored for one year before being consumed.

The Queen's College brewhouse is a stone building 50 feet long, with graduated stone roof tiles. The date of its construction is not known, although its enormous roof beams suggest a great age. On the ridge are two large louvred housings, with a wooden louvred window in the end gabled wall. These louvres were formerly controlled by a simple vertical pole with wooden dowls between each louvre, fixed to the inside. The capacity of the wooden mash-tub was four quarters and the copper was built into a high brick structure with furnace and ash pit below, the overall height exceeding 12 feet. Access to the rim of the copper was by a flight of wooden

The copper fire being dampened down in Queen's College brewhouse in the 1930s.

stairs to the staging about 5 feet high with a further set of open steps leaning against the outer wall; this gave access to the open-topped copper. A wooden water tank was formerly the cold liquor tank at high level. The lead and wood pump, consisting of a wooden bucket working in a lead barrel with leaden pipes, was used to raise the water; this was built in about 1500.

Two coolers with wooden troughs to them, only a few inches deep, were made of deal. They held 216 gallons. During the 1920s a removable copper coil connected to the cold water supply was used to assist the cooling process. At this time the casks were sent to Burton-on-Trent for cleansing and also supplies of malt, hops and yeast were sent from this town each month. Brewing tools used were a narrow wooden shovel for removing grist from the vat. A rake was used to remove the hops and a strainer stood in the cooler, also to remove the spent hops. A wooden funnel with a copper tube was to assist in the filling of the casks by hand ladling. The ladle was also used to remove the beer from the fermenting vessels. A copper bucket with a narrow spout was used to 'top up' the casks following the overspilling of the yeast from the top bung-holes. An all-in-one wooden shovel with a looped handle was used for measuring and scooping up malt.

Brewing ceased at the outbreak of war in 1939 but even in 1935, some additional beer was being purchased from a Birmingham brewer. The costings for the January 1939 brew were:

4 quarters of Malt @ 90/-	=	£18-00-0
25 lbs of Hops @ 3/- a pound	=	£ 3-15-0
Yeast 14 lbs	=	7-0
Excise Duty	=	£60-4-5
		£82-6-5

Quantity brewed		
9 × 36 gals	=	2,592 pints
Allow for wastage,		say 92 pints
Leaving 2500 pints to sell at 10d pint	=	£104- 3- 4
Estimated profit on Brew, 1939		£ 21-16-11

The reason why brewing ceased in 1939 seems more likely to have been due to the poor condition of the plant, and not necessarily due to labour shortage. A quotation from Wilson and Scotchman Ltd of Keyford Works, Frome, Somerset, dated 21 November 1941, stated: 'Two new vessels in English Oak. One 7'3" bottom diameter × 6'10" top diameter × 3 feet deep inside, hooped with steel hoops F.O.R. Frome in sections, for £25. One 6'0" bottom diameter × 5'7" top diameter × 2'8" deep inside, hooped with steel hoops etc, for £22. We could send a man to pull down old vessels and fix the new for £9. Could do work in January next (1942).' The firm reported that the two brewing vessels were decayed and beyond repair. The same firm re-quoted for the above renewals in May 1945, but this had risen to £160 plus £20 labour for taking down and refixing new vessels. Nothing was evidently done about these works, although estimates were made in 1945 for brewings. These were a total cost of £145 10s 0d for 2,500 pints, to be sold at 1s 4d a pint: a total of £166 13s 4d. The profit thus accrued was estimated to be £21 3s 4d.

In 1949, Mr C.K. Mill, Managing Director of Arthur Guinness and Son, Dublin, wrote on 10 November, offering to rebuild the two vats as they had suitable wooden staves at Dublin. Evidently Mr Mills' son was at the college and had passed on the sad fact that their own 'home-brew' was no longer available. Again, in October 1953, calculations were made for the same quantity of brewing based on material costs supplied by Morrell's Brewery. The retail price in 1953 of 2s 9d a pint was 'to cover Buttery expenses and wastage which is high with home-brewed in warm weather'. The total cost was estimated at £319 3s 4d, with a revenue of £343 15s 0d, giving a profit of £24 11s 8d. Even this failed to galvanize the governing body into a positive decision to reinstate the brewhouse. Instead a decision was taken to have a bottled beer produced, an 'Audit Ale' during the 1960s. This was brewed and bottled by Bass, Ratcliff & Gretton, Burton, for Mitchells & Butlers, Birmingham, in a half-pint bottle size only.

An elaborately decorated buffalo horn used for drinking on ceremonial occasions belonged to the founder of Queen's College, Robert de Eglesfield, as did a silver trumpet. A boar's head salver dating from 1668 is also used on college 'Gawdy Days'. Stored in the vaults along with these college treasures are twelve silver-mounted double-handled mugs. A coconut shell, which was washed ashore fifty years before the discovery of America, was made into a cup used by the provost of Queen's. A silver candel cup dated 1663, a lion tankard that can be whistled through a mouthpiece in the bottom when empty – hence the expression, 'whet your whistle' – are further highly valued relics of the college. A three-pint tankard dating from 1700 has a series of pegs which marked the measure for each successive drinker. A sconce cup was presented to anyone who misbehaved, they had to drink one quart of beer right off in one go; if successful the others in the group had to drink a pint! This custom was abolished in 1927. An amusing china cup discloses a realistic frog in the bottom when all the beer has been quaffed. On the underside is the following quotation: 'Tho' malt and venom seen untid, Don't break my pot, or be affrighted.' For the drinking of Chancellor Ale special slim tall glasses were used. Quite evidently, drinking home-brewed beer at Queen's College was an art form, with all the requisite trappings. This happy custom, lasting for six hundred years, is unequalled anywhere else in the country.

With the closure of the college brewhouses over the forty years from 1880 to 1920, with the exception of Queen's College which lasted until 1939, supplies of beer were made by local common brewers, such as Hall's and Morrell's. It is likely that one or two of the very large Burton brewers also supplied beers, such as S. Allsopp & Sons and Bass, Ratcliff & Gretton. These two firms were very active in this period as they were able to speedily make deliveries throughout the country via the still developing railway network. Draught beers in wood casks would be supplemented by bottled versions, particularly from Burton, of their stronger beers. After the Second World War, the Bass Group of companies obtained a virtual monopoly of supplying bottled beers to Oxford colleges. Bass, Ratcliff & Gretton or Bass Worthington brewed Audit Ales for All Souls, Nuffield, Balliol, New, Exeter, Trinity, Lincoln, University, Magdalen, Wadham and Merton. Most of these bottled Audit Ale labels were oval, black and white, with the College name on the top half and details of the brewer on the lower half. The typeface used was Old English Gothic. Bass Mitchells & Butlers, Birmingham, brewed and bottled for All Souls (also an Old Ale), Merton, Magdalen, University, Christchurch, Exeter, New, Wadham and Trinity.

Osney Abbey, founded in the early twelfth century, which owned land on the western side of Oxford adjoining the city wall and straddling the main road to the west, decided to sell this land for development in the early fifteenth century. This area had a number of islands and was navigable up to the New Bridge. In 1452 the monks built the first brewery in this locality and leased it to a common brewer, later converting the premises to a malthouse. This was later to become a part of Morrell's Brewery. From about 1800 it remained in use as a maltings by the brewery until sold to the university authorities in the 1950s. After the dissolution of the monasteries the lands of Osney Abbey were given to Christ Church College as an endowment in 1546. In 1563 a chorister at the cathedral, one Robert Linke, took a lease on what is now Morrell's Brewery and here built the first brewhouse which he sublet. The archives of Christ Church College indicate that several leases were made, initially to Thomas Kenton, then to his widow who sold the business to Richard Tawney – all these changes of ownership occurring in the early to mid-eighteenth century. Richard Tawney's eldest son, also called Richard, inherited the brewery with his younger son Edward, a maltster, acquiring the disused brewhouse that had been built by the monks in 1452. Ownership came into the Morrell family via James Morrell, an Oxford lawyer who acted on behalf of the Tawney brothers. It was Mark Morrell's sons,

James and Mark, who entered into partnership with Edward Tawney in 1797. Today, Morrell's still have a very close relationship with the university, maintaining the close links fostered two hundred years ago. The old emnity between 'Town and Gown' has long since been forgotten. What greater compliment to the colleges could a brewer give than to name his products after them? A bottled Light Oxford Ale, College Ale and Castle Ale have been produced with a variety of different labels during the past fifty years. Proctor Ale, Varsity and Buttery Ale were all popular draught beers in the 1930s, ranging in price from £13 4s 0d and £16 4s 0d a barrel, against the weaker Ordinary Ale, priced at £6 18s 0d. The present range includes Varsity Bitter, Graduate Bitter and College Ale, all cask-conditioned draught beers, and Friars Bitter, a keg beer. This brief account of Morrell's Lion Brewery, although now the only common brewer in Oxford, does illustrate the development from monastic brewing to a small twentieth-century regional common brewer.

A custom that only died out during the 1950s was the visiting of inns in the city by the proctor with 'Bulldogs' or college policeman who would ask students, 'Your name and College, Sir?', the purpose being to prevent their visiting and drinking in public houses. Before the war, The Gardener's pub was the only one in the city of Oxford to have an insurance scheme to pay the fines imposed by the proctor. Members paid one penny extra on each pint, and the pub paid the college fines.

The bursars of New College, Oxford, Thomas Monpesson and Richard Crosse, gave a receipt for £130 in connection with the building of a brewhouse, dated 22 December 1697. Prior to this, Warden Woodward had decreed on 4 December 1663 that at all times, excepting at audit time, only small beer was to be in college. William of Wykeham had founded the college on 30 November 1379 and over several hundred years, rents were derived from numerous properties to endow the college. As early as 1638 a lease on the yard of the Trillocks Inne, later called the Newe Inn, and on the Saracen's Head, later the Lenwade Bridge Inn, at Great Witchingham, Norfolk, was made until 1841. The Three Tuns in Oxford had a series of leases from 1654 up until 1850. At Newton Longville, Buckinghamshire, the Fox & Goose Inn was conveyed to New College in 1849 by farmer John Short of Shenley, for the sum of £1,200. In London, The Coopers Arms, Silver Street, was leased during the period 1847 to 1898. These and many other properties ensured that the college finances were kept in the black with their rents being paid at audit time. The level of rents paid at the turn of the century in London are indicated by those paid by Hoare & Co. Ltd, for the George Inn, Fenchurch Street; the first year's rent to the college was £150 and for the subsequent 79 years of the lease, the rent stood at £300 a year.

The high academic standards of the medieval period were not only centred on Oxford but were also shared with Cambridge. These two leading universities were composed of numerous colleges spread throughout each of the towns. Shared with these two towns were the earlier origins of monastic education at Canterbury, Winchester and Windsor. Benedictine and Augustinian monasteries had to send at least one in twenty of their monks to university, where they would be further educated in theology. They lived together in groups of ten Benedictines, and only four or five of Augustinians. Accommodation was in hostels or inns; in Cambridge this was an early feature of the town.

As one of the two greatest seats of learning in this country, Cambridge University's founding goes back as early as 1240, when there were no purpose-built premises. The scholars and students lived and worked in rented rooms in the town, usually local inns. By 1280 there were thirty-four hostels in use, several of the inns being used exclusively for academic purposes. Each hostel had its Master and some had halls, chapels and gatehouses. The first of the Cambridge colleges to be founded was Peterhouse in 1280 under the will of the Bishop of Ely, Hugh de Balsham. Here there was a master and six fellows. During the next seventy years saw the establishment of seven colleges, with the Chancellor of the Exchequer, Harvey de Stanton, founding Michaelhouse in 1323. The magnificent King's

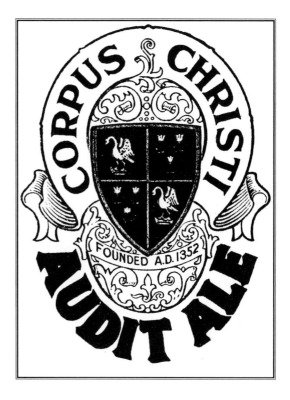

College was founded by King Edward II for thirty-two scholars in 1336. Years later a house in Milne Street was converted into Clare Hall. Pembroke Ganville was established in 1347, followed by Trinity Hall in 1350. Corpus Christi College was founded in 1352 and completed in 1378 and was the last to be built for some seventy years due to outbreaks of the plague. The town of Cambridge was badly hit by the plague in 1349, 1361 and 1368, reducing the population by a third over a period of some forty years. The Peasant's Revolt in 1381 sacked two of the colleges, Corpus Christi and Great St Margo. As early as 1336 the University exercised jurisdiction on the brewing trade as a petition made by the chancellor: 'that on the demand of the Chancellor, the Mayor and bailiffs should make trial or assize of the bread and ale'. However, the scholars wished to exercise their ancient privilege and it was restored.

The Benedictine monks founded Buckingham College which was the first hall to house students. This was deemed necessary due to the lax discipline of the monks, as they were consorting with women of the town and practising other unseemly traits. Once again a bishop of Ely was closely involved in the affairs of a college. In 1496 Bishop Alcock suppressed the bankrupt nunnery of St Radegund, the refectory became the hall and the prioress's rooms the Master's Lodge of Jesus College. In 1662 John Strype, a scholar of Jesus College, wrote to his mother and assured her that the food was good and sufficient: roast meat at dinner and supper every day except Friday and Saturday as these were still fast days when only fish and pudding were served. A second course was served on four evenings a week at high table only. He did not find it necessary to go to the buttery for extra bread and

ST. JOHN'S COLLEGE, CAMBRIDGE

AUDIT ALE

beer except at breakfast. Jesus College had a similar religious background to the site of St John's in that it was founded on the site of the Hospital of St John. It also had a large brick court and gatehouse, as does King's which has a Tudor coat of arms supported by the 'Beaufort' antelopes, Tudor rose, portcullis and crown: Christ Church also has a similar magnificent heraldic ornamentation.

Henry VI built Queen's College in the early 1440s to match his endowment for Eton College close by to Windsor Castle. It was built of red bricks imported from Holland and originally had a provost, 70 Fellows, 10 priests, 16 choristers and 6 clerks. In the late nineteenth and early twentieth centuries it was enlarged, when it had 10 Fellows and 100 undergraduates, but after 1918 it had more than doubled: a similar development had also taken place in the other colleges. The northern wing was the chapel, on the east there was the central gatehouse and on the south and west a hall, library, lecture rooms and chambers. The kitchen, bakehouse, stables and a brewery were in a side court. These stables and the old brewhouse were reconditioned as two common rooms in 1935 as a memorial to Dr Fitzpatrick the Chancellor. The Queen's College brewhouse was built in 1533–4 and had been demolished by the late 1950s.

Trinity College was founded by Henry VIII in 1546 following the dissolution of the monasteries and his accruing considerable monies as a result of selling them. The bursar's accounts of 1566–7 indicate the presence of the brewhouse, but a new brewhouse was built on a new site during the period 1606–12, a third replacement was made in 1822–5, and this building remains in existence. In Gray's *Cambridge Revisited* published after the First World War, he mentions that a house for the brewer was adjacent and that it was shortly to be demolished. Gray further refers to the daughter of one of the brewers, who was born in Trinity College, being buried in Mill Road cemetery.

On the accession of the Catholic Queen Mary it meant that there was a purge on Protestants and the Cambridge trio of Cranmer, Ridley (a distant relative of the Chelmsford brewers of that name) and Latimer, all perished at Oxford. Queen Mary was followed by the Protestant Queen Elizabeth I in 1558 and another purge in reverse took place. The Queen visited Cambridge and there was much rejoicing with plays and exhibitions, and large quantities of wine and beer were consumed. Sir Walter Mildnay founded Emanuel College, and Sidney Sussex was established on the site of a Franciscan friary. Typical of the standards required to be upheld by colleges was the regime practised by Caius whose day started at 6 a.m., with lights out at 8 p.m. It was forbidden to gamble or visit taverns in the town, go to cockfights and bull baiting or to have long hair and wear silk clothes.

King's Hall (later incorporated into Trinity) converted part of a house into a brewhouse with leaden boilers, mash-vats, coolers and other vessels. Magdalene brewhouse was built between 1625 and 1629 and was still in existence in 1959. The brewhouse of Corpus Christi was pulled down in 1823. On a visit to Cambridge common brewers in 1890, the author Alfred Barnard, who produced four volumes on breweries and malting companies, stated that: 'All Colleges had their own brewhouses.' At Clare College rebuilding took place in 1521 following a fire at the Master's Lodge and treasury, the quadrangle taking fifteen years to complete. At the south end of the west side was the kitchen and butteries which were built in 1523, next to which was the hall, built a year later. The south range was begun in 1640 and took two years to build, then came the Civil War. The north range was the last section to be built which included a hall and butteries to serve it, with a kitchen and library.

College brewing had ceased at Cambridge before the start of the twentieth century and to replace their own home-brews, colleges took supplies from a number of local common brewers. The ordinary daily beer drunk would probably have been of a weaker quality, equivalent to 'table beer'. However the other stronger beer brewed for special occasions was the 'Audit Ale'. This was given to the tenants of the colleges when they came to pay their rents as part of the endowments to provide for the running expenses of each college. On quarter days it was the custom for these tenants to bring the money owed together with a gift, such as a chicken or goose or maybe some home-made farmhouse cheese, and these gifts were given to the college bursar at his office. These food gifts were to supplement the Audit Feast at which liberal quantities of the strong Audit Ale were consumed. The beer was of a dark colour and similar to barley wine. Of the colleges giving up their own brewing, it is likely that their recipes were given to the chosen local common brewer so that he could emulate the type of beer that had become a long tradition. An early trademark registration of four bottled beers was made by Mr P.L. Hudson of the Pampisford Brewery, Cambridge, on 7 January 1892. They were the Cambridge Dinner Ale, the Cambridge Audit Ale, the Cambridge Pale Ale and the Cambridge Stout. Mrs A.M. Bullwait, née Hudson, wrote in August 1970 and confirmed that she was born at Brewery House in 1899 and that her mother was the second wife of the founder, Mr Hudson, who died when she was fourteen in 1913, in her own words 'we did brew that "Trinity Audit Ale" at one time'.

Dales' Gwydir Street tower brewery in Cambridge.

Lacon's, the large Great Yarmouth brewery, took over one large and several smaller breweries in Cambridge during the 1890s and a publicity booklet published in the early 1960s stated that: 'Lacon's association with the University began towards the end of the nineteenth century, when the Vice-Chancellor granted wine licences to a number of newly acquired public houses in the city. Soon afterwards Lacon's were brewing their Audit Ale for many of the Colleges, each College having its own individual label.' The style of labels for colleges invariably had the name of the college with its coat of arms, often in full colour. Henry Pegg's Benet Brewery, Cambridge, produced an Audit Ale for Peterhouse prior to that brewery being acquired by Fremlins in 1929. Dales' Gwydir Street brewery in Cambridge which is still extant, a typical small tower brewery, produced Audit Ales for Pembroke College as well as for sale to the general public in their public houses. This firm was taken over by Whitbread in 1954 and continued to supply a bottled Audit Ale for some time, although this was bottled and brewed by Wells and Winch, Biggleswade Brewery. This production ceased in about 1980. Greene King of Bury St Edmunds, Suffolk, acquired Cambridge brewers Bailey & Tebbutt in 1924, and produced a bottled Audit Ale which was available until 1983. This may have been based on the Cambridge brew which was produced there until the 1950s. Lacon's were the most prolific brewer and bottler for the Cambridge colleges.

Education and theology were an integral mix for many centuries, and the teachings of Christ dominated the daily life of students. Not only in the university colleges of Oxford and Cambridge were the layout of the buildings in the accepted quadrangle design. These courtyards were also to be found at Winchester and Eton Colleges. Whereas King's College, Canterbury, previously referred to, was a direct and integral part of the monastic life surrounding the great cathedral, both Winchester and Eton Colleges were founded on new sites. The earliest of these two great institutions of learning was Winchester College. Founded in 1382 by William of Wykenham, Bishop of Winchester, it still has many attractive mellow brick and flint buildings dating back to the fourteenth century. The Old Entrance to the college from College Street consists of a buttressed porter's lodge which leads into an outer courtyard from which the adjacent brewhouse can be accessed. This was built in 1394. The chimney which served the copper furnace is built of stone abutting the archway of the porter's lodge, with the long roof line broken by a tiled and pitched roof vent on the ridge; this allowed the steam and brewing vapours to be expelled and the beer to cool. An early

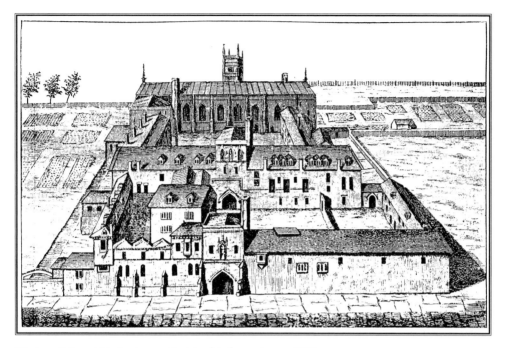

Winchester College with its brewhouse to the right of the front archway, c. 1772.

engraving dated 1772 clearly shows the brewhouse and in *Winchester Illustrated*, published in 1905, it confirms that brewing was still taking place. There was a mezzanine timber floor on which the cooling trough was situated below the roof vent, supported by heavy timber beams and posts which limited the headroom. Racking of casks and stillioning took place on the ground floor, beneath a section which was lath and plastered below the first floor timbers. An abundant water supply could be relied upon, as just east of the porter's lodge a fast-flowing stream eminates from the River Itchen via the cathedral deanery gardens and Wolvesey Palace. In 1620 the warden was instructed to keep the key of 'the outer door by which entrance is made into the cellar'. This was evidently required because previously the pupils had been allowed unrestricted access to the brewhouse and allowed to consume as much beer as they required. The third Lord Shaftesbury told his father in 1689 that there were scarcely any Winchester students 'that escape ye Mother vice of Drinking, the Predominant of ye Place', but New College, he thought, was not really much worse than other colleges.

A table of the beer brewed yearly in Winchester College is revealing in that, in 1709, each chaplain consumed 70 quarts of beer weekly and each servant 21 quarts, and that the latter allowance was considered insufficient. Similar allowances were made to other staff, though the total consumption accounted only for 472 of the 820 hogsheads brewed annually; 44,280 gallons per annum, or 23 barrels per week. The 140 pints allowed the chaplains each week would no doubt have included their households which consumed 20 pints a day. Each scholar and quirister was allowed 3 pints daily but, in 1712, it was noted that there was a wastage of beer amounting to one hogshead a week. In 1739 one of the fellows declared that the warden, who in 1709 had been content with his allowance of 70 hogsheads, 'annually claims and enjoys 104 hogsheads of Beer, which after a more profuse consumption in his lodgings than can well be imagined enables him at the end of each year to sell to the Bursars as much as, at a very low and moderate valuation, he receives £20 in money for'. Hence, by 1766, the supervisors pointed out that a better management of the beer would enable the college to improve the scholar's food. A resolution of 21 April 1808 stated that day labourers should receive beer money instead of beer, but in all probability they received both. A quirister's daily allowance at this date had increased to 4 pints, while the nurse enjoyed 6 pints daily. Certainly during the period 1820–8 the scholars were able to draw as much beer as they wished but that food, such as bread, cheese, butter and meat (both beef and mutton) was carefully measured and regulated. As part of this liberal consumption of beer, 'the bedmakers used to carry every evening into each of the seven chambers a huge "nipperkin" of beer to last all night'. Beer was consumed at breakfast, dinner, supper and 'beer under your bed'. This happened in the days when beer was the only authorized drink, long before the introduction of tea and coffee and even after their importation, the cost was prohibitive. During the 1860s it was reported that juniors were instructed to carry down from hall full jorums of liquor, which they concealed under their gowns as a formal mark of respect for the prohibition inacted. Some pupils added raisins, rice and brown sugar, and this sweetening may have been to disguise tainted or sour beer. The lax management in the brewhouse not only caused wastage but probably some poor quality brews. It was noted in 1872 that the college had been spending £350 a year on beer for the scholars, which equated to £5 annually on each boy. The *Hampshire Chronicle* reported on 4 March 1789 that the 'populace were not remarkably inebriated', after the cathedral and Winchester College gave 'many hogsheads of strong beer 'to celebrate the return to health of King George III. Today the brewhouse looks much as it must have done for some five hundred years, although nothing remains of the brewing plant or tools and of course the pupils no longer have the benefit of their beer allowance; nor does the cricket team receive 'beery' sustenance as it once did.

King Henry VI decided on the site for Eton College, so that it was close to his birthplace and favourite residence, the castle. He acquired the site close by the River Thames in September 1440. Henry Sever was the first provost. The king had lands in France at this time and several abbeys were endowed to the college such as Fecamp, Fontenoy and St Stephens at Caen, with the largest Benedictine abbey supervised by Herlouin Bec. Many of these original endowment deeds are still held in the magnificent college library. Local lands in both Buckinghamshire and Berkshire, with fishing rights on the River Thames, further supplement the revenue.

The king visited Winchester College for several days in July 1441 to see how the school was administered and William Waynflete, the headmaster for more than eleven years, was induced by the king to resign in order to organize the burgeoning Eton College. It was intended that it should be modelled on the lines of Winchester and so some five or six scholars, two commoners and a few day boys went from Winchester to Eton. The King's chief architect for the construction was William de la Pole, Earl of Suffolk, who left the practical details to his surveyor, John Hampton, with William Lynde the clerk of works in February 1441.

The interior of Winchester college brewhouse in 1910.

The brewhouse is situated behind the chapel in its own yard backing onto the Library Hall, and some 60 feet from a small tributary of the River Thames. The present building is two storeyed with dormer windows, now housing an art gallery and the college boilerhouse. Two rainwater hopper heads date from 1714 and to the east side of the yard, the library and cloisters date from 1720. It is therefore apparent that this fine building supersedes a previous one, probably built on the same site. The layout, with quadrangles and cloisters including a bakehouse, garners, stables and hayhouse in addition to the brewhouse, is similar to that at Winchester College.

In the 1750s Sam Smith was the brewer on an annual wage of £13 0s 4d with John Atkins to assist him for £12 0s 4d. John's additional duties included keeping the watercourses and sluices clear for just 10s per year. In 1757 Sam Smith authorized the expenditure of £1 for Ash to hoop the barrels, while in 1754 the cooper's bill was for £4 2s 10d, a quite considerable repair or renewal bill. Six leather jacks were purchased for £1 16s 0d in 1754, two years previously these had cost £2 14s 0d and a Mr Bidle, cooper, presented a bill for £5 12s 0d. The year of 1758 records that the butler was paid £9 8s 11s for one brewing of Small Beer and that the total cost of twenty-seven brewings of Ordinary Beer and twelve Hogsheads of Strong Beer brewed between 1 September and 1 April, cost £255 14s 4d. It was further noted in the account ledgers that 'for the future 36 of hops be allowed for each

Brewhouse yard at Eton College with the eighteenth-century brewhouse on the right.

brewing of Strong Beer and Election'. Throughout the eighteenth and first half of the nineteenth centuries, several tenant farmers had supplied both barley and malt in lieu of part rent. Previously in 1752 a written instruction indicated that 'Hops not to exceed 16 1bs to each brewing of Ordinary 28 to Strong with 34 for one brewing of Election'. 'There were 29 brewings of Ordinary Beer at 42 of malt each brewing and 18 Hogsheads brewed after Strong Beers also 3 brewings of Strong Beer at 72 to each brewing also brewing of Election Beer at 74 which makes malt £157 6s 0d.' It is apparent that the 'Winchester Bushel' measurement was in use for some time; this dates from King Henry VII's time and consists of a carved stone bowl measuring 8½ inches deep with a diameter of 19¼ inches. A similar one is at Northampton, but this is dated 'E.R. 1601'.

A History of Eton College, 1440–1910 by Sir H.C. Maxwell Lyte, KCB says: 'The College brewhouse, which in former days had supplied beer to Kings and Nobles, bore an indifferent reputation at the end of the 18th century.' In a parody on Gray's Ode, written 'on a near prospect of Eton, in 1798', a colleger derides the quality of the beer:

> *Pint after pint you drink in vain,*
> *Still sober you may drink again,*
> *You can't get drunk in Hall.*

Bearing in mind that the common and day pupils would have been receiving second or third brewings of Small Beer, it is no wonder that their expectations of getting drunk were limited! Scanty food supplied by the college, such as the staple bread, cheese and soup, had to be supplemented from other sources. It was normal for pupils to obtain their breakfasts at private rooms hired in the town of Eton, lower boys were made to bring 'cans of beer' from the Christopher Inn at their own peril. A bar in the window of Lower Chamber was loosened to permit extra provisions to be passed through. The provost originally had seven fellows and seventy scholars, this figure has increased to over a thousand today.

During the mid-1850s the brewer was a Mr Carter who was paid £14 0s 4d. In 1853 his under-brewer was Mr Bird who was responsible for the sluices and was paid £10 10s 4d. The clearing of the sluices would have been essential in order to dispose of the spent hops and other sediments from cask cleaning, while the spent grains would have probably been given to tenant farmers as animal feed, although there is no apparent charge for this in the accounts. As a comparison of wages, the butler and baker were paid the same as the brewer in 1853, while the groom, under-cook, verger and porter were paid the same as the under-brewer. The gardener was at the bottom of the scale at just £8 per annum, while the laundress was paid £30.

The year 1855 had the highest expenditure on beer brewing which was £815 5s 9d, but the average annual brewings were twenty-two barrels of Ordinary Beer and three of Strong and Election Beer. In the mid-eighteenth century the annual average cost for brewing was £190. The account ledgers give details of all expenditure, broken down to previous years brought forward, plus acquisitions of coal, malt, hops and beer. In 1852, 'Malt bought by the Bursar for the expense of this year' cost £367 10s 0d, 'hops bought by the last year's Bursar for the expense of this year' cost £39 8s 4d (5 cwt, 2 qrs, 121 lbs) brought forward, in addition to 7 cwt, 1 qrs and 21 lbs used in 1852 for:

8 Brewings @ 40 lbs per brewing	2 cwt	3 qrs	12 lbs
14 half Brewings @ 20 lbs ditto	2	2	2
2 Brewings of Ale @ 66 lbs each	1	0	20
Extra to Strong and Small Beer		2	20
Weight of Pockets			25
	7 cwt	1 qrs	21 lbs

The Brewers' Allowance of Coals which he is not to exceed is 10 cwts to each Brewing which was all spent.

	7 tons	10 cwts	0 qrs	0 lbs
2 Brewings of Ale	1	—	2	—
Scalding Casks		9	—	—
	8 tons	19 cwts	2 qrs	0 lbs

A brewers' labourer was paid £2 18s 0d in 1852 with an additional item for sundries at £1 10s 6d, making the total cost for the years' brewing, £609 15s 3d.

The Strong and Election Beers were evidently brewed for the provost and fellows in their allowance, also by implication at election time for the college officers. It is probable also that the stronger brews would have been used at the dinner following the annual rents paid by tenants, as there is mention of such dinners in the 'Audit Room' in 1853. Unlike Oxford and Cambridge universities, the strong beer was not named Audit Ale. From 1854 there are several annual notes that 'The Provost took in lieu of his allowance of four hogsheads of ale at £4 11s 7d, total value £18 6s 4d', this seems to imply that he was not happy with the beer quality and preferred to take the cash value.

For the year 1873 there appears the first entry of purchases of beer from an outside supplier, namely S. Allsopp & Sons of Burton, with a total expenditure of £234 17s 0d, with work being carried out in the brewhouse by Thergold for £1 10s and Carter, sundries of £1

2s 6d and £1 0s 6d, and others amounting to a total of £5 6s 3d. In the following year Allsopp's account was for £419 12s 6d with some returned beer deducted. Evidently Samuel Allsopp's beer was popular. In 1875 the total sum of £545 6s 0d was expended, dropping over the next five years to an average of £265 a year.

A small single-line entry in the account ledgers for 1880, reads 'Sale of Brewery Plant. . . £60 6s6d'. This is somewhat confusing as a sale poster dated 10 August 1881 advertised: 'Eton College – brewery plant etc. – to brewers, coopers, metal dealers and others. Mr G.C. Hetherington is honoured with instructions from the Provost and Fellows to sell by auction without reserve, on Wednesday, August 10th, 1881, at one o'clock for two o'clock at the College Brewery, the PLANT comprising: "Capital stout copper, inside measure 7'9" x 4'5"; the brickwork and furnace to ditto; 3 Wooden Liquor-Tank lined with Stout head inside measure 8'8" x 6'9", depth 2'0"; Hop Back 10'2" x 5'7" depth 22"; Stout Oak Mashing Tub inside measure 7'5" x 3'4"; Stout Oak Under-Back 6'2" x 3'6"; Stout Oak Working-Vat 8'1" x 3'2"; about 48 stout Butts and Hogsheads in good condition; copper and lead pipes; 3 Powerful Force Pumps copper taps; Iron Malt and Hop Strainers: 3 Rousers; Capital Stillion; Tun-Bowl; Waste-tubs; Wood-Work of small loft etc."'

It may be that following a fire, which was not an uncommon occurrence, some of the plant was sold locally such as brewing tools and a malt grist mill not mentioned in the above inventory. Coupled with what was evidently a declining quality of their home-brewed beer and the rising popularity and widespread distribution of Allsopp's beers, the final cessation of brewing at the College in the early 1880s was almost inevitable.

Haileybury College at Great Amwell, Hertfordshire, was built specifically for the sons of civil servants living and working in India. No doubt the intention was that the graduates would be favourably disposed to working for the East India Company. The estate of Haileybury was purchased in October 1805 for the sum of £5,900. In March of the following year an estimate and design for the college was received from William Wilkins, of Caius College, Cambridge. The design was for a large quadrangle of buildings costing £50,855 and this estimate and design was accepted. Work moved forward at a rapid pace; on 12 May 1806, a foundation stone was laid by Edward Parry, the Deputy Chairman of the East India Company. The school's original name was The East India College, and this remained in use for some fifty years. An Act of Parliament abolished the college on 16 July 1855: 'An Act to relieve the East India Company from the obligation to maintain the College at Haileybury.' The principles of the college were said to be: 'An Institution conducted upon Christian religious principles may reasonably be expected under the favour of Providence, to be productive of a benign and enlightened policy towards the Native Subjects of British India, to improve their moral condition and to diffuse the happy influences of Christianity throughout the Eastern World.'

Following the Indian Mutiny in June 1857, and the fall of Delhi on 27 October of that year, celebrations took place at the school with considerable relief; parents' safety being uppermost in the boys' minds. A last sermon was conducted in the school chapel by Henry Melvill on 22 November 1857. The college had accommodation for 100 pupils and the buildings were set in 55 acres of grounds. An auction was held in London on 30 August 1861, and the college and its grounds were acquired by the British Land Company, evidently as a development speculation. This company sold the estate in 1862 and following some alterations, teaching recommenced in 1863.

The old East India Company's Haileybury College, with the former brewhouse situated to the right-hand corner.

Above the central porticoed entrance on the front elevation was the library, with the school chapel on the left. To the right was the dining hall and next to it, one of three kitchens. A larger scullery, pantry, knife-room and tea-house, divided the kitchen from the brewhouse. This was in the front right-hand corner and measured 15 feet by 30 feet. In front of the brewhouse was an enclosed yard which would have been for cask cleaning and storage. In the right-angled corner of the quadrangle was situated the water pump, and in the return side wing adjacent to the brewhouse was the servants' hall.

Wrexham Lager Brewery, North Wales, was the first lager brewery to be built in this country, in 1882. In a town already well endowed with breweries, the company had great difficulty in selling its new style of beer. Unlike the other common brewers in the town, the Wrexham Lager Brewery Company had no tied houses initially. It was therefore necessary to find a market for its light and dark lager and so the management turned to exporting its bottled lager. Agents were set up in Glasgow, Edinburgh and Dublin, with a store in Manchester. Hotels and clubs throughout the country were supplied and, at the turn of the century, 80 per cent of the company's business was exported. Among the many small accounts which the company acquired was to supply their lager to the Bromsgrove School, Birmingham, in the 1890s.

Malvern College celebrated its centenary in 1965 with a bottled Centenary Ale. The colourful label consisted of an oval picture depicting the college on a black background surrounded by a red and blue border. Malvern College was written in white lettering and Centenary Ale in gold, with 'brewed by Bass, Burton-on-Trent' below. A neck label, dated 1865 and 1965 in similar colours on either side of the college's colourful coat of arms, made this an attractive commemoration of the event. Similarly, the University of Birmingham Guild of Undergraduates commissioned the local brewery, Mitchells & Butlers, to bottle a beer for their use during the 1960s. Despite the recent interest in premium bottled beers during the 1990s, there have been no bottled beers produced for any academic institutions during the last five years. The last to be brewed was for Imperial College by Charles Wells of Bedford, in 1987. Somewhat unusually one of the few retail brewers who bottled a beer for a university was G.E. Cook & Sons Ltd, Tidings Hill Brewery, Halstead, Essex, who had a small chain of off-licences. During the 1960s a high-rise university campus was built at Colchester and one of these high-rise blocks is depicted on Cook's 'Unibrew' label. The brewery ceased brewing in 1974, probably one of the last retail brewers to survive.

'A Noggin of Strong Ale, M'Lord?'

omestic brewing has been carried out in the most humble of houses to the grandest in the land. Today the home-brewer brews for himself at home and this is now quite a popular hobby, with specialist manufacturers providing equipment and materials. However, this aspect of today's 'home-brewer' is not within the scope of this book. But, on the other end of the scale, there is one large manor-house and one stately home that continue to brew in the traditional ways of old. These shall be looked at in detail later.

Domestic brewing was once an important industry, mainly catering for the needs of country folk who often lived beyond the radius of the local brewer and their delivery round. It was also very much cheaper: it was reckoned in the 1820s that home-brewed beer prices were a quarter of those in an alehouse. William Cobbett of Kensington, with his usual vitriolic tongue, said, 'we may prepare for the making of beer in our own houses, and take leave of the poisonous stuff served out to us by common brewers'. He went on further to comment that 'a family uses 2 quarts of beer every day from 1st October, to the last day of March inclusive; 3 quarts a day during June and September and 5 quarts a day during the months of July and August, and if this be not enough it must be a family of drunkards!'

William South, a husbandman of Writtle, Essex, had an inventory made on 3 July 1658 and 'In the Buttrey' he had, 'four brewing vessels, three runlits, one halfe hgshd, one beerstal, one funnel, two bowls and some other implements, valued at one pound and twelve shillings'. Charles Clark, of the same village, on 20 December 1659, had the following inventory of his 'Buttrey': 'One great Ireon pott 8/-; one hogshead, one halfe Hgshd, 2 Brewing Vessels, one Keeler, one Cheesestand and a Beerstall, £1 10/-; one letle Ireon dreaping pann 2/-; one Kneading trough 1/6d; One Bushel and a halfe peck 4/-; one Mustard quarne, 2 old Sives, 2/6d; one pair Bashits, & their Cuppleings, 3/-; one old Brass Kette, 5/-.' In other inventories from the area, one household had a 'best beer butery' and 'the small beer butery', in which there were hogsheads of beer and beer stalls. This last inventory gave the more usual use of a buttery as a cellar, where both draught beer and bottled beer were stored. The draught beer was placed on the 'stalls' or stillages at a height of 12 to 18 inches, this allowed a jug to be placed under the beer tap for dispensing. It is apparent from the description of Charles Clark's buttery that he not only used it for the storage of beer but that he also brewed there. It is possible that he made his cheese there too. In 1726 John Hillyard, a Writtle bricklayer, had a buttery in which he had one hogshead and two kilderkins of beer. He had his own brewhouse and this contained 'one small old brass boyler for wort, two tubs one cowl and a kneading trough', valued at 14s 6d. Other tradesmen at about the same time such as the miller, John

Godfrey, had in his own brewhouse 'one coper, one kettle and tubs, valued at £1 16/-'. John Day the elder, a carpenter in Highwood, a neighbouring village, had 'one small copper, four tubs, one bras cettle, other small things, £1 5/-'. A more elaborate brewhouse was that owned by Margaret Allen of Roxwell. Her inventory taken on 16 May 1724 listed the following: 'Brewhouse 1 Copper, 2 Mashing tubs, 1 Underback, 1 Cooler, 3 Wort Tubbs, 1 Hopp sive, 2 tap hoses, 2 Jetts, 2 stalls with ye copper bars. £10 2/-.' From the extent of the equipment in this brewhouse it suggests that above average quantities for a normal household were being brewed. Margaret Allen may therefore have been retailing some of her beer. Quite why the Sheriff of Hull was forbidden to retail beer in his own home in 1452 remains a mystery. In the following year he and his wife were given crimson cloaks for their office at the town's expense so perhaps they did receive some sort of compensation for this.

It is important that mention be made of the home-brewing being carried out at the cradle of the Industrial Revolution in Coalbrookdale, Shropshire, as the early developments of industrialization were to play a major part in the demise of small-time brewing. Not least of these influences was the use of coal and iron in making water-pumps, metal tools, steam-powered engines, all of which revolutionized the brewing industry. This influence extended from the mid-eighteenth century into the twentieth century. By 1796 there were at least nine large firms and twenty blast-furnaces in the Ironbridge Gorge area, and the ironmasters rapidly laid down 'L' shaped iron plateways for their flangeless wheeled wagons. In 1802 the Cornish engineer, Richard Trevithick, had built his locomotive at Ironbridge to haul coal and these iron trains replaced human labour and horsedrawing. All the intense activity in the mines and at the iron furnaces required a large labour force. The mine owners also provided some cottages for their workers.

Carpenter's Row consists of eight cottages which were built in 1783 and have a brewhouse at each end of the terrace to the ground floor. Built of local bricks and tiles with quarry-tiled floors, the copper was to the rear with the furnace flue shared with the next-door cottage's living-room fireplace. The cottages consist of a front door with a single front window, behind which is the narrow winding staircase to the two bedrooms upstairs. In the case of the two cottages adjacent to the end brewhouses, they had an additional bedroom over the brewhouse, measuring 15 feet deep by 11 feet wide. Off the ground floor living-room was a small pantry. From the front elevation one may discern the smaller windows of the brewhouses from those of the cottages.

Charity Row was built for widows but differed from Carpenter's Row as the brewhouse was detached. Access to the rear brewhouse, which was also the washhouse, was via a back door. There were five rows of these terraced cottages which had accommodation for thirty-four separate families. In the 1830s the Coalbrookdale Company built New or Upper Row at nearby Horsehay, and these consisted of twelve cottages for the principal workmen. The company also built thirty-two cottages for brickworkers – six at Pool Hill and eight at Frame Lane – with a further eighteen at Sandy Bank Row. The kitchens measured 14 feet by 12 feet with a large coal-fired range made locally, a pantry, and upstairs two bedrooms; the brewhouse was again detached. Living conditions were very cramped, with more than five people living in most cottages. Besides Carpenter's Row, School House Row in Coalbrookdale also had a brewhouse at each end of the terrace of ten cottages. These also had an additional bedroom above the ground floor brewhouse, which measured 13 feet square. School House Row was demolished in 1960 and sadly several of the dwellings in the very confined space of Carpenter's Row are now boarded up.

Engine Row consists of six houses built in two blocks of two and four. These were built at around the same time as Carpenter's Row. The brewhouse was originally small, measuring 10 feet square, and situated on the left at the back of the rear block. This was later incorporated into the living-room, and a new brewhouse constructed on the left-hand end. This was clearly evident from the lower ridge and eaves, the simpler style of the chimney-stack and the differing pattern of the two windows. A small lean-to store abutted the brewhouse which measured 13 feet in depth by 14 feet 9 ins metres to the front elevation.

Numbers 44 and 45 Wellington Road, Coalbrookdale, had a front living-room and rear scullery from which a staircase led to the bedrooms upstairs. On the left-hand end a single storey lean-to brewhouse served both dwellings, measuring 7 feet to the front elevation, by 10 feet 6 ins in depth. Projecting to the rear was the single flue chimney-stack serving the brewhouse copper furnace. As with most of the other Coalbrookdale dwellings, the brewhouse served the dual purpose of washhouse. Across the Coalbrookdale valley, with the works at the bottom, is situated Tea Kettle Row, high up on the hillside opposite Carpenter's Row. Set into the steep wooded hillside, these six terraced cottages seem incongruous as immediately below them is the very grand Rose House, family home of the Darby family. The brewhouse which served Nos 31 to 36 Tea Kettle Row is set into the steep hillside behind the cottages. A narrow service alley-way gives rear access with the detached 12 feet by 19 feet brewhouse situated behind Nos 34 and 35. To its right side a narrow staircase leads to the higher domestic level. Previously in front of these steps was the water-pump. A central door led into the brewhouse with an oven immediately opposite the door on the rear wall. On either side were two boilers or coppers of about the same capacity. Below the larger of the two shuttered front windows was a water-butt. Unlike the previously mentioned cottages, Tea Kettle Row was not built by the Coalbrookdale Company and predates them by some forty years. There is evidence of several building stages although the front elevation has some unity, with a common roof line. Possibly prior to the large rear brewhouse being built, the six dwellings used a small lean-to brewhouse adjacent to the left-hand end, No. 36. The last known brewer was Isaac Jones who was a resident in the 1920s.

Wages were paid on alternate Saturdays and this was referred to as the 'Reckonings'. After work the labourers would gather at a suitable beerhouse and while waiting to be paid, clocked up on the slate the drinks they owed. Sundays were for the family and a good hearty meal but come Monday and the men went back to the inns again. In 1843 it was recorded that a twelve-year-old said of this custom, 'I

One of several cottage brewhouses still extant in the Coalbrookdale area; this is Tea Kettle row.

can drink one and a half pints of strong beer'. One wonders then just how much beer the labourers must have drunk, having worked such long hours in strenuous working conditions and often under intense heat.

For cottage brewing, a 20-gallon pot, a mashing tub that also answered for a tun-tub and a shallow tub for a cooler – costing about £2 in the 1820s – would suffice. A 9-gallon cask of beer could be brewed from this equipment. Between three and four bushels of malt were required to produce a strong beer using this plant. A correspondent of the day commented: 'Beer into a cask is an hour's work for a servant woman, or a tradesman's or farmer's wife. No work was too heavy for a woman in any part of the brewing process, otherwise I would not recommend it to be performed by women, who though so amiable in themselves, are never quite so amiable as when they are useful; and as to beauty, though men fall in love with girls at play, there is nothing to make them stand to their love like seeing them at work!'

A Sussex farmer, Mr Ellerman, stated at a House of Commons Committee Meeting in the first quarter of the nineteenth century, 'that forty years ago [1780] there was not a labourer in his parish that did not brew his own beer, and that now there is not one that does it, except by chance the malt be given him'. The reasons for this dilemma was blamed on the high taxes on both malt and hops, and the lowering level of labourers' wages. In 1632 these were 4s a week with a skilled carpenter earning a further 2s a week. By 1655 the labourer was earning on average another shilling a week while the carpenter was now earning 10s a week. Living standards declined in the 1820s and 1830s, despite a large population growth. Labourers' wages were reduced to 6s a week and much of their work had become seasonal. With the Enclosures Act previous access to common land and woodlands was denied the common man, he could no longer obtain free kindling wood. With these minimal wages, the working-class man had to find 5d for a quart of beer; it had now become a luxury.

With the seasonal nature of employment for most of the labourers in the latter part of the eighteenth century, they at least were able to earn one shilling a day in summer and 1s 8d at harvest time. Hard times came again for the agricultural workers with the onset of the agricultural depression during the 1870s. Grain was being imported from America and consequently the grain-growing areas of the south and east were hardest hit. Many labourers left the land to work in the new industries springing up everywhere with the result that landworkers' wages started to rise. Still, their living conditions were unsanitary and harsh with dampness in their cottages accepted as normal. Throughout this period the only workers to be permanently employed were the horsemen, carters and ploughmen. The horsemen were always the 'top men' and with the dairymen and shepherds, they at least had a permanent roof over their heads and some security for their families.

At the turn of the century, when motor vehicles were starting to be used, the lorry driver could expect to be paid £1 17s 0d a week, a labourer £1 5s 0d and the horsemen £1 7s 0d a week. From the mid-1950s several craftsmen preferred to be independent, among these were thatchers and hedgers. There were also itinerant harvesters, haymakers, fruit-pickers and, of course, the seasonal hop-pickers. For many small farms, and also a few public houses, an itinerant brewer also offered his services. This practice died out at the beginning of the last war but I did have the great pleasure of meeting one of these characters, Mr Eddy Dale. I first met him by chance at the Cock Inn, Beazley End, Essex, in 1993 and he told me that he had brewed at Patten's Farm and also at the Red Cow Inn which is now closed. He also said that 'he had brewed a bit at home' but as he was now well in his eighties, he had forgotten the old brewing recipe. Eddy had been a horseman and then he drove a tractor, but later in life as he slowed down, he was often paid only a small wage for his brewing, but was given a good hearty meal and free beer, of course!

Agricultural prices for both malt and hops rose, just as with other products. A bag, or pocket, of hops cost on average £2 10s 9d in 1781, while a quarter of malt in the same year was £1 10s 0d. Ten years later the hop price had risen to £4 14s 1d and malt was 40s a quarter. In 1801 the price for a pocket of hops was £5 2s 8d and malt was 63s. Malt held its price for the next thirty years or more, as a result of the depressed economy. The one bright spot on the horizon for the farmworker was harvest time. The *Vale of Evesham News* reported on 10 September 1870: 'The farmers in this neighbourhood have gathered their friends and employees together to rejoice with them at their ingathering of harvest. The good roast beef of Old England, the foaming home-brewed, and the smoke of the fragrant weed were most liberally supplied, and the jovial toast and song went round which made the very walls resound with the mirth of those within.' It sounded all very jovial but the dark clouds for the labourers would be fast looming with little work available in the winter.

In Norfolk the custom was to give the reapers a good breakfast at around 11 a.m. This would be plum cakes with caraway seeds and a drink of beer. A good dinner with plum puddings and beer was served at four in the afternoon. In the West Country, cider was the preferred drink but elsewhere, beer was king. Several types of containers were used to take the beer out to the fields, at both haymaking and harvest time. Stoneware pitchers were used for a very long time, as were the small wooden coopered casks holding only a few pints. Later, glass bottles of beer were used and many of these found their way into ditches, hedgerows and streams. Appropriately enough the old banner of the National Agricultural Labourer's Union had a very visual sign. To one side, a fine wooden cask of beer stood proud with the words, 'United – We Stand'. On the reverse side the same wooden barrel is seen exploding into pieces with the words, 'Divided – We Fall'. This surely brought the truth home!

Most brewhouses at farmsteads were detached, this was a simple fire precaution particularly when the buildings were timber-framed. Many of these outbuildings had a shared purpose, the most common was its use as a washhouse, often with a secondary copper. These coppers were always built into either a brick or local stone furnace. The outbuildings were also used as the bakehouse, referred to in medieval times as the 'backhouse'. Many such combined brewhouses are still to be found throughout the country. Richard Brown of Horsefrith Park, a yeoman farmer of Writtle, Essex, had an inventory made on 4 June 1713. The farm had a dairy, a backhouse, used in this case as a cheese-making room, a barn, carthouse, brewhouse and a malthouse. Fields consisted of 'mowing ground' of 75 acres, 14 acres of barley, 6 acres of wheat, one field of 12 acres under wheat and barley, 14 acres of oats and barley and 26 acres of bullemon. Livestock consisted of 38 couples of sheep and lambs and 37 sheep, 2 bulls, 24 fatting cattle, 40 cows and calves and 16 dry cows; 8 horses and their harnesses with one breeding mare and 2 colts; one sow and 10 pigs. In the brewhouse there were two small coppers, one mashing tub, one cooler and other brewing utensils, valued at £5. Over the brewhouse was a storeroom which housed some wood, weights and scales and an 'old kneading hutch'. In his cellar Richard Brown had eight hogsheads, two half hogsheads, drink stalls and some bottles. A further five old hogsheads (probably empty) and a stall were in the 'small beer buttery'. In the malthouse was 'All the malt, a screen, a bushell, and wire for the kiln, some sacks, rakes, forks, and other implements belonging to husbandry'. For this farmstead of some 150 acres and its livestock, Richard Brown probably employed about six or seven permanent farmworkers, with anything up to an additional ten at hay and harvest time. The fact that he had his own malthouse and his 20 or so acres of barley, suggests that this malting of barley was a profitable part of his business. With these acreages of barley he would have also been supplying other farms and houses with malt for their own brewing.

Shingleford Farm, Tillingham, Essex, is a timber-framed cottage dating from about 1500, but the first known brewing on site was in 1875 when Henry and Hannah Hawkins purchased the 70-acre farm. Henry died in 1909. For a fee of 4s paid at the local post office, Henry had licences to brew for domestic consumption in 1893 and 1897; brewing ceased there in the early 1920s. John Rayner Hawkins, the son of Henry, took over the farm on his father's death, and his two sons, Thomas Henry and Robert Walter Hawkins continued the business into the 1990s. In November 1940 a stray German bomb knocked down the brewhouse chimney which was on a lean-to building to the right. The copper was taken out in the 1950s as were the oak fermenting vats. Malt and hops were supplied both by the local small common brewer, Gray & Sons, Chelmsford, and H.T. Eve and Co. of Maldon supplied the malt. James Liddiard of Great Baddow was also a supplier of hops. These last two firms were typical of small local suppliers throughout the country who for several hundred years supplied the raw materials to many a home-brewer in cottage and farm.

Gorrell's Farm, Highwood, Essex, has been owned by Wadham College, Oxford, since at least 1800 and probably even before that as the timber-framed farmhouse, barns and brewhouse date from the early eighteenth century. The present tenants Mr and Mrs Joseph Horsnell took over from Mr F.J. Horsnell who was born in 1926. In 1891 a Mr Staines was the tenant and before him it was a Mr John Ralph. The detached timber-framed brewhouse, measuring 15 feet by 18 feet, has a store area of 7 feet 6 inches by 15 feet. At the opposite end is the large brick-built chimney-stack which incorporates a washhouse copper on the left side, a bakehouse oven in the centre, with the brewing copper on the right. John Ralph had an inventory made on 18 January 1858 and in the buttery there were 'two Puncheons, 1 Puncheon and contents, 2 Hogshead Casks an 18 gallon cask; a 9 gallon; 3 drink stalls; Linen drier; 2 pieces of board; Saw and sundry pieces of iron. In the Brewhouse, 5 swill tubs in yard, 3 brewing tubs, Hog form; Deal Table, Sundry tubs and baskets, 2 hen hips, Cheese knife, 7 Corn Sacks; Sundry wippletrees.' Brewing had ceased by 1926 and probably even several years before that date. Today the inside of the brewhouse is lined with laths and lime plaster and the chimney-stack is used for the straw stubble central heating boiler.

Brewery Farm, Polstead, Suffolk, has white-painted walls with two windows on either side of the central entrance door with a single dormer window over it, all beneath a neat straw thatch roof. This is all that now remains of the original Brewery Farm. However, that may not be strictly so for, still living in this lovely cottage, are the ancestors of the Edward Lilley who used to brew on this farm. The farm had about 100 acres, mainly growing peas, beans and barley, the latter was sent to several of the maltings in the neighbouring village of

A typical eighteenth-century farm brewhouse at Gorrell's Farm, Essex.

Boxford. At one time there were twenty-two maltings but by the turn of the century there was only one owned by Mr Kemball. Another malting at Peyton House was demolished in 1922. One of Edward Lilley's employees was George Everett who lived in Butcher's Lane, Boxford, opposite Mr Kemball's malthouse. He started work on 1 January 1907 on his fourteenth birthday as a 'lad' on Mr Lilley's farm. He was paid 2s 6d a week but at harvest time, with all the additional work, he received 10s a week. In 1911, at the age of eighteen, he had a pay rise to 9s a week. A year after the First World War broke out he joined the army and returned afterwards to work for Mr Lilley until 1931.

Mr Lilley would brew three sacks of malt each week but during the summer months he would have three large brews in a fortnight. His customers were nearly all private and on other farms and larger houses to which Edward Lilley did all the deliveries, no doubt to ensure that he got paid for his beer and also to obtain further orders. Mr Lilley did all the brewing himself but the manual labouring of preparing the malt and cleaning of utensils and brewing vessels was done by George Everett. George recalled several years ago that either Mr Kemball or Mr Mason of Kersey delivered the malt to Brewery Farm. George and his brother Jack were required to grind the malt and there was a hand mill, rather like a clothes mangle, with two wood rollers. A hopper above was filled with the malt and allowed to trickle between the rollers, thus crushing each grain. A device allowed the speed to be controlled and how fine the grist should be. Evidently it took the two brothers two hours to grind the malt, discharging it into another sack. George's comment was that Mr Kemball's malt 'was just nice' and easier to grind but sometimes Mr Mason's malt was 'on the tougher side. You had to get the rollers close, and then that was harder for us to turn.'

One of two coppers, complete with wooden lid, at Gorrell's Farm.

Jack's job was to wash out and scour the wood casks, the racking of the beer from the vats was done by Mr Lilley. The home-brewed beer was left in the casks for at least a week before drinking and evidently, according to George, Mr Lilley was generous with his beer to his workers, particularly at harvest time. Good generous quantities of home-brewed was a fine incentive for the hard work and long hours of harvesting. The brewhouse boiler also doubled up for the weekly washing of clothes. Strangely it seems Edward Lilley never drank his own beer nor smoked, although on at least one occasion when George caught him, Edward's reply was 'Ah, that's one I had given me'. The Everetts also brewed their own beer, a domestic tradition which the brothers inherited from their father as in many other cottages. They always brewed for harvest time despite the ample quantities from Brewery Farm, but there was not beer in the home all year round. George recalled that if his father managed to have a little surplus cash then he would buy a couple of bushels of malt and make another small brew. Their recipe was a bushel of malt and a pound of hops and this would make between 18 and 20 gallons of beer. July was the month when they usually brewed and this would start around 2 a.m. in the morning. The copper was lit to boil the water then the malt was put into the mash-tub and stirred with one gallon of hot water and two of cold. A wooden masher was then used to stir it up, a long handled wooden tool with an open cross-branched square griddle at one end. Around 5 or 6 a.m. the liquid was drained off into another tub with a piece of sacking to cover it, this was left for about four hours. The copper was then boiled again for the second mash, utilizing the same malt grist. This second wort was boiled up with the rest of the hops and finally produced a weaker version of the first brew. These brews were evidently not as bitter as present-day beers but George observed that it 'was a lovely deep amber colour'. George also remarked that he liked to drain off a mugful after the first mash and before the hops were added, the sweet wort very much to his liking.

Surrounding the thatched cottage were several barns of which only two remain. They were all timber-framed with weatherboarding treated with bitumen. All of these had pantiled roofs, including the small one to the left of the cottage, which linked with the two-storeyed brewery. In front of the brewhouse and partly in front of the cottage was a large thatched weatherboarded barn with a stable-type door. The brewhouse was situated on the left of the cottage and was built of brick with one entrance door near the centre. At the extreme left end there was the water hand-pump enclosed in a wood ducting which protected the lead water pipe up to the top floor, the entire ducting projecting above the roof line reminiscent of a chimney-stack. To the left-end gable there was a single flue brick chimney-stack above the roof ridge. From the entrance door to the right-hand end to the top floor and partly to the ground floor were adjustable wooden louvres. On entering the door into the brewhouse, on the right were two shallow lead-lined cooling trays, hence the ground floor louvres to allow cooling air to penetrate and warm air to be easily dissipated. To the left there was a copper with another above it, with both furnace flues discharging into the chimney-stack. On the ground floor there was the mash-tun and above it, on the platform shared with the second copper, was the fermenting vessel. A wooden open staircase led up to the platform. An interesting design of brass thermometer made by Dring & Fage of 56 Stamford Street, London, with a scale from 0° to 235°, is still treasured by the Lilley family as is the old wooden mash paddle and narrow wooden malt shovel. Coal for the coppers came from Moys of Colchester. The goodwill of the business was sold to Greene King & Sons Ltd, Bury St Edmunds, Suffolk, in 1925, no doubt so that the large regional brewer could acquire the farming and country house accounts, and possibly a few public houses supplied by Mr Lilley who had been brewing since at least 1885. Mr Hugh Lilley informed me that, unofficially, brewing was only done on a small scale for a while by his grandfather. Sadly the old brewhouse no longer remains, only the name of Brewery Farm denotes the whereabouts of this Suffolk cottage industry.

At Knighton Farm, Newchurch, on the Isle of Wight, a brewhouse constructed of yellow bricks under a Welsh slate roof was built in 1826. The original farm cottage dates from 1692 and has a thatched roof, a common feature for older properties on the island. The detached brewhouse of a single storey is linked to the main house. It has also served as a bakehouse in the past, but more recent use had put the copper to heating pigswill! The later building of the brewhouse in the early Victorian period ties in with the development of the farm, when the additional workers would require their beer as part payment for their labours. On a somewhat grander scale was the late eighteenth-century brewhouse built at Smedmore House, Dorset. The bay-fronted house dates from about 1710, with further additions made fifty years later. The core of the house is Jacobean and to the rear of the property, on the eastern side, are the late eighteenth-century walled gardens, courtyard and brewhouse. This measures about 20 feet by 23 feet, it has no windows but two doors opposite each other, one leading to one of the walled gardens. Sir William Claville was the owner of this house, being knighted for his services in Ireland. His descendants retained Smedmore House in direct line until 1833. Since that time the house has been in the Mansel family and has passed from father to son through four generations. Steventon Grange, Berkshire, is a typical house of the period. An inventory taken in 1324 indicates that there was a chamber and hall, a pantry and a buttery, larder and kitchen and a brewhouse and dairy. Evidently two Benedictine monks lived here with their several lay servants, as indicated by the number of kitchen utensils. There were twenty plates, dishes and saucers of wood, all stored with cooking pots and pans in the kitchen. It is therefore likely that the brewhouse catered for a maximum of twenty people, far more likely though would be a figure of ten or twelve people.

From the diary of Sir John Wittewronge of Rothamsted Manor, near St Albans, Herts, written in 1694, can be appreciated the volume of his spring brewing:

March 16th. Tunn'd a pipe of strong beer and four hoggsheads of small brued with 22 bushells of malt and 6 pounds of hopps: the pipe stands next the courtyard in the old Seller.

March 23rd. Tunn'd the 2d pipe from the courtyard with 22 bushells of malt and 6 pounds of hopps and four hoggsheads of small beer with the pale malt.

March 30th. Tunn'd the 3d pipe from the courtyard and 4 hoggsheads of small beer with two and twenty bushells of malt and 7 or 8 pounds of hops.

The Wittewronge baronetcy was created on 2 May 1662 and became extinct on 13 January 1771. Sir John was born in 1618 and died at the age of eighty. A John Bennet derived Rothamsted Manor from his cousin, Thomas Wittewronge, the last of the line who died in 1763. He was succeeded by his nephew, John Bennet Lawes, the first baronet of Rothamsted, a JP created on 19 May 1882. Sir Charles Bennet Lawes assumed for himself and his issue the surname of Wittewronge by Royal Licence, 18 April 1902.

Old Shoyswell Manor at Etchingham, Sussex, built in the sixteenth century, is a typical tile-hung timber-framed house. It is reputed to have been a hunting lodge of King Henry VIII, although the name is taken from the Shoyswell family who owned it from the 1250s to the end of the seventeenth century. In his will dated 1580, Thomas Shoyswell bequeathed among other items to his widow Dorothy, 'free liberty to bake and brewe in the bakehouse and brewhouse for her owne necessarie use and to drye her clothes upon the hedges and bushes about his manor house of Shoyswell'. It sounds as though things could have been a little better for the widow Shoyswell.

The Lordship, a fifteenth-century moated manor house with its dairy on the left and the brewhouse in the right-hand gabled wing.

Set in the middle of the typical English village near Buntingford, Herts, stands the manor-house called The Lordship, Cottered and its adjacent farm buildings close by the parish church. The Lordship is a timber-framed house dating back to the fifteenth century, its earliest owner being a John Fray. The house is set in its own spacious grounds with the remains of its moat forming a 'U' to the rear of the house. A central porch gives access to a central hall with several molded timber arches, to the left is the old sitting-room set with oak panelling probably from the eighteenth century but with the original carved oak fire-surround. Behind this is a passage which leads to a room at the end which has a large brick-built chimney-stack – this was the old brewhouse. The old brewing copper and its brickwork have now been removed, but some fifteen feet outside is the covered well complete with winding gear which still survives. To the rear there is a store and the old dairy while a previous tool house, which led off the brewhouse, has now been incorporated into one timber-studded room. At the other end of the building is the similarly studded kitchen with secondary entrance door and a small winding staircase leading off from a lobby. The overall size of the brewhouse measures 12 feet by 20 feet and the large double flue-stack probably also served the bakehouse. The nearby storeroom could either have served as a cheese store, adjacent to the dairy, or possibly as a dry store for the brewhouse and bakehouse. A few miles to the east there is another ancient manor-house, also with its brewhouse now incorporated into the living accommodation.

Alswick Hall, Layston, Herts, stands isolated on sloping ground, this timbered seventeenth-century manor-house facing west towards Buntingford about a mile away. The hall stands on a partly moated location, the remains of the moat now forming a lake facing the

Alswick Hall, Hertfordshire. The central chimney stack served the brewhouse.

front elevation – the site is believed to have been the site of the chapel of Alswick. The timber-framed building is built on small brick foundations under a handmade tiled roof. The original 'T' shaped plan has the vertical section facing east, the main block is 71 feet long by 17 feet wide with a central doorway, to the south is a stone-paved hall with a wide seated fireplace which backs onto the parlour at the southern end. To the northern side of the entrance is a large kitchen which also has an inglenook fireplace. A short passage from the hall has a winding staircase leading off it from the intersection of the 'T', this stair enclosure has one window and is gabled. A massive double-faced chimney-breast has a three-arched fireplace in the hall, to the eastern projecting wing the other side of the fireplace previously served a brewhouse; this measures 15 feet by 18 feet. Beyond the old brewhouse are two rooms with terracotta floor tiles which were previously the dairy. Tudor brick chimney-stacks are set diagonally and the external elevations of the hall remain much as they have done for several hundred years. To the north of the hall is a very large Victorian barn which forms part of the farm development, the property now being approached via an avenue, past tied postwar farm cottages. The isolated site of the house necessitated the brewhouse to cater for the needs of the small community that lived here and were dependent on their farming.

Llanaeron House, Llanaeron, Dyfed, was designed by John Nash, the renowned architect, who was commissioned by Colonel William Lewis to build the fine house and its service courtyard in 1794–5. Apart from minor additions the house remains true to Nash's designs and as such is a unique property now owned by the National Trust.

The house is pre-dated to Tudor times by the Parry family when, in 1689, Anne, the heiress of Llewelyn Parry of Llanerchaeron, married Hugh Lewis of Plas Cilie Aeron. This match united two parkland estates into one, amounting in 1873 to 4,397 acres. The present house is a neo-classical villa, with colour-washed roughcast walls and deep-eaved slate-hipped roofs. The two storeys are in a square plan with the kitchens, scullery, butler's pantry and housekeeper's room connecting to a service courtyard and quadrangle. This includes the servant's bothy, cheese and dairy rooms, smoke and meat curing rooms, boot and laundry rooms and the brewhouse in the far corner. The courtyard to both the service area and the detached stable and farmyard are beautifully cobbled in herringbone patterns of elongated pebbles. The service buildings are constructed of rubble stone with double-hipped slate roofs, the brewhouse has two windows to the rear north-east elevation and one facing into the courtyard from which access is made. Within the brewhouse are two large stone vats, divided by steps with a furnace beneath each vat; these measure approximately 4 feet high and 4 feet in diameter.

Colonel William Lewis died in 1828 and his son John inherited the estate, with Mrs Corbetta Lewis dying just three years later. Major John Lewis married Mary Mettan, twenty years his junior, in 1841 at Barwell, Leicestershire. Major Lewis died in 1855 without an heir, his widow running the estate until her death in 1917 at the age of 104. On her hundredth birthday, a special dinner was served at the Feathers Hotel, Aberaeron, which had been built on Lewis family land and 300 guests were brought to the coastal town by a special train on the Great Western Railway. The estate passed via the female line to the Boultbee family and then the Lewes family. Due to family debts it is evident that the house was not altered and so it is that this unspoilt Nash house has been passed down as a rare example of an early Nash design. In 1940 Captain Lewis's son, John Powell Ponsonby Lewis, inherited the estate and on his death in 1989 he had bequeathed the entire property to the National Trust.

In 1859 there were eleven domestic staff there, with the butler earning £40 per year and six maids carrying out various duties on an average wage of £8 a year. On the farm there were seven men who were paid 1s 11d per day; in the gardens, a further six men were paid similar wages with the head gardener paid £42 a year. Estate workers, who included a keeper, carpenter, mason and labourers, amounted to seven with daily wages ranging from 3s a day for craftsmen to 2s 6d for others. The staff worked an eight hour day and were also paid overtime. The total number of staff in the latter part of the nineteenth century amounted to thirty-one. They would have consumed around 80 gallons of beer a week with probably a further 10 gallons a week consumed by the family. On special occasions when there were house guests this figure would increase, as would the estate staff's requirements at harvest time when casual labour was employed. At these times the brewhouse would be producing around 120 gallons a week.

Continuing the journey northward, while at the same time reviewing the estates of nobler families, Shibden Hall, Halifax, is reached. The close-timbered façade, with diagonal timbers and mullioned oriel windows to each of the gabled bays on either side of the entrance porch, denote the early date of construction by the Otes family. William Otes was in residence in about 1425 and his granddaughter Joan should have inherited the property but litigation ensued. However, Joan's husband's influential family, the Saviles, won the court action and had moved in by 1504. The Saviles made their mark on the property as denoted by the recurrence of the family armorial device of three owls, seen in ceiling bosses and a glass window. Shibden Hall passed into the ownership of Sibel Savile and her husband Robert Waterhouse in 1522, he being a lawyer and MP for York. The Waterhouses owned the estate until 1612 and it was sold to Samuel Lister in that year in order to stave off bankruptcy. Samuel was a cloth merchant with four children, two sons marrying into the Waterhouse family. Shibden Hall survived the Civil War. Several more generations of the Listers lived at the hall, with Anne Lister inheriting it in 1826 on the death of her uncle James. Anne Lister was devoted to the house and made several improvements until she died in Georgia, her body being returned to Halifax for burial. In her will, Shibden was left to her Welsh cousins with Dr John Lister and his family taking up residence in 1855 and using the house as a surgery. On his death in 1867 the house came into his son John's ownership, but once again the threat of bankruptcy loomed and so, in 1923, his friend Mr A.S. McCrea purchased the park and the reversion of Shibden Hall for the people of Halifax. John died in 1933 and two years later it was opened as a museum, still open today and managed by the Calderdale Council, Leisure Services Department.

An inventory of 1677/8 has the following item: 'Item in Ye brewhouse one copper brewing vessel £2.10.00.' Later in February 1718, James Lister paid 'Mr Rookes & James Tattershall my servant for 800 of Bricks 16/-' and 'John Johnson & his partners being Bricklayers, for mending low Kitchen Chimny & setting brewing lead etc at Shibdenhall 18/-'. This second item suggests that after forty years of brewing, the lead, possibly either pipes or linings to a tun or coolers, required replacement. The brewhouse, which still remains, is near the threshing room and dairy but the equipment seen today in the brewhouse is not original, the items having been removed from the White Bear Inn, Norwood Green, Halifax, and re-erected by the museum staff in 1953. In March 1720 the records of Shibden Hall record that

James Lister paid 'Mr Joseph Holmes, by his son, for malting 4 quart of Barley at 6/- & for the Excise, 15/5¼d', clearly indicating that an outside maltster carried out the malting, probably of barley, from the Shibden Hall estate. Somewhat unusually hops can still be found in the area and these possibly came from the hop seeds found in the dregs of casks when they were being cleaned out. Yorkshire was not a commercial hop-growing area being too far north, so the hops used in brewing on the estate would most likely have come from the Herefordshire and Worcestershire area. Requests for consignments of hops were frequently made by Yorkshire families to relations and agents in London, the supply from the more fertile and mild climate of the south producing the finest quality hops from the counties of Kent, Surrey, Sussex and Hampshire.

Stackpole Court, Pembrokeshire, had plans for a new brewhouse and dairy drawn up on 19 January 1843. The instructions of the architect, Mr Ashton, were: 'In order that the beer may be conveyed by a pipe from the brewhouse into the cellar, it will be necessary to fix a lift pump on the upper stage, by which the beer may be raised to the mouth of the pipe, which should be so high as to give a good fall to the barrels in the cellar . . . for this purpose (if it is found necessary) the pump may be worked from a stage raised 2 or 3 feet above – or the head of the pump may be kept up and handle lengthened. The center flue of the stack to be 1'6" square opened within the roof with the brewhouse to carry off the steam from the copper over which there may be a hood with a funnel.' The copper was supported on three brick piers and stone lintels, an underback was situated beneath the mash-tun. The copper was 8 feet in diameter and the mash-tun 6 feet in diameter. There were three coolers measuring 7 feet by 10 feet with two louvred windows to the north elevation and three to the west. The underback measured 6 feet in diameter by 4 feet 6 inches high and the mash-tun was 4 feet high. On the top of the slatted roof is a louvred turret with a weather-vane surmounted by the Earl's coronet. The beer line to the cellar commenced in the brewhouse with an upright pipe, it then descended underground to the washhouse courtyard, from thence the pipe carried along passageways above the door heads to the cellar. Provision was made about two-thirds along the way for cleaning the pipe which was about 290 feet long. The fall of the ground is 10 feet in 155 feet in an east/west direction. The brewhouse was built adjacent and at right angles to the larder and the previous scullery was formed into a cheese room. The brewhouse yard measured 25 feet by 15 feet and was in the right angle formed by the new brewhouse to the larder, with the new cheese room on the third side opposite the larder; the fourth side was the washhouse drying ground.

The Georgian mansion was largely rebuilt in about 1854 following a previous rebuild in 1735, it had been fortified and damaged in the Civil War. It was built on the site of an earlier Norman castle, the Lorts having owned the estate since about 1608. In 1689 Miss Elizabeth Lort, the sole heir, married Sir Alexander Campbell (of Cawdor) whom she met at a fashionable London ball. Their son, John, inherited the estate in 1715. The house was demolished in 1963 but the brewhouse block remains today, as does the stable block which is converted into residential flats. Stackpole was a medieval barony which took its name from a stack or inlet off Broadhaven and embraced the parishes of Stackpole Elidyr, Boshertson (formerly Stackpole Bosher), St Petrox and much of St Twyndls. The barony was governed from the previous castle described as 'the castell of Stacpooll or court of Stackpooll' in

The large detached brewhouse and dairy at Stackpole, Pembrokeshire.

1674. The lands surrounding the castle included home farm together with the deer park. As early as 1188, when Elidyr de Stackpole and his wife were the owners, they were criticised by a young man of their household saying, 'Why are you afraid to spend this money when your lives are so short and the money you are hoarding will go to others?' He also gave the best food and drink to the farm labourers and household servants saying that they should enjoy them as the fruits of their labour.

The Earl of Halifax who previously lived at Hickleton Hall, Yorkshire, sold the estate and house to the Sue Ryder Charity and consequently moved to Garrowby, near York. Having been well pleased with his own beer at Hickleton, it was decided to transfer all the brewing plant and tools to his estate at Bugthorpe. An old cowhouse with a granary above was considered a suitable venue for his new brewery and with the guidance and supervision from Mr Ross, the head-brewer at Samuel Smith's brewery, Tadcaster, the transfer was made. The first brew at Bugthorpe took place on 9 November 1989, with Wilf Dorsey as brewer, a retired estate forester for the Earl of Halifax at Hickleton Hall for some thirty years.

Bugthorpe brewhouse is built of red brick in two storeys under a pantiled roof, the top floor granary having access via an external staircase; this was removed on the conversion. The reconstruction of the brewing plant was done by Samuel Smith's brewery under the supervision of Mr Paul Smith. The original copper was built into new brickwork and has a bottled gas heating unit. The copper mash-tun, built by Thomas Ryder & Co. of Manchester, is situated on the ground floor beneath the wooden grist bin and hopper on the top floor. An ex-dairy cooling unit is fixed to one side of the mash-tun. This vessel is also used as the fermenting vessel. A perforated paddle with a wooden handle is used, as are several other copper samplers. A new small copper coil which can be easily removed is used during fermentation, so that if the wort starts to overheat or if it gets too cool, then either cold or warm water is passed through the coil to assist fermentation. Samuel Smith's supply all the malt made from Halcyon barley, and Golding and Fuggles hops are used. The brew capacity produced is 100 gallons with an OG varying between 60 to 70. Water is from the mains which is pumped out of bore holes on the chalk wolds to the east, and a pound of gypsum is added. The beer is racked into six firkins and five kilderkin aluminium casks appropriately designated 'Earl of Halifax'; it is intended that all the casks will be the smaller size. The brewing takes place once a year in September and is aimed to be a personal service to the Earl's shoots on his estate. The Earl of Halifax's brewery is believed to be the only private estate brewhouse still producing its own home-brewed beer in England. The Garrowby estate comprises some 18,000 acres in trust through the Halifax Estates and the Halifax Family Trust.

The village of Hickleton, in the guise of several different spellings, was mentioned in the Doomsday Book. Before the dissolution of the monasteries the land was owned by the priory of Monk Bretton but following the disbandment of the monks, the lands passed through many ownerships. During the reign of Queen Elizabeth, Judge Rodes purchased the manor of Hickleton and built a large mansion for his younger son Peter. The property soon passed into the Jackson family in about 1600 who retained the manor for three generations before they sold it to Sir Michael Wentworth of Wooley in about 1705. A descendant of Sir Michael evidently preferred the Hickleton area to Wooley and built 'a very handsome house a little to the south of the old mansion which he suffered to go into decay'. The present Hickleton Hall was therefore built in about 1740. For financial reasons the manor was sold in 1828 to Sir Francis Lindley Wood of Hemsworth and remained the family residence until the death of the 2nd Viscount Halifax in 1934. Edward, 1st Earl of Halifax, made his home at Garrowby and Peter, the 3rd Earl Lord Halifax still lives at Garrowby.

During the last war the hall was requisitioned by the military authorities and in 1947 many of its contents were sold. It became a girl's school until it was sold in 1961 to the Sue Ryder Foundation who are currently the owners. Garrowby was acquired by Sir Francis Lindley Wood before Hickleton Hall and was to all intents and purposes a shooting lodge. On the death of Charles, the 2nd Viscount, in 1934, the hall was closed down but the brewhouse at Hickleton continued to brew once or twice a year to serve the needs of the family and estate workers. On the outbreak of the Second World War, all brewing ceased until the end of hostilities in 1945. The brewhouse finally closed down in 1989 but before that final stage is reached, there is much to tell about the 'Hickleton Brew'.

In the village there were two home-brewers in May 1919, the year that Clarence Hellewell started work at 'The Hall'. Clarence's reminiscences of his time, first as assistant brewer from 1926 to 1935 and subsequently as head brewer from 1935 to 1989 at Hickleton Hall shall be recalled. The two home-brewers were Mrs Middleton who lived at No. 38, and the other was Mrs Adams, the wife of the hall's butler; she referred to her brew as 'stout'. An amusing story was told by Clarence about Mrs Middleton in her latter life as a widow when she became increasingly dependent on other people for such things as kindling sticks and logs for her fires. She was most generous with her home-brew to anyone who helped her, but plainly her beer production became less successful and she would apologize by saying 'the beer is not quite as good as it should be as it didn't work very well'. One day she was helped in some way by Henry Heptenstall who was Lord Halifax's brewer at the time. He knew all there was to be known about home-brewed beer, but was also blunt in his manner of speech. He was evidently quite a terrifying character, known as

'Owd Arry', but for all of that a kindly man. On the day that Owd Arry delivered whatever he was taking to Mrs Middleton, she asked him if he would like a glass of her brew. His stock reply was 'niver been known to refuse' and the glass of beer duly arrived with the inevitable and fully expected remark that 'the beer was not quite up to standard'. Owd Arry was well prepared for this and in his cruelly blunt way said: 'Well, I'll tell tha' wot Mrs, they allus say it's a pity to set owt to work as isn't able!' Whereupon he drank up his beer, wiped his mouth on the back of his hand and stumped off up the garden path, no doubt leaving Mrs Middleton laughing in the doorway, as they were old friends. According to Clarence Hellewell's recollection, there were at least three other houses in the village that had brewing coppers, but they had not been used much by the outbreak of the First World War.

The brewhouse is a rectangular limestone building believed to have been originally erected as a gardenhouse or bathhouse at the same time as the hall and stables by Godfrey Wentworth in about 1740. It is most likely that it was converted into a brewhouse when Sir Francis Wood, father of Charles, 1st Viscount Halifax, moved to Hickleton from Hemsworth High Hall in 1829. The local stone-built building is situated to the north-east of the hall and measures 38 feet by 17 feet, with a blue slate hipped roof and a louvred ventilator sited over the brewing copper. The building is decorative in appearance with a string course at intermediate level. There are three rooms with a central door on the east side and opposite a central window on each side, all having been built up since its original use. In one room all four corners are concave recesses which may have been provided for tightening bolts on metal hoops to a large, coopered, water storage vat. At a height of about 15 feet a ceiling has been provided and the walls painted. Water for brewing came from a spring at Loscoe Pond, being pumped up into a tank situated in the loft of the brewhouse over the original open cooling tray. This water supply also served Stotfold Farm who received its supply by a horse-drawn water cart. This cart had a single coopered 100-gallon barrel with a bung on the top, from which a wooden chute was placed from to underneath a tap at a higher level from the water tank. Brewing took place ten times each year, 200 gallons being brewed at each session of five consecutive Wednesdays in March and October. Before brewing commenced all the equipment and plant had to be thoroughly cleaned and the estate joiner, George Wakefield, had to remove one end of each of the two 110-gallon casks so all signs of dead yeast could be removed. In addition to the 2,000 gallons of beer produced each year, the brewhouse had a double-strength beer referred to locally as 'ale', this being brewed normally only once a year or as an extra brew for special occasions. The brewing copper last used at Hickleton was a replacement of the previous one of the same dimensions which had worn paper thin. The replacement was made in the early 1930s and was supplied by Darmons (blacksmiths) and jointly fixed with George Ball, head of the estate stonemason's department. The mash-tub was wood coopered and made by Whitworths Son & Nephews Brewery at Wath-on-Dearne and was deteriorating and becoming unfit for use by the beginning of the Second World War, so this was replaced by a copper of the same size with a capacity of 279 gallons when full. This was supplied by Thomas Ryder of Manchester for the cost of £75. In the period leading up to the 1930s fermenting took place in the cellars of the hall, and a similar sized coopered cask was made and supplied by Whitworth's Brewery. As it was larger than the door opening it had to be erected in the cellar.

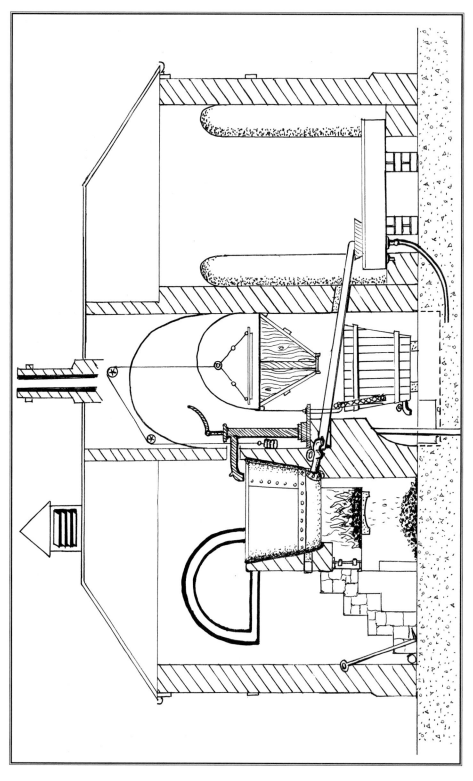

Elevation of Lord Halifax's brewhouse at Hickleton Hall, Yorkshire.

Malt, hops and yeast were supplied by Whitworth's Brewery, also wooden casks such as the two 110-gallon casks; other replacements included several hogsheads. This brewery company went out of business in 1958 and up until this time their head brewer, George Bayliss, a friend of Mr Clegg, who was at that time Lord Halifax's estate agent, gave technical brewing advice. The Wath-on-Dearne brewery was a common brewer owning 170 public houses which was acquired by the renowned Tadcaster brewery company of John Smith's. At some unspecified time the brewing materials were supplied through Carter Longbottom, ironmongers in Doncaster, probably due to the fact that the hall butler, Mr Adams, ordered groceries and other items from this firm. Following the closure of Whitworth's Brewery, the materials were supplied for a few years by Clarkson's, a small brewery in Barnsley, who were also acquired by John Smith's. Mr Clegg the estate agent was also a director of Clarkson's brewery. John Smith's also supplied materials, to be finally followed in 1984 by Theakston's of Masham, North Yorkshire.

Because of the many months between brews, often six to seven, the wooden casks deteriorated and tended to dry out. This necessitated regular repairs until it was no longer viable to do so and the Memel oak previously used in these casks was no longer available. Mr Mutch, who had by now replaced Mr Clegg as estate agent, instigated the purchase of metal casks which proved easier to clean and required no repairs. This changeover took place in the mid-1980s.

Lord Halifax paid 4s to HM Customs & Excise for a Private Brewer's Licence during the 1950s, which permitted the brewing of beer of an annual value in excess of £15, for the consumption by farm labourers employed by him. This licence permitted the holder to brew beer on his premises for his own domestic use, but the beer was also chargeable with duty. There were a number of spoilt brews at Hickleton Hall, certainly in the time of Clarence Hellewell, who kept appropriate records. No doubt his predecessors, the Heptonstall brothers, never kept any records. In 1955 the Customs & Excise were approached by Dibb & Clegg, solicitors acting for the Hickleton estate, with the view to receiving a rebate for the spoilt beer. The reply indicated that 'the current law dealing with spoilt beer is the Customs & Excise Act 1952 Sections 263 (3) and (4). You will see that these two sub-sections of the act only allow us to deal with spoilt beer claims received from Brewers for Sale. The current position is identical with that existing prior to the passing of the 1952 Act, the old Acts were these of 1880 and 1915.' Ten years previously, on 31 December 1944, the same solicitors had requested the basis of calculating the duty on beer brewed by private brewers. The Customs & Excise reply was thus: 'Duty is not charged, in the case of private brewers, on the actual produce of the brewing, but on a theoretical quantity which it is assumed any brewer can produce from given brewing materials at a standard gravity of 1055.' In the case of the materials used at Hickleton – i.e. malt – the brewer is deemed in law to have produced 36 gallons of beer (1 barrel) for every 2 bushels of malt used, and from the quantity so obtained, an allowance of 6 per cent for waste is made and duty charged on the net. Thus for the Hickleton brew, the calculation is as follows:

Materials used 1 Qr Malt	=	8 bushels
Produced @ 1055° OG	=	144 gallons
Deduct allowance 6%	=	8 gallons
Charged with duty	=	136 gallons = 3 brls, 28 gals
Duty @ £14.6.5½ per standard barrel	=	£54.2.2

The standard Original Gravity of 1055° used by the Customs & Excise was exceeded in most brews, with the exception of that on 22 June 1954 when it was only 1049.92°. The average gravity over the last thirty years was 1064°, with the highest original gravity of 2000° being achieved in 1944 followed by the March 1982 brew of 1073°. The year of 1965 was not a good one for Clarence Hellewell as he had two failed brews, the first was a special brewing on 27 May for Lord Irwin's twenty-first birthday party when 108 gallons were put down the drain. A hurried replacement brew was done on 17 June and proved satisfactory. Again, on 9 September, the brew failed, possibly due to the brewhouse being too cold. A further brewing took place on 1 December 1965 and four each of kilderkin and firkin casks were racked satisfactorily.

Besides the special brewing for Lord Irwin's birthday, another 'special' was brewed on 22 June 1981 to celebrate Prince Charles and Lady Diana's wedding. On 15 May 1984 a later brewing was done for a function at Garrowby when 300 guests attended. The last brew at Hickleton Hall was carried out by Clarence Hellewell on 9 March 1989, assisted by Ken Linley, when 100 gallons were brewed. The cost of 168 kgs of best Pale Ale Malt was £55.40 and 4kgs of 1988 hops was £15.50, plus VAT, making a total cost of £209.52 – 26 pence per pint! There was of course no duty paid.

The story of Hickleton Hall brewing is best told by the late Clarence Hellewell in his own words: 'My career as a brewer started in 1926 when I was twenty-two years old. I was sent to help two old brothers 'Owd Arry' and 'Owd Ted' Heptenstall who were the last surviving members of an old Hickleton family. I, being comparatively young, they seemed terribly old to me, but really they were only in their early sixties and were, and had been all their lives, estate workers, generally as farm hands. All I could gather about the brewing was that they had inherited it from their ancestors of the same name, who were long since dead. They were very proud of their skill as brewers and of course were looked upon by the rest of the community as being people of a rather higher intelligence than the ordinary bloke, the very fact that they could brew beer put them on a plane of their own. They knew it too and took advantage of the fact by keeping all knowledge of the process entirely to themselves. Looking back now I think they had decided to take their knowledge of brewing to their graves, and they nearly did. Both had a son each but neither worked on the estate and had no intention of ever doing so. This meant there was no one of the family to follow the Heptenstall brothers as brewers, therefore they had made up their minds that brewing at Hickleton would end with them and, as I said earlier, it nearly did.

'When I first was sent to help them they were both beginning to get worse for wear with rheumatism particularly Owd Ted. After helping them for a few years he had to finally call it a day, and I had to spend more time with Owd Arry. What I used to do in the first place was to clean out two huge wooden casks, each holding 110 gallons, which would contain that week's brew. The estate joiner, George Wakefield, had previously taken out one end of each cask so that the insides could be scrubbed and cleaned. When I arrived they [the casks] would be out in the yard in front of the brewhouse laid on their sides. I used to crawl inside with a scrubbing brush and a bucket of hot water, giving them a thorough scrubbing out to remove the white dead yeast which clung and stuck to the sides as the level of the liquid went down with the drawing of the beer from the tap near the bottom. Incidently the casks were more of the shape of an airship, and stood on their ends. As I say, they each held 110 gallons, making sure they held all the brew which amounted to a little above 200 gallons. The brewing, including the fermenting period, was a week's process almost. We brewed always on Wednesday and put it in the casks [called racking] on the following Tuesday, when two more empty casks would be brought out of the cellar then the process would be repeated. This we used to do five times in the spring [March] and five times in the autumn [October] making ten brews per year, meaning the consumption was around 2,000 gallons per year. In fact for some reason or other I helped to brew eleven times one year! It [the beer] was used extensively in the Hall, of course, and was on the table every day at lunchtime. The outside staff, farmworkers, joiners, masons, gardeners, in fact any of the estate workers, while not having an everyday issue, yet did very well out of it.

'There were what were known as "beer jobs". The farm workers were those who were directly attached to the estate by working on the house farm of about 70 or 80 acres which were farmed by the estate for milk, butter, bacon, etc., under the jurisdiction of a foreman who was known as the farm bailiff. This gentleman's name was Thomas Cocking. Other departments got beer allowance for sundry hard or dirty jobs such as carpet-beating, chimney-sweeping at the Hall, haymaking at harvest time, tree felling and numerous other jobs. The issuing out of the beer was in the hands of two people. For work connected with the Hall the butler used to draw it out of the extensive cellars under the Hall, while the outside staff were served by Owd Arry. One particularly dirty job was the farm threshing days, when liberal amounts would be consumed and supplied twice a day at about 10.30 in the mornings and 3.00 in the afternoons. The threshing-day beer was always most welcome, especially if it was a hot day. This was a job when it was a case of all hands on deck, as it was an understood thing that all departments gave a hand with that except, of course, the Hall servants.

'At the drinking time we all gathered round Owd Arry who described himself as the "boiler art" and with a twinkle in his eyes he used to say, "t' boiler art sups fost, last and int middle". The thing which used to nauseate me was that there was only one drinking vessel which was either a battered tin half-pint mug, or a part of a cow's horn which had been sawn off in its widest part, a wooden bottom fixed in somehow (I never could find out how!) and this left a vessel about the size and shape of an ordinary half-pint tumbler. Either of these depending on which Owd Arry picked up first was used for everyone, passed round in turn. I am not ashamed to say that I shuddered as it came to me, possibly after a chap who had been chewing tobacco a few minutes earlier. Ugh. However, there only seemed to be me who bothered about it, and I never said anything.

'On brewing day, after I had washed out the casks, I helped with whatever was taking place, my work getting more and more as Owd Ted became less able to get around with his rheumatism, until finally he had to call it a day and give up. This meant that I had to be present all the time on brewing day, even to the early morning start of the process which began at 2.30 a.m. The reason for starting at such an unearthly hour was to allow for two lots of water to go onto the malt before say, 7.00 a.m. when the real work began. The two lots of water were required to get the 200 gallons. The malt absorption of the water meant that when the mash-tub was full there was only 100 gallons of liquid to run off. What happened then was the first lot was run out of a tap in the bottom of the mash-tub, then the tub was filled up again to get the final required amount. This all had to be done before 7.00 a.m. The amount of materials to brew what we called "beer" was a quarter of ground malt, 7 or 8 lbs of hops and 5 or 6 lbs of yeast. We also had one week's brew during the session that we brewed double-strength for special occasions and never saw daylight outside the Hall. This we called "Ale", heaven knows why! I never really knew the purpose of this as the "beer" was strong enough for the ordinary use and the "Ale" was just too strong for anything. I can't think why or where it was used. It was so strong as to make wine glass measures quite sufficient. I could never get on with it. I always felt I wanted a knife and fork to it! I think by the look of the half-full glasses left on the dining-room table after it had been served, that there was far more wasted than drunk.

'As I became more and more involved in the actual process of brewing I was required to come for the 2.30 a.m. start and to stay with Owd Arry until the end of the process. In spite of this, all I could learn about it was what I saw! This of course was very important, but I realized in after years how little I really knew about it. I have already stated I think the Heptenstall brothers thought the brewing would end with them, therefore I was told very little, other than what I asked about. Quite candidly I did not know what to ask! Therefore I was finding out little or nothing about the part of the process which mattered.

'We, Owd Arry and myself, were allowed a hot dinner on brewing day which was brought from the Hall. I used to look forward to that as it was a lovely meal of meat and vegetables cooked by the Hall cook (Mrs Burbridge) who of course was at the top of her profession. This we took into an adjoining building where there was fire and long table with a couple of chairs. It was really the saddle room or harness room. There would be whips, saddles, bridles and harnesses with silver-plated metal parts all on brackets on the walls which were lined with matchboard to keep the things off the walls, so avoiding as much dampness as possible. Although the horse population had dwindled, horse-drawn carriages etc. were used quite often in spite of the fact that Lord Halifax owned a 1914 Rolls-Royce car. Yet a splendid pair of blacks [horses] and a riding pony were kept until well into the 1930s. We would enjoy our dinner, then Owd Arry having been up for most of the previous night and now warm and full of dinner would usually drop off into a snoring sleep. I was young and not tired like he, so one particular time I thought I would write down all I could think about that might be useful if ever I had to be responsible for the brew myself. I never thought I would be, but that was to come as a surprise and indeed a shock a few years later.

'I remember writing those notes very well, at the same time keeping my eye on Owd Arry who had passed away into slumber and was building his snoring into a shuddering crescendo, like the organ in St Paul's Cathedral, crashing out the last verse of 'Onward Christian Soldiers' in double ff! Anyway, with a last terrifying roar it blasted him back into wakefulness and his bleary eyes gradually focused on me. I could not help laughing although I loved him. He eventually realized where he was and it wasn't long before his eyes started to twinkle, though seventy-three or seventy-four he didn't wear glasses. He had tiny warts hanging on his eyelids which seemed to wobble when he laughed, which was quite a lot. He, like most old men of his day, sported a moustache and what had once been a black beard, but now liberally mixed with grey. He was, all in all, a delightful old man but like lots of those old characters they either liked you or they didn't, and let you know according to which every way you happened to be in their favour. However, on now being fully awake again he said "Wot's tha' writin'?" I replied, "Nowt much," and stuffed my notes into my pocket, little knowing how important they were going to be.

'A few years later, about 1935, we were well into our spring brew, in fact we had one week's supply of materials left or I should say materials for one more brew [week's process] when Owd Arry was taken ill and had a stroke. Something had to be done so I said to the butler, Mr Adams, "What are you going to do?" and he promptly said to me, "You will have to do it!" In my ignorance (which is what it amounted to) I felt no lack of confidence as to whether I was capable of doing it or not. If I had known then that, in spite of my notes, how little I knew about the complete process, I should never have dared to tackle the job! I knew nothing about the fermentation side of it which is one of the most vital parts of the process, nor did I know anything about temperature etc. for the ferment. This had never been showed to me as I had never had anything to do with it after the brewing day. I little realized how important that stage can be, in fact the fermentation is all important. If that is not correct then you might as well begin again.

'Still I carried on but mercifully the Hall closed down after the death of Charles, 2nd Viscount Halifax, and brewing was cut down to once a year, sometimes once in two years. This carried on up to the war when we didn't brew for four years, in fact I thought it had ended altogether. After VE Day, Mr Clegg, who was the estate agent proper, said to me, "Have we any beer left?" I said we had the greater part of a hogshead [54 gallons] left but I didn't know what it would be like, as it had been on tap for 2 years! He said, draw it all off and bring it into what had been the army NAAFI, the army having left for the D-Day invasion in 1944. I duly drew it off and examined it sceptically, it looked terrible and in my opinion was "bloody awful", cloudy and tasted like vinegar. I didn't say anything and Mr Clegg called all the workmen left on the estate together and anyone else who was around and invited them to come for a drink to celebrate the end of the war in Europe. It would be mid-afternoon when the festivities began and, as the beer was poured out by Mr Clegg at a little window through which meals etc. had been served during army days, I watched anxiously as to the effect the (in my opinion) horrible stuff might have upon those misguided enough to drink it. However, there were no complaints and there must have been some alcohol left in it as the conversation got louder and more enthusiastic, which made me think people will "sup owt" if it is called beer and free of charge! Personally I restrained myself with no difficulty, apart from a token part-filled glass in front of me and which I deposited into the drain at the first opportunity, or rather when everybody else was too happy to witness my sacrilegious act. Quite candidly I was glad to see it out of the way. It must have done some good as everyone went home in good spirits.

'It was some little time before we brewed again as the Earl of Halifax was finishing his time as the British Ambassador in America. In fact I thought brewing had ended but on completing his term he soon started to enquire about the beer again, and once again my worries began. We brewed again about a year later then at intervals of two years up to 1963. While through experience I was obviously getting the brew a little better, try as I may I could not get the finished product to clear and I could not understand why, or how to correct it, with the result that after about three weeks or a month after each brew when it was nice to drink but still not clear, it began to "work" again in the casks, because the cloudiness was in fact yeast, and started a secondary ferment, especially in warm weather. I had no means of knowing where I was going wrong, but with each brew my worries returned as try as I might I could not think why I wasn't getting it right.

'Mr Clegg called in a gentleman called Mr G. Bayliss, who was head brewer to Whitworth Son and Nephew, a small local brewery at Wath-on-Dearne. It seemed Mr Clegg and Mr Bayliss were old friends of army days. Mr Bayliss duly came over to give us what advice he could, but gentleman that he was, he didn't know quite what to do or say to me without interfering and also he did not know what I wanted to know, as he knew I was in charge of Lord Halifax's brewery and no doubt put me on a pedestal which I was really unworthy to occupy. He examined the beer we had on tap, I would say about two months old, drew a glass out of the cask currently on tap, held it up to the light, took a mouthful out of the glass then spat it out again. I gather this is how people taste things, by rolling it round in the mouth and not swallowing it, thus leaving the taste behind in the mouth. I, in my anxiety, thought he spat it out a little quicker than he might have done. As I watched, fascinated at him examining the glass of liquid which resembled cloudy pond water, I am sure tadpoles would not have been out of place in it! After an uncomfortable pause during which all my brewing life flashed before me, he respectfully suggested we let them take it away and filter it for us. My heart rose, feeling sure that was what was required for this brew at least. We had between 50 and 60 gallons left which they took away, filtered and put into clean casks. I have to admit that when it came back it was considerably better, but it didn't satisfy me.

'Mr Bayliss was very good to us and persuaded Mr Clegg to let them make all kinds of copper vessels and other utensils for us which would help. For instance all our tubs, tanks etc. had been made of wood, i.e. Memel oak which was beginning to be increasingly difficult to get hold of and what was available the breweries needed all for themselves. I refer in the main to our mash-tub and fermenting tub, both of the same size, also all the casks were made of wood. The fermenting tub was replaced by a copper one made especially for us by Thomas Ryder and Co. of Manchester on the instigation of Whitworth's (Mr Bayliss) who also helped us in a number of other ways by making us copper sieves, a coil to put into the fermenting vessel during the ferment, and suggested to Mr Clegg that he get a small refrigerator to cool the brew as we ran it from the boiling copper, whereas previously we had to run it all into a long shallow metal tank and let it cool as it wanted.

'The length of time this part took depended, of course, on the weather. I shall always be grateful to Whitworth Son and Nephew for the invaluable help they gave us, particularly with the replacement of the wooden mash-tub for the copper one. This eventually became both the mash-tub and fermenting vessel, the previous fermenting tub having been in the cellar under the Hall where the beer was stored in the days when Lord Halifax lived in the Hall. In fact the tub mentioned had to stay there as it was much too large to go through the cellar door and had to be built down there. When helping Owd Arry I always thought the cellar was an impossible place for the ferment to take place as where the vessel [tub] stood was overhung with black cobwebs which inevitably would occasionally plummet down into the fermenting wort. I remember enquiring about the questionable cleanliness of this, only to be told they would all come out when the yeast was skimmed off. I suppose that was true but I wasn't unduly impressed, I still thought it was not quite right, but being as I had nothing to do with that part of the process I had to be satisfied with the answer given. Mercifully I only had one brew myself under those circumstances as we left the Hall in 1936 and converted part of the brewhouse to use as a cellar. The cellar under the Hall looked a splendid sight after a brewing session with around ten or twelve of these huge casks standing

Staging to the copper on the left with the grist hopper suspended above the mash-tub.

in a row. The cellar was rather a horrible place, dark and damp, dirty and full of cobwebs, but reasonably warm and I suppose an ideal place to keep beer, though its appearance belied the fact. It was used for no other purpose but for the storage of beer. An underground tunnel led from there to what (in my opinion) had been an icehouse. It [the ice] would have been taken off the local ponds or lakes in the Hall grounds to be used in summer time to pack around things which required keeping in those days, there being no such things as refrigerators.

'The method used for the storage of the ice was that the building I have described as the icehouse, which was a place about 14 or 15 feet square, had a deep hole in the floor of about 10 or 12 feet deep with a side door at the bottom. The ice was put into this hole and covered over with straw or something similar which minimized the wastage by being below ground and covered up. Access to the ice was through the tunnel to the side door mentioned. The beer cellar and the larder being on the same level and, although I never saw this process in action, I would think there would be a door connecting the beer cellar with the larder. This would mean that ice could be conveyed through the tunnel into the larder without having to be taken above ground level. As I say I never saw this in operation as it had ceased to be before my time, but that is my assumption as to what took place and I don't think I would be far wrong.

'After the war ended I was rather surprised when Lord Halifax decided to resume brewing. Although I was glad in one sense to feel that he intended to keep the old practice going, yet I was sure that all my worries were to return as indeed they did. At intervals of sometimes two years I brewed with varied success and almost, in my opinion, near failure at times. It proved to be my old enemy, the inability to get the finished product to clear. I felt so helpless, not knowing what to do and so anxious to get things right. We found that though not clear it was getting better, but far from what I knew it ought to be, yet I was powerless to know what to do to correct it. Mr Clegg, the estate agent and director of a brewery in Barnsley, suggested he asked the head brewer, Mr Thackeray of Clarksons Brewery, to come over and advise me what to do. He duly arrived but didn't help me very much, taking samples away for examination the result of which I never heard. On reflection (many years later) makes me realize that he was too respectful to suggest that I didn't know how to brew! This, strictly speaking, was the main trouble as I know full well now but at that time I was using the little knowledge that I had acquired which was sadly lacking in the most important parts of the process. I still think that Mr Thackeray should have been able to tell me what was wrong but, as I say, I feel he didn't want to show me up. However, nothing of help was forthcoming from that source.

'I tried various ways of my own to improve the beer but with very little success. Lord Halifax used to have one or two barrels taken for use at Garrowby and he always gave a barrel for the annual presentation evening in the Village Club when he and Lady Halifax came to present the prizes for the Garden's Competition. This was always arranged in October just after our autumn brew, consequently the beer was as good as it could be under the circumstances; in other words it was still cloudy! There was never any complaint, everyone was too respectful but I was always glad when the function was over. On one occasion of a visit to Hickleton, Lady Halifax said to me that the beer they had at Garrowby seemed to develop white bits floating on top of it. This I knew was what was called 'wild yeast' which was really dead yeast that had worked out of the beer and was, of course, the result of it being cloudy. The cloudiness being yeast I had the idea then of decanting all the beer that was taken to Garrowby in the hope that the bits would be left at Hickleton after running it through muslin to filter it. This didn't help and my worries increased.

'We carried on like this until 1963 when the matter was finally brought to a head. Mr Clegg said to me, "Lord Halifax [Edward, 1st Earl] wants to see you about the beer, and it is in your hands as to whether we continue brewing or not." My heart was racing as I went into Lord Halifax's sitting-room. He was sitting near the fire reading his newspaper as I nervously presented myself, with Mr Clegg just behind me. Lord Halifax greeted me with his usual kindly smile and told me to "pull up a chair". This I did, and Mr Clegg did the same. I felt like, I would suggest, a poor victim laying his head on the block to await the executioner's axe! After a short pause Lord Halifax said, "Clarence, you haven't got your beer right." I thought that was the understatement of the century, but it was the voice of doom for me, yet I found myself experiencing a certain relief in the fact that this could be the make or break. Lord Halifax turned to Mr Clegg and seemed to address us both and said, "Do you think we should continue to brew?" As I hadn't then had an opportunity to offer my explanation one way or the other, I took the opportunity to answer before Mr Clegg, and said while I would agree that if there was no way of improving the beer, then as far as I was concerned I would say by all means end the brewing altogether, but I felt that it would be a great pity to end a tradition which had been going on for generations. I thought Lord Halifax seemed relieved at my saying this, because he turned to Mr Clegg and said, "What can we do to help Clarence, as I think we must carry on with the brew." Mr Clegg said he had been thinking about the matter himself and he thought he would ask the head brewer of the Barnsley Brewery to come over and supervise a brew or two. While I was not wildly enthusiastic about the prospect of someone else telling me what to do, yet I realized it was the only way we were to get to the bottom of things.

'The head brewer's name was Mr John Clark and thus began an association which lasted until 1976. A good deal longer than was really necessary, but Mr Clark had found himself a nice little sideline and therefore hung on to it after we could have managed very well without him. I used to tell him our requirements regarding malt, hops, yeast, etc. and he directed his brewery to prepare and supply some. In all fairness to him he did not interfere in our methods at the beginning but felt his way a little, as I realized he had very little idea as to what we actually did. Our first brew under his jurisdiction was not an unqualified success, as he had his own ideas as to the quantity of water we should need to allow for malt absorption, loss during boil and fermentation. He produced a water meter to measure how much we should need in the copper to allow for everything. He, of course, was feeling his way and was sadly out with the quantity. He said the meter was at fault, at least it got the blame for the fact that we only produced about two thirds of what we should normally have done. I told Mr Clegg about this but I couldn't help but notice that Mr Clark did not rush in to take the blame but allowed "Clarence to take the bucket back" so to speak.

'However, this first effort with Mr Clark taught me a lot, both about the brew and Mr Clark himself! The first and most important factor was that I found out my most serious fault, if one can call it a fault, the way to clear the beer which had haunted me throughout my brewing career. He didn't say anything about it until a day or so before we put the brew into the casks. Then he produced the answer "finings". I had to admit I had never heard of such things. I say "things" because they consist of a horrible looking, and smelling, liquid which I understand is out of the swim bladder of the sturgeon fish. It is a grey slimy liquid which is obviously heavier than the beer and takes all the cloudiness down to the bottom with it as it sinks, leaving the beer clear and bright. This was the answer to all my main worries and I knew that subsequent brews could only get better. This proved to be the case and I shall always be grateful to Mr Clark for having to show me this, as I am sure he wouldn't have done if he could have helped it but, as with all the processes, he had to leave it to me or stop at Hickleton all the time which he had no intention of doing and in fact was not able to do, being in charge of the Barnsley Brewery.

'I began to dislike his manner with me as I realized he wasn't telling me any more than he had to and only answered my questions as briefly as he could, because he could see that it was not going to be too long before his services were not required. I sensed this, knowing that he couldn't hide the things from me, as I knew too much already and only wanted to see what he did and all my worries were over, but he did the best he could to delay things in that direction. It was not all success with Mr Clark, but once again Clarence was left to carry the can! This happened in May 1965 when we learned we were to have a special brew. I say special, it was to have been brewed the same, but it was an extra brew, to celebrate the twenty-first birthday of Lord Irwin, the son of Lord and Lady Halifax. The function was to be held at Garrowby for about 800 people. All the usual materials were ordered and the same procedure for the mash etc., but when we came to the fermentation we found that something was definitely wrong as it was not fermenting properly. I summoned Mr Clark who was not in the habit of attending the mash at 2.30 a.m. He usually arrived mid-morning. He had done his mid-morning visit which should have been sufficient and he brought the yeast with him for us to put on in the afternoon as we were letting the hot wort over the fridge. I knew there was something wrong with it and when Mr Clark arrived for the second time he seemed to think my fears were unfounded and suggested we went ahead with it. This we did but I was right, something (I still do not know what) was wrong with it. We had put it into the casks and later on when we came to draw it out through the tap, it was what is known as "ropey" meaning it ran out like oil. Mr Clark on seeing this told us to throw it away and we should have to brew again. Time was getting short as it was now mid-June and the function was to be held in July. Mr Clark said I must have had my mashing water too hot and had scalded the malt. I thought I must be slipping if I had, as I was always so careful to get my water heat dead right at the required temperature of 160°. I had used what is called a stick thermometer which is like a walking stick with a thermometer fixed in the middle. The way it is used is to put it into the hot water and the mercury registers whatever heat it might be and when it is taken out of the water does not sink down again as it cools but remains where it is until it is bumped on the floor, after having being read of course. I told Mr Clark that I had been most careful about getting the temperature right, and suggested that perhaps the thermometer was faulty? He didn't think it was, but agreed to take it back to the brewery for testing. Incidentally it had come from there in the first place. Mr Clark thought it was much handier than the one I had already and indeed so it was, if it had been in order, as it proved not to be!

'I never saw it or its like again! Having been absolved from blame I made preparations for brewing again. I think Mr Clark didn't quite know what to do himself, for some (unknown to me) reason, he decided to rush in another brew and brew it almost double strength, heaven knows why, but this is what we did and housed it in casks borrowed from the Barnsley Brewery as there wasn't time to get our own cleaned again. This time with our own thermometer all appeared to be well, in fact as far as the brew was concerned, all was well except in my own mind it was going to be far too strong to be palatable. The great day arrived. I went over with the beer (100 gallons) the day before, to see it set up in the marquee, four casks at each end. I was also anxious knowing that it was sheer alcohol, being at the strength that it was, and I couldn't help wondering what effect it would have on the innocents who were to dispose of it.

'I stayed overnight with Horace Atkins, the head joiner at Garrowby, while Mary my wife came with the Hickleton contingent the next day. Came the function and the result! There were bodies laid all over the place, of the unwise who thought they could drink beer, and I'm sure they could in the ordinary way, but they had not allowed for the awful effect of the Hickleton brew! As I was leaving the field with my wife and friends on our way to where our coach was parked, we noticed a little chap in an army greatcoat lying on the grass near the marquee with a chair at his bottom, also lying on its side. He was completely "blindo" and didn't care whether it was Christmas or Easter. We all went over to help him up but he was beyond redemption. However, we picked him up and set him back on his chair again after asking him if he was all right. He was quite incapable of speech of any kind, in fact his eyes could not focus properly either. As I say we straightened him up as best we could and left him to his or other people's devices, confident he would not lack attention when it was needed. Looking back at him as we boarded our coach, I could see that that attention would not have to be long delayed, as it had been raining, the ground was soft and his chair legs were sinking into the ground. My last sight of him as we left was that he was listing heavily in the opposite direction to the way in which we had found him!

'Some days later we heard from the estate agent at Garrowby that the carnage was considerable, insofar as they had to go round gathering them up to see them safely off the premises, but I had a good deal of satisfaction in the knowledge that a good time was had by all. We ourselves were not without our casualties, one in particular who, but an hour earlier, had clapped me on the back congratulating me on the excellence of my brew, asked the coach driver as we were approaching York on our homeward journey to be allowed off the coach and, as he was being assisted by two chaps who had their arms around him, he expressed a wish to be put down and allowed to die! I would think that his wish would be expressed with all sincerity on seeing the helpless condition he was in. By the look of him I would say he was at the stage of the worst conditions of seasickness. I myself am no plaster saint and I keep an open opinion on such activities but I can't help thinking that when things are free some people can't control themselves and act with moderation out of the window. However, I was quite happy that my part of the business had proved successful and that was all that mattered, because the home-brew was so important an item if it had not been right the whole happy function would have largely been spoilt. However, the people who mattered, Lord Halifax, and the reason for it all, Lord Irwin, expressed satisfaction on the brew along with lots of others too. There had been a number of functions in my early days when I was just the brewer's assistant and when the home-brew was very much in evidence and had not been as good as the one just described at length but I knew, and resolved myself to see, that I would do my utmost to improve it still further and I can say with confidence that subsequent brews have proved that to be correct.

'As the years and the brews came and went I began to wonder how much longer Mr Clark's services would be required because he had long since ceased to be very much help to me regarding the actual brew, in fact on one occasion he was away on holiday in Scotland when the brew took place! He took no part in the proceedings whatsoever, other than to order our materials which was the least of our worries. However, to be involved in some way, he gave me instructions that I should ring him on the telephone on the evening of brewing day to tell him details of gravity, temperature, etc. What he would have done if things had not been right I don't quite know! However, as regards his existence as our "aide", circumstances and himself solved the problem for us. He became puffed up with his own importance, like the bull frog in the fable, and expressed disatisfaction in his remuneration for his services, which were actually in kind not money. He didn't seem to be able to see that we could manage very well without him and, I understand, called at the office of Dibb and Clegg, Barnsley (where he resided) and practically demanded further reward. Mr Mutch had asked me several times if we really needed him and I had to admit while he was still useful, we could manage without him, in fact had done just that for years. Mr Clark was told quite firmly that we were grateful for his help and advice in the past, but Clarence could now manage on his own. He was also told that he could stay on in his now advisory capacity but on the present terms only. I understand he went off with a flea in his ear and I would think in a fearful rage too, though I have no proof of this, other than the knowledge that he was a very short-tempered man.

'However, while he was considering his position, circumstances came to our aid in the fact that John Smith's decided to close the Barnsley Brewery and supply their pubs in this area from Tadcaster. This gave us the opportunity we were looking for as obviously we needed our materials from other sources. Mr Buckley of Dibb and Clegg had already approached T. & R. Theakston Ltd of Masham near Ripon. I felt a little sorry for Mr Clark here as he had practically fixed up for John Smith's to supply us from Tadcaster. So this was the end of Mr Clark's reign for which I was thankful. I thank him for showing me what the reason was for my beer not clearing and for numerous other items such as an electric pump, sachrometers and various other utensils which made our task that much easier. I told him that I could never remember seeing any finings during Owd Arry's days, but the beer was always clear. He said they must have used finings but I clung to my story that I had never seen or heard anything about them. The only thing he could then think about was something I had told him about a practice which I saw but could never understand. What had happened was that in Owd Arry's time, when the beer had finished its boil in the copper and was ready to run into the cooling tank, we used to strain off the hops through a sieve placed on top of the cooling tank. Owd Arry used to say to me, "tha' must save a bucketful of them 'ops to put in't barrels next week". This I used to do, wondering what for? I would collect the said bucketful of the wet steaming hops and put them into a cupboard with a sack over the bucket to keep out the dust.

'These were kept until the following Tuesday (we always brewed on Wednesdays) when the fermented beer was put into the casks. At this stage the bucketful of the wet hops, now a rather horrible mess, was starting to decompose with fustiness. A small quantity of this "mess" was put into each cask along with the beer. Mr Clark said he had heard that something of that kind had happened in the dawn of beer-brewing and that was the only thing he could think about which might have been used as a clearing agent. I couldn't help as I had not been told what the wet hops were for but the whole idea was in complete opposition to cleanliness and was just the thing to encourage the development of bacteria. It is one of the mysteries that the old brewers did take to their graves but one thing I am certain of is that they had a good reason for this practice and I never heard tell of them having beer that "went off", but that was understandable in one sense as it was highly unlikely that they would have told me or indeed anyone else other than their boss if they had had some "go off".

'So we shall have to leave that question unsolved. It would seem to be against all the ethics of producing good beer, which is something I have always striven to do and I think finally succeeded in doing. I would hesitate to offer advice to anyone else as there are so many things that are involved in the production of beer, such as the quality of the malt for instance. Every harvest or crop of barley may be slightly different, some better than others according to a good or bad harvest. Yet when one goes into a pub for a pint of beer and finds it good, one would expect to go into the same pub say six months later and order a pint and expect it to be just the same, as indeed so it would be, for the simple reason the breweries have scientific methods whereby they can make it the same every time, whether the quality of the malt is the same or not. With our equipment we were at the mercy of so many things, quality of materials, weather, lack of any way of knowing whether quality is good or bad. For instance we also mash at 160°F. At a brewery the brewer would test a sample of malt and if it was a little below standard, would say that to get the greatest extraction we must mash at say 162°F, or perhaps 158°F according to the quality of the malt. We have no means of knowing whether the quality is good or poor, so we have to mash at the same water temperature every time, consequently our brews are always slightly different in taste.'

From Clarence's own description of his brewing for Lord Halifax it is evident that he fully upheld the fine traditions of his employer and acted true to the family motto of 'Perserverando'. Although brewing has now ceased at Hickleton Hall, the present 3rd Earl, Peter, maintains the brewing traditions for, at his residence at Garrowby, brewing is carried out once a year using the old copper mash-tun and fermenting vessels recovered from Hickleton Hall. Long may Lord Halifax continue as the sole landed gentry to brew for his own use, in the once common manner of all estates.

SUMMARY OF HICKLETON BREWS, 1946–89

Date	OG	Labour	Coal	Haulage	Hops	Malt	Yeast Quantity	Galls	Licence	Duty	Per Pint Gross Cost	Per Pint Cost Net
May 1947		5.14.3	1.0.0	1.1.0	3.12.0	11.5.0		171	4/-	81.3.3	1/7	5d
Oct 1947		5.5.9	1.10.0	1.10.0	4.1.0	11.6.0		180	4/-	81.3.3	1/7	4½d
March 1949	1072°	7.12.7	2.0.0	2.0.0	3.19.10	12.11.0	1/6	171	4/-	103.4.9	2/-	6d
March 1951	1063°	9.6.9	2.0.0	2.0.0	4.10.11	15.8.0	2/6	200	4/-	105.13.3	1/9	5d
Oct 1952	1058°	7.19.10	2.0.0	1.10.0	4.11.0	17.1.3	2/6	200	4/-	105.13.3	1/9	5d
June 1954	1049°	10.8.1	2.0.0	1.10.0	4.16.3	15.18.9	3/-	198	4/-	90.19.0	1/7	5d
April 1956	1061°	13.4.2	2.0.0	2.2.0	4.18.6	15.6.3	4/-	198	4/-	105.13.3	1/10	6d
Aug 1958	1060°	16.19.4	2.0.0	No Charge	(C) 3.6.0	(D) 8.8.8		104	4/-	60.12.8	2/2	8½d
Nov 1961		(A) 27.12.7	2.0.0	No Charge	5.0.0	12.0.0		153	4/-	86.9.2	2/2	9d
Sept 1964		(B) 22.1.6	2.0.0	No Charge	No Charge	No Charge		100	4/-	(E) No Duty	7d	7d
9 March 1989				15.50p	55.40p			100	4/-	No Duty	26p	26p

Last Brew	Combined Cost of £50.00

NB   (A) and (B) Labour costs include gratuity to Mr Clark

         (C) and (D) For Aug 1958, indicates malt and hops supplied and charged by the Barnsley brewery

         (E) Customs & Excise duty repealed by Reginald Maudling, Chancellor

Hickleton Hall's copper being taken away for delivery to Garrowby, Yorkshire.

For ten centuries the great Traquair House in Inverleithen, Peebleshire, has stood in the border region beside the River Tweed and is home to the descendants of the Stuarts of Traquair. The house is a part of Scottish history, playing host to Mary, Queen of Scots in 1566 when the Traquair House home-brewed ale was served. It has much of interest, including twelfth-century manuscripts, glass, silver, books and pictures, it also has a priest's room and a complete library dating from the 1750s.

In 1739, a 200-gallon copper had been installed at a cost of £8. It is probable that soon after the visit of Bonnie Prince Charlie to the laird in 1745, brewing ceased. From that date until 1965, the brewhouse lay dormant but intact. In that year, the 20th Laird, Peter Maxwell Stuart, reopened the brewhouse. He had inherited this fine house in 1952 and had renovations carried out. For seventeen years, Peter Stuart did the brewing himself but with growing numbers of visitors to his house it became necessary for him to have a brewer. The first to take the job of brewmaster was Ian Smalley. In 1965 production was about 2,000 bottles, all individually numbered, with only occasional brewings. This gradually increased to once a month and today there are two brewings a week. Each gyle is only of 4 barrels (144 gallons). Peter Maxwell Stuart died in 1990 but his daughter, Catherine, continued the business, increasing the awareness of their special bottled beer and even exporting it. Before Peter died he had trained Ian Cameron to be his second brewer.

The brewhouse is situated below the family chapel and measures 8 feet square. The adjacent fermenting room is slightly smaller and has a cobbled floor. Brewing commences at around six in the morning and lasts for another thirteen hours or so. Pale malt and roasted

The famous Bear gates guarding the approaches to Traquair House have been closed since 1745 when the last person to pass through them was Bonnie Prince Charlie. Over 200 years later the Traquair Brew House upholds family custom by producing to the ancient recipe its unique strong ale.

Traquair House Ale

A potent liquor brewed by the Laird in the ancient Brew House of the Oldest Inhabited House in Scotland.

barley from Thomas Fawcett & Sons, West Yorkshire, are placed in the unlined oak tun, this is fused with spring water from the estate. The copper, dating from 1739, then receives East Kent Golding hops to the wort. Fermentation then takes three days in the unlined oak vats. Traquair House Ale is strong, at 7% ABV and is resistant to the wild yeasts likely to be present from the wooden vessels. This is despite their all-day cleaning after each brew. Around 400 barrels are brewed each year with August (too warm) and January (water freezes) being the only months in which brewing does not take place. A draught beer called Bear Ale at 5%, named after the famous gates that have remained closed since Bonnie Prince Charlie's visit, is available locally and in Glasgow; it has been brewed since 1982. A few 'special bottlings' have been produced with the 100th brew being commemorated on 4 October 1978. A royal silver jubilee and the laird's own silver wedding were commemorated, as was Catherine's twenty-first birthday. In 1987 a 400th bottling took place on the anniversary of the execution of Mary, Queen of Scots. The bottling is done by the Belhaven Brewery in a brown bottle; 'specials' have been in white enamelled bottles, whereas the normal Traquair House Ale has a green on white label.

The magnificent house and estate of Chatsworth, at Bakewell, Derbyshire, known as 'The Palace of the Peak', was built for the first Duke of Devonshire between 1687 and 1707, with later additions by Wyatville between 1820 and 1830 for the 6th Duke. However, the house was begun by Sir William Cavendish (the family name) as early as 1552, and after his death it was continued by his widow, the renowned Bess of Hardwick, who had four husbands. Sir William Cavendish came from the delightful village of Cavendish in Suffolk and was one of King Henry VIII's commissioners for the dissolution of the monasteries. Bess also built Hardwick Hall near Chesterfield, which remained in the Cavendish family until it was taken by the government in 1957 in lieu of death duties and then given to the National Trust.

The 4th Duke, a prominent Whig politician as was his father, served the country as prime minister from November 1756 to May 1757. He made considerable changes to the parkland and decided that the house should have a new western approach necessitating the demolition of the old stables and offices. James Paine, architect, was commissioned to build a new stable, coachhouse and brewhouse quadrangle to the north-east of the great house, completing this work in 1762. The two-storeyed building was built in the same grand style as the house, with the mellow sand-coloured stone relieved with heavy round-headed arches and quoins, and an impressive archway with the ducal coat of arms in a pediment, all surmounted by a clock tower cupola. Paine was also responsible for altering the course of the River Derwent and for building a new bridge over it. The nearby village of Edensor was partly raised so as to give a clear view but in 1775 an inn was built (now the estate office) to accommodate sightseers. What remained of the village was enclosed to become an integral part of the park as it is today. These works were designed by Lancelot 'Capability' Brown, the most renowned landscape designer. The 4th Duke married Lady Charlotte Boyle, the heiress of the 3rd Earl of Burlington, and brought further estates into the Cavendish family wealth, including Londesborough Hall, Bolton Abbey, and Burlington House and Chiswick House in London. Devonshire House, in Piccadilly, London, was burnt down in 1733, but was later rebuilt. Chatsworth Park consists of 1,100 acres, surrounded by a further 12,000 acres of farmland, woods and moorland.

In 1858, Messrs Jepson supplied pale malt and fine Kent hops, also soda-water bottles and seltzer water. The malt, delivered on 6 May 1858, was ground on 14 May at a charge of 9s 6d for thirteen loads. During the same month A. Gregory supplied 32 lbs of barm (yeast) at 3d per pound. The brewing was carried out by William Dale who invoiced His Grace, the Duke of Devonshire, for nine days of brewing at Chatsworth at 2s per day; his invoice dated 18 May totalled 18s. On 31 December 1858 William Dale signed a receipt from the Duke for 'nine pounds, seventeen shillings and sixpence, being one quarter's wages for attendance as Brewer & Cellar Man at Chatsworth House'. The beer cellar, which is still intact, must be one of the grandest in the country. It is built of stone in the form of a tunnel with the walls dissected with shallow arches, thus forming pillars. Within each of these arched recesses are wooden single cask stillages with a continuous stone stillage on the other side. However, the grandest aspect of the beer cellar is the three remaining 100-gallon wooden beer barrels. Each of these, and there were at least five, have a most detailed carving of the Duke of Devonshire's full coat of arms on the entire barrel end. This consists of a circular shield with three stags' heads surrounded by the garter and the motto, 'Honi soit qui mal y pense', the family motto, 'Cavendo Tutus', below. On either side are stags rampant and a ducal crown surmounting the crest helmet, surely the most elaborate beer barrels ever!

A beer pipe led from the brewhouse to the cellar and a tale told by John Oliver, the assistant controller to Chatsworth House, relates that one day when working with an old friend he said, 'come and look 'ere, and I'll show you summat not many folk know about'. With that he scraped some soil to one side with his boot and exposed a 2-inch lead pipe which had been bent up and had a wooden plug driven into a hole which was drilled into the top of the bend. 'This is t'pipe that leads from t'brewery to t'beer cellar, and this is where young lads in t'gardens used to tap off t'ale on its way down. Young uns out a brewery would tip un off, thee'd say, "get ya buckets ready a three o'clock on Friday", and sure enough down

The Chatsworth beer cellar with the armorial beer casks on wooden stillages.

the ale 'ud come, then thee'd all meet up in t'stokehole for a good drink later.' Knowing how canny many of these understairs staff were there is no doubt that this practice was repeated in many another large country home. Brewing at Chatsworth ceased sometime between the two world wars.

Shugborough, at Milford, near Stafford, has been in the possession of the Anson family since 1624, when William Anson purchased it. Thomas Anson, the great grandson of William, was MP for Lichfield, the first of several Ansons to represent the constituency for a hundred years. Thomas enlarged the seventeenth-century house by adding the linking buildings and several classical temples and monuments in the extensive grounds. He was financially assisted by his younger brother George who was the renowned Admiral Anson. He had accumulated the spoils of war against the Spanish and, on his return after four years in 1744, invested much of his money to make Shugborough as it is today. On his death in 1761, a childless widower, he left much of his wealth to his brother. Thomas Anson died twenty-eight years later and his great-nephew inherited the estate. In 1806 he was created Viscount Anson.

Once again the house and grounds were remodelled, this time by Samuel Wyatt who built the Ionic portico to the east frontage between 1794 and 1806, and the three-storeyed projecting feature to the garden elevation. This first viscount, who married Anne the daughter of Thomas William Coke of Holkham, Norfolk, was the first of five succeeding Thomases, the second being created Earl of Lichfield in 1831. No doubt with the encouragement of his father-in-law, Coke of Holkham who was a great reformer of the agricultural system, the 1st Viscount had his own home farm built along the lines of the most modern theories of the day. This was Park Farm, designed by Samuel Wyatt and built in 1805; previously the land had been farmed from earlier buildings known as White Barn Farm. Park Farm is sited close to Stuart's Temple of the Winds and the main house. The design was based on Holkham's famous farm improvement theory, with a quadrangle in which the farm manager's house is situated opposite the entrance and two long side ranges. One range contained the cattle sheds and stables while the other had a water-powered mill and the farm brewhouse. The water mill was used to grind the corn of which a part was given to the local poor people. In the centre of the yard were poultry houses, a dovecote and pigsties. There was also a malthouse listed in an inventory of 1817 and in 1827 Mark Smallman was the maltster working for an annual salary of £36 8s 0d. This farm was considered in its time to be the most up-to-date, incorporating all the latest ideas in management, advice having been received from Nathaniel Kent who had also planned farms for George III at Windsor Great Park. The Park Farm brewhouse would have supplied the needs of the thirteen farm workers, also the eight staff of the hunting establishment and an additional twelve building workers. These thirty workers would have required about 100 gallons of beer a week with an additional increase of another 30 gallons for casual labour at harvest time. The Park Farm consisted of some 2,000 acres of which 300 acres were normally given over to barley for the estate malthouse and brewing requirements. There were 100 cattle and 17 oxen used for ploughing and 30 heavy horses, with a further 1,700 Southdown sheep. The steward, Mr Wheelock, supervised this large farm and had farm labourers working for him for 10s a week and a daily quantity of free home-brewed beer.

A second brewhouse had been built earlier, in the 1760s, as part of the service wing to the mansion house. This is built of brick with stone dressings with a cupola above the pedimented central archway. A clock and bell are dated 1767 and this indicates the date of construction, the architect probably the local master mason, Charles Trubshaw. The brewhouse is at right angles to one end facing the midden yard. An inventory made in 1842 gives some indication of the contents of the brewhouse: 'large hop bag, cleansing sieve, 2 wood scrapers, copper pump, 2 mash rules, large mash-tub, 22 tubs of different sizes, 5 pails, 2 tun dishes, 2 lade gawns, 2 benches, pair of small steps, 4 beer shoots, 4 casks of different sizes, 2 trucks, 2 beer coolers, copper of 432 gallons, with lead and underwork, copper 200 gallons and underwork'. The butler, Benjamin Purser, was required to oversee the brewing process in 1827. The title of 'butler' originates from the person who looked after butts of ale in the cellars, likewise the term 'buttery' indicates the place of storage of both beer and wine, and in some cases actually the place of brewing. The butler's accounts for 1863 show the following items:

20 Oct-6/ – paid for yeast for brewing
31 Oct – £1.3.3d paid to Mr Ash for brewing and cleaning
10 Nov-6/ – paid for yeast for brewing
24 Nov – £1.1.0d paid to Mr Ash for brewing and cleaning

The butler had an assistant to do the actual brewing, and in 1803 one Benjamin Bishop, who worked in the estate garden nursery, was paid £1 for twenty nights' work watching the brew. Six years later he was paid 10s for six days' brewing. The brewhouse was strictly the preserve

Shugborough's renovated brewhouse interior.

of male servants, as the housekeeper stated in the 1820s that neither she nor any other female servant ever visited the brewhouse. Clearly the process of brewing was cloaked with secrecy and it is for this reason that nearly all the old brewing recipes have been lost for all time.

Shugborough's beer was brewed in several strengths, a strong beer for use by the family and their guests, and a weak 'small beer' of a much larger quantity for the daily beer allowance of all the employees. This beer allowance was a gallon a day for manservants and about half that for women. In 1827 there was a total of 107 staff, with 82 male and 25 female. These staff were split, with 70 outside staff to 37 inside. Providing a plentiful and wholesome beer supply was considered the duty of a caring and efficient household.

In the previously mentioned inventory from the early 1820s it shows that Shugborough's cellars were full to the brim with almost 12,000 gallons of beer and ale, clearly indicative of the extent that visitors were entertained. One of these was the young Princess Victoria who stayed for three days in which 450 gallons of ale were consumed! 'Old Tom' is one of the beers mentioned in the inventory and this evidently was a strong beer named after Thomas Anson. Apparently there were times when beer was purchased from a brewer in the neighbouring village of Great Haywood, possibly as a result of a shortage of their own home-brewed beer at Shugborough, due to a defective brew or a large number of unexpected guests. The dowager Lady Lichfield was also evidently partial to a bottle of Bass from the famous Burton-on-Trent brewery. The 2nd Viscount Anson was owner and master of the Atherstone Hunt and he entertained many of the famous and fashionable sporting celebrities of the time.

Purchases of materials are recorded, and even transfers of malt from the estate farm were noted so that in September 1809, 40 buckets of malt were recorded as costing £30. In 1812 the sum of £119 13s 0d was paid for hops. In 1815, 795 buckets of malt were purchased costing just under £400. The brewer's report for December 1848 shows that 83 buckets of malt and 79 lbs of hops were purchased, and that 1,197 gallons of beer were brewed.

The brewhouse is a brick two-storeyed building linked to the ornate stable block and is now a museum; domestic houses, coachhouse, laundry and kitchen abut the mansion house. The brewhouse may have started life with some other use, such as an additional stable room with hayloft, built between the main stable block and the coachhouses. There is a step up into the building with the local blue-brick floor laid upon another floor. The building retains several wood louvred windows and some of the old brewing plant, this includes the coopered mash-tub and fermentation vessel. The cellars in the mansion had been liable to flooding in the past and it is known that drains from this area led directly into the junction of the two rivers, the Trent and Sow. The drain from the brewhouse, however, leads to a soakaway in the midden yard, it is therefore likely that at times of cleansing the brewing plant and casks, flooding would have taken place here. The soakaway would have had to be cleared of silt (and debris such as grains and hops) on quite a regular basis. Within the mansion house cellars there were two very large coopered storage vats appropriately named 'Lord Anson' and 'Lady Anson' dating from the 1840s, and probably able to hold several hundred gallons each. There would also have been many coopered casks of conventional sizes standing on stillages, ready for drawing off the ale and beer.

By the time the 3rd Earl of Lichfield, Thomas Francis Anson, was in residence, beer drinking was declining in favour of tea. The 3rd Earl, born in 1856, once again brought the Anson family together with the Cokes of Holkham and Thomas married Lady Mildred Coke, daughter of the 2nd Earl of Leicester of Holkham, Norfolk. The third Thomas made himself very unpopular by closing down a number of alehouses on his Staffordshire estates and it is thought that he was responsible for the closure of the brewhouse. The servant's beer allowance was replaced in the 1880s with between 8s and 10s per month which was also to cover their washing money. Consequently an age-old tradition died out but, as a result of this action the brewhouse languished moribund for many years, leaving something of its past to be seen today.

Fortunately the Staffordshire County Council entered into an agreement to administer the estate for the National Trust in 1960 and decided to open a county museum in the stable block and service wing. As part of the policy to show the public the 'workings' of an estate, the farms produced cheese and butter samples and the brewhouse was opened, with minimal alterations to allow the public to pass through. Early in 1987 staff from Shugborough visited Hickleton Hall, the previous residence of the Earl of Halifax, where his brewhouse was about to be removed. The intention was to seek advice on the proposal to recommence estate brewing at Shugborough. Technical advice was given by the head brewer of Samuel Smith's of Tadcaster, Mr Ross, and the project 'came alive'. Plans were drawn up and passed in June 1989 and work commenced, including the purchase of a stainless steel vessel which would double up as a mash-tun and fermentation vessel. This was clad in timber to give a feeling of more authenticity for the period; it was also enhanced with a copper lip and hoop. A brass cased electric pump was installed to pump back the wort to the copper, some 10 feet higher. Previously this would have been done by a manual pump lifting at least 100 gallons, quite a tiring job. As the brewhouse fittings were being removed from Hickleton Hall, the opportunity was taken to acquire the cast-iron fire doors and fire box for heating the copper which was placed inside new brickwork. All this construction work was concluded with a grand opening introducing Shugborough's first brew appropriately named Lord Anson's Ale on Friday 28 September 1990. This historic occasion was marked by a pottery tankard with a red shield reading 'Lord Anson's Ale'. Sadly this revival of estate brewing was short-lived, although the brewhouse may still be seen by members of the public.

The quantity and liveried appearance of staff was just as important as the continued glorification of the houses in which the landed gentry and aristocracy lived. With the continual social round of entertaining, the gentry had to uphold their place in society and be seen to be doing so. Staff numbers remained fairly constant in the larger houses for a considerable period, as may be seen at Calke Abbey. In 1737 there were 25 staff and in 1910 there were 27. However, only a decade later a depression had set in. The effects of a terrible First World War had changed this lifestyle. No longer were the great houses able to have large numbers of cheap labourers and this factor inevitably brought about the rapid decline of the old way of life for the gentry.

The baronetcy of Calke Abbey was created on 8 September 1626 for the Harpur family, Sir Henry being the first baron. His grandfather, Sir Richard had died in 1573 but before that the Augustinian canons had lived a communal life at their priory here since the twelfth century. The original Elizabethan courtyard house was modernized into a Baroque mansion by Sir John Harpur, to be continued by his son, Sir Henry, who altered the house into its neo-classical style at the end of the eighteenth century. On completion of the house, very grand stables were built by Sir John between 1712 and 1716 to the design of Burton mason, William Gilks. Beyond the stableyard is the smithy yard which has a dovecote above the blacksmith's shop. On the north-east corner of the stable block are the old slaughterhouse, bakehouse and the brewhouse. Early records of brewing at Calke are to be found in a sixteenth-century agreement between Robert Baynbrigge, Esq. of Calke and William Summers, yeoman: 'In consideration that William Summers shall to his best ability well and truly serve Robert Baynbrigge as Cooke, Brewer and Baker in Robert Baynbrigge's house and not depart from service without special leave or licence, Robert Baynbrigge sets to William Summers all that tenement or Cottage and housing belonging to it joining upon Gilborrowe lease'. A further Article of Agreement dated 1621 between Robert Baenbridge and Henry Harpur indented for the sale of Calke, which included 'all brewinge leades, milke leads pumpes of leade Conduits and conduit pipes Cesternes of leade and all Andirons in the house. All brewing vessels bedsteads tables formes wooden stooles not cov'ed with any kind of silke or stuffe.' Possibly due to an increase in the domestic staff at Calke and an increased demand for beer, also the deterioration of some of the brewing plant, a new brewhouse was constructed in 1743. To enhance the validity of the second point estate accounts show that Thomas Bancroft was paid for hanging a new brewing copper in 1738–9. In the same year work was carried out to the brewhouse by Thomas Minion, evidently repairs to the structure. The mason, Mr Chambers, was paid £149 15s 6d, 'for building the new Brewhouse', shown in the accounts for December 1743. The account book for 1746 reads 'Paid him [Mr Sills the plumber] his Bill for ye Year 1743 (ye Brewhouse Built) £116 0 0'. The plumber and mason were not the only craftsmen to benefit as Thomas Minion was paid £41 14s 0d in 1744 for, among other things ' . . . new Iron Works for the new Brewhouse'. The new mash-tubs, working tuns and hogsheads were supplied by Palmer the cooper who was paid £43 on his account entered in the account books for 20 November 1744. He was later paid £4 4s 0d in 1751 for casks 'to keep the beer in'. It was not unusual for tradesmen's and suppliers bills to be submitted once a year and so the apparent lengthy time delay between the construction and completion of the brewhouse, in 1744, and the accounts recorded in 1746 was normal 'credit' trading for the landed gentry. The brewhouse which exists today at the northern right-angled corner of the outbuildings quadrangle, which has the stables in the southern end, cannot be identified for certain as to being on the same site or form as that of the brewhouse built in the 1740s, this range of outbuildings dating from 1712–14.

On entering the brewhouse one is immediately faced by the mash-tun which is constructed of vertical oak staves held together by wrought-iron bands, with overall dimensions of 6 feet wide and 4 feet 6 ins high, with a slight narrowing towards the base. A moveable cover and a false wooden bottom are almost standard equipment, but at Calke the false bottom boards are not perforated in the normal manner. Beneath the false bottom boards there is a lead-lined hole of 3 ins in diameter, the whole tun supported on wooden joists at a height above floor level of 8 feet 3 ins on brick walls of two course thickness. It is most likely that a wooden underback was originally sited beneath the mash-tun. The original copper, now missing, was built into the circular brickwork, now stained with verdigris, clear evidence of its previous existence. Beneath the copper, which was fixed in the brickwork, was the furnace with cast-iron opening door and grate to the furnace, and a small tunnel at the base from which the ashes could be racked clear and which would have assisted the air flow to the fire. A flue from the furnace was built of brick into the wall behind the copper,

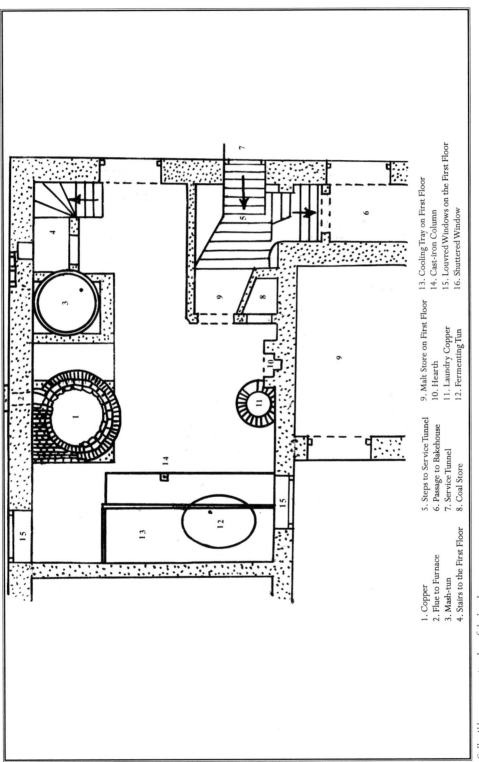

1. Copper
2. Flue to Furnace
3. Mash-tun
4. Stairs to the First Floor
5. Steps to Service Tunnel
6. Passage to Bakehouse
7. Service Tunnel
8. Coal Store
9. Malt Store on First Floor
10. Hearth
11. Laundry Copper
12. Fermenting Tun
13. Cooling Tray on First Floor
14. Cast-iron Column
15. Louvred Windows on the First Floor
16. Shuttered Window

Calke Abbey, a composite plan of the brewhouse.

also with a cast-iron door to allow the draught to be regulated. The chimney-stack is on the outside of the wall. At Calke, as was the normal design for a brewhouse, both the copper and mash-tun had access via a flight of stone steps in the north-eastern corner of the building (very often wood open-tread stairs were used). The steps lead to a staging which allowed direct access to the malt and hop stores, thus enabling the easiest and most convenient manner of placing the raw materials into the process plant; at Calke this staging floor no longer exists. This same floor also gave access to the cooling trays. Evidence of this floor is suggested by the holes in the walls where previously were fixed the supporting joists on both walls, as well as a cut beam jutting out from the corner of the wall. The cooling trays are sited to the west wall on a wooden platform which is supported by a cast-iron column and wooden rafters. As with much of the other plant, the cooling trays are built of wood staves, forming troughs of 5 feet wide by 15 feet long and of a shallow depth, and were originally lined with lead; later types were built of copper only. A smaller trough, now collapsed, was most probably used for the smaller quantities of ale and stronger beers brewed. To assist the cooling process there are two louvred windows in the north and south walls.

Below the cooling troughs on the elevated staging is an oval fermenting tun, 1.9 metres wide, 2.85 metres long and 85 cm deep, similar in construction to the mash-tun, and supported on several brick piers. The position immediately below the cooling troughs allowed for the wort to be drained below into the fermenting vessel, where the yeast was added. A similar vessel would have been sited below the now collapsed smaller ale-cooling trough, this was 4 feet in diameter and 2 feet 7 ins deep. Both tuns have holes in the sides in which cocks (either wood or brass) would have been inserted to allow the beer to be drained off for racking. Next to the fermenting tun is an open iron tub, measuring 2 feet 4 ins in diameter and 4 feet deep, with tapering sides towards the base all set in brickwork of an overall height of 1.2 metres with a furnace beneath. Next to this there is another hearth with a chimney and it is most likely that this was to provide heating in the brewhouse, enabling brewing to take place all year round. Adjacent to this hearth and to the right of the service tunnel is a brick enclosure which was the coal store. The tunnel is an unusual brick-built one which leads to the several cellars under the north wing of the house. It runs for 234 feet below the courtyard, before turning ninety degrees and running a further 130 feet to the north side of the house where the four cellars are situated. Each cellar is named, 'Labourers', 'Servants', 'Harvest' and 'Abbey', and access to the tunnel was gained via stone steps, down which the casks of beer had to be lowered before being rolled along the tunnel. Several cast-iron grates set along the length of the roof of the brick tunnel provide a limited amount of light and ventilation. A short distance along its length a further set of stone steps lead up to the old bakehouse, situated in the adjacent room to the south of the brewhouse.

The liquor supply to the brewhouse was served by a branch off the main service supply indicated on a plan dated 1897, but prior to this it is likely that a well with a hand-pump in the vicinity of the service courtyard would have served both the brewhouse and bakehouse. In the brewhouse itself two pumps had been installed for the sum of £9 4s 6d by George Mugleston, a glazier, on an invoice dated 9 July 1773. At this date Moses Taylor was both the brewer and baker, utilizing surplus yeast from the brewhouse in his baking. Malt was supplied by a Mr Boltsby who was paid £48 for supplying 280 strike of malt in 1741; two years later a Mr Barker was paid £68 13s 4d 'for malt delivered for Sir Henry's use'. In 1745 a payment was made to Ralph Sherys, a butcher, on 29 May: 'Pd him also for 531 stke Malt deliv'd in the year 1744 charged at 3/- per stke, and the butcher allow'd Sir Henry 2/- per strike for his Tyth Barley which is according to the common custom of 1/- per strike in Exchange Barley for Malt £79-13-0.' Hops were supplied by a Mr Stray of Nottingham, with two entries of deliveries in 1744 and 1745 amounting to £53 15s 0d.

Both ale and beer were brewed but by the nineteenth century ale consumption had considerably declined. In the 1730s single hogsheads of ale and beer were 'tapt', usually every other day, with twice as many tappings of ale to beer (tapping at this time referred to the amount consumed as against brewed). A hundred years later, in the early 1820s, it is recorded that in December 1821 there were 198 hogsheads and 3 kilderkins of beer brewed and 19 butts of ale. A year later it was 116 hogsheads of beer and 4 barrels, 1 kilderkin; in December 1824, 126 hogsheads of beer were brewed and only 16 butts. Large quantities of ale and beer were kept on stock in the cellars in the period between 1832 and 1838, up to 29 butts, the consumption being between 1 to 2 butts every two or three weeks. Consumption fluctuated considerably in most large households, particularly with an increase at Christmas time and again at harvest time in August/September. It is interesting to note from the Calke records of 1738 that bottled ale regularly appeared such as 'between 8th March and 17th March, Bottled Ale 2 doz; Spent'. Further records indicate that between the years 1737 and 1739, both 'Milde and Small Beer Expended'. This entry appears to be the only one that gives some idea of the type of beers brewed but, in addition, strong ale or beer would be brewed for special occasions. Most of the ale and beer was stored in the 'Servants' cellar, with the 'Labourers' and 'Harvest' cellars also in use. On 18 May 1825, 288 gallons of ale and 126 gallons of beer were put in the 'Harvest' cellar.

The consumption at this time was about 5 hogsheads per week, mainly by the farm labourers and house servants, while ale consumption was restricted to the discerning tastes of Sir George Crewe and his family, other than at harvest time. The normal free allowance to all servants and outdoor staff was three pints a day and a similar quantity would be given as part payment to casual labourers. Some beer was also sent to London, such as on 14 August 1836 when a half barrel was dispatched. The Harpur Crewe family did not have a London seat, but they did own Warslow Hall, near Buxton in Staffordshire. When staying there it is probable that beer or ale would also be dispatched, along with many other household items and some of the house staff.

Brewing appears to have ceased in 1873, probably due to several varied reasons, not least that the number of servants and staff had declined and that the old traditional methods of brewing, including that of ale, had been superseded by technical advances and a larger brewing capacity, hence cheaper beer from many common brewers. Both Ind Coope, the Burton brewers, and Offilers of Derby, supplied beer after this date. The transport of beer was facilitated by the opening of the Melbourne railway station in the 1860s.

Sir William Petre was born in 1506 and at the age of thirty-three he was granted by letters patent 'The Manor of Ingatestone, Mountnessing and Fryerning belonging to the abbey' on 15 December 1539. This was as a result of King Henry VIII dissolving all religious houses that had an income of less than £200 in 1536. Sir Petre immediately demolished the old Abbey and built the existing Ingatestone Hall. A brewhouse and buttery were built on the south side of the base courtyard, to the right of the entrance gateway. The gateway has a one-armed clock and below this was the brewer's chamber into which the clock weights descended. The brewer worked on a part-time basis, however, the Petre family records held at the Essex Record Office in Chelmsford indicate that by 1552 brewing was quite a large concern. There were brewings every two weeks, other than at harvest or festival times when a weekly brew was necessary. The two weekly brews produced on average 32 kilderkins and the buttery was capable of holding 40 kilderkins (720 gallons). In 1552 there was a total of thirty-two brewings producing 18,432 gallons. With the estimated additional harvest and festival brews, the total production was in the region of 20,000 gallons for the year. The cost of this brewing was about £75. For the Christmas of 1547–8, 10 kilderkins of 'household beer' or 'single beer', which was a low gravity beer equivalent to the old monks single 'X' beer, and half a hogshead of 'March beer', a stronger brew, were left over after the festivities! In August of 1547 three quarters of malt were sent to East Hornden Farm for brewing by a Mr Cornelis; a month later he delivered back to the hall 8 hogsheads of what was apparently a stronger hopped beer. It is recorded that there were two hop kilns 'near by' in the records of 1552. It also notes that 4 hogsheads were sent to Aldesgate House and that the Ingatestone Hall supplies of beer were short, maybe due to the illness of the brewer, thereby necessitating purchase of 14 kilderkins from a Thomas Ramme, a local brewer, at a cost of 19s 10d for small beer. Ten years later it was noted that Harrison's wife, of Radwinter, brewed 200 gallons for 20s as against the Ingatestone brewer's charge of 20s for 252 gallons.

In the inventory taken in 1600, the beer cellar had '8 beer stalls, 2 half tubs to stand under the taps, a tilter, a shelf for the jacks, beer stools, 2 oyster tables and a pail with an iron baler'. There was also a lock and key to the courtyard door. The brewhouse had a 'great' copper, mashing vat, the 'yealdinge' vat (for fermenting the wort) and hop baskets, also a sweet wort tun, the cooler, the 'chunke' into which the wort ran, the 'cowles yeast' tubs, jets, skeps, troughs, the 'rowers' to stir the grain, the pulley used for raising casks, a 'stuke' hooped with four iron hoops , a 'shavell' (small spade, probably wooden) to take up the 'graynes', a leaden trough, two roundlets (wooden casks) for yeast storage, and a 'tunnel' to fill the casks. Two cask sizes were used, the kilderkin of 18 gallons capacity and the hogshead of 54 gallons. The typical quantity of malt used in the year was 11 quarters and 2 bushels.

Anna Maria Barbara, wife of the 8th Lord Petre, wrote instructions in 1740 for the estate brewhouse management: 'if there bee forty in family the expence of this office may probably bee computed att about a hundred pound a yeare the price of malt is for the most part about halfe a crowne a Bushell wch in some parts of England is called a Strike and holds eight gallons and a halfe and wch I take notice of to avoid mistakes because that mesure wch they call a Bushell in some parts of the North holds twice as much the common allowance of malt is 12 Bushells to a hogshead of March Beer 8 Bushells to a hoggshead of Ale and 2 Bushells to a hoggshead of Small Beer and 'tis probable that one week with an other you will consume about three hogsheads of Small Beer one hoggshead of March Beer so that the weekly consumption of malt will bee Six Bushells for the three hoggsheads of Small beer, eight bushells for the hoggshead of Ale and three bushells for the fourth part of the hoggshead of March Beer in all seventeen Bushells of malt a week wch (reckoning the malt att halfe a crowne the Bushell) comes to £2-2s-6d. But because it is the custome in many places to take a hoggshead or two of Small Beer from the same quantity of malt that makes each hoggshead of ale or March Beer, if this bee practized it will Lesen the expense of that Article for Small Beer wch with other good managments may bring the whole yearly change of malt Drink within the compas of one hundred pound tis both the best husbandry and the surest way to have always good malt Drink to Brew as seldome as possible Sir Robert Howard who was a great manager and nicely curious in his malt drink never brewd but twice a year in October and in March and tho it bee an uncommon thing to keep small beer so long his was extremly pleasant very clear and not stale wch was preserved from being so by putting about 2 pound of hopps into each hoggshead of Small Beer. It is not only a very creditable thing to have always good small beer but it likewise saves a great deal for drink that is fresh and clear goes twice as farr as when it is new and flatt besides when this happens servants will thro away a great deal to hasten the broaching of a better hogshead if the water bee good it will require the Less quantity of malt to make the brew strong and that wch brews well commonly washes well too spring water very seldome happens to bee good for ether purpose but where no other can be had it may be very much mended by keeping it five or six dayes in the Brewhouse before they make use of it and the water bee never so good in its kind, the keeping of it in the hous for some time before they use it is an advantage to it an other good husbandry is to have the copper that Boyles the water of the Largest size: for the same fire make the water boyle if it were twice as much by whch meanes twice as much beer is made with the same expence of fire, any sort of coal being cheaper and much more convenient for that purpose than wood: besides there is a way of hanging the copper, and placing a little iron dore att the mouth of the furnace to shutt in the heat (wch cannot bee where they brew with wood fires) wch contrivance makes a very small quantity of coales serve the turn and without wch double the quantity would beer consum'd, if there could bee any communication by troughs or leaden pipes betwixt the Brewhouse the Sellar it would save a great deal of Labour in the tunning besides a great deal of drink that spilt and wasted by having the Sellar and brewhouse open to all commers on those dayes whereas if it were conveyed by pipes, one man in each place would tun all the drink without wast or trouble any sort of Liquor is esteemed more wholesome out of the vessel than out of the bottle and because the old fashioned hoggshead will not preserve the drink fresh to the Last, some curious observer invented a sort of vessel that stands upon the narrow end, shapd almost like a sugar loafe as in the margin being broad att the top the scum (wch keeps in the Spirit of the Liquor) does not break as in the old fashioned vessels, but rather groes thicker the nearer it comes to the bottome by wch manner the Drink continues fresh to the Last wch makes these sort of vessels very convenient especially for small brew for the use of your owne table it is esteemd an advantage to the malt to lett it bee grownd four or five dayes before it is make use of and there are many new inventd sort of malt mills, but for such a family as yours none will bee so proper as the old fashiond one drawne by a horse.'

This delightful description certainly throws more light on the practice of estate brewing in the eighteenth century, not least for highlighting both ale and beer and the use of hops, which in this case indicated that they were locally grown. Ingatestone Hall has many underground springs and culverts which disperse the water, all indicated on a map, so it is apparent that the water supply was adequate for brewing such quantities. It should be remembered that because of the untreated water supplies, large quantities of small weak beer were consumed instead of water. In 1800, however, the 'West Rouge' of buildings, including the brewhouse, were pulled down. Brewing, which had been taking place at Ingatestone Hall for the Petre family for 260 years, had finally come to an end.

Possibly unique in this history of brewing was the permission granted by the Duke of Northumberland to the Alnwick Brewery Co. Ltd. That small brewery was permitted to display His Grace's full coat of arms on their letterheads with a 'ribbon' which read 'Brewers by special appointment to His Grace the Duke of Northumberland'. This common brewer was registered in 1890 and ceased brewing in 1963, at which time it owned twenty public houses.

The Duke of Northumberland had acquired Alnwick Abbey in 1765 from the Allgood family, who had been the owners for fifty-five years. The duke also owned Hulne Priory, only a few miles from Alnwick Abbey. Hulne was the first Carmelite convent in this country, and is one of the finest monastic ruins in the north. The principal entrance was by the gatehouse which had the guest hall to the west and beyond this were the brewhouse, bakery and other domestic offices. In the reign of Elizabeth they were purchased by Thomas, 7th Earl of Northumberland, but he was executed in 1572, thus losing the property. This was subsequently repurchased in the early part of the seventeenth century by the Earl of Northumberland. The seats of the Duke of Northumberland are Alnwick Castle, Warkworth, Kielder and Prudhoe Castles, all in Northumberland. Titles of the Percy family include Baron of Alnwick and Baron Warkworth of Warkworth Castle, etc. Warkworth Castle ruins are impressive, with a substantial keep which had a large beer cellar and buttery on the west side with two wine cellars to the east. On the sloping inner ward was situated the large brewhouse and laundry at the foot of the motte. A large curved arch still leads into this area which measures 48 feet long (east/west) by 23 feet wide. Immediately south of the brewhouse was the church facing into the large outer ward. On the eastern side was a long range of stables with a large wellhouse in front. A piped water supply probably ran from this well some 230 feet to the brewhouse. On the west side of the outer ward was the hall, kitchen, larder and buttery. To the southern boundary was a solar and chapel abutting the great gate tower, with its bridged access.

Charlecote House, Warwickshire, is a superbly preserved Jacobean house and estate, completed in 1558, a date found on heraldic glass in the hall. Thomas Lucy was knighted in the house in 1565 and it is the park where William Shakespeare is alleged to have been caught poaching deer. There is a very fine Elizabethan gatehouse built of mellow red bricks and stone quoins; it has two octagonal towers with ogival-shaped lead cupolas. There are equally fine and distinguished rooms in the house, particularly the library, but perhaps of special interest are the excellently preserved service wing areas. The scullery and kitchen with their stone flag floors and scrubbed tables and dressers are complete with every tool used a century ago. In the outbuildings, which are contemporary with the Tudor house, is the laundry which is at the end of the west wing of the stable buildings. The laundry is complete here too, with water-pump and two brick-enclosed washing coppers.

The coachhouse and carriagehouse contain vehicles used by the Lucy family in the nineteenth century and include a wide variety of nine horse-drawn coaches. The tack room is equally evocative of the past. Of particular interest is the superbly preserved brewhouse. It is complete with all the brewing equipment with two brick-enclosed coppers and their massive brass valves. Coopered tuns and a cooling tray clearly indicate a typical late eighteenth-century brewhouse layout. Barley grown on the estate was malted in the village and returned to the brewhouse. Cellars under the house stored the beer in wooden casks. At the time of George Lucy's death in 1845, a valuation was carried out in July of that year, this revealed that there was 4,630 gallons of beer and ale in the cellars. This beautiful and most interesting property is now in the ownership of the National Trust.

Charlecote Park brewhouse with its two coppers, mash-tun and cooling tray.

The gracefully elegant town of Woodstock, Oxfordshire, is renowned as the birthplace of this century's greatest politician, Winston Spencer Churchill, at Blenheim House. Fletcher's House in Park Street, which leads to the triumphal arch entrance to Blenheim, is now a museum of the Oxfordshire County Council. In 1279 Adam Bennett held a house in Park Street on the corner of Brown's Lane, now long gone. He also owned the site of the Marlborough Arms Hotel. In 1526 a house in the proximity of the museum belonged to a Thomas Fletcher and, by 1581, Joan, his widow, had quit-claimed to her son Henry. Before 1609 Alderman Thomas Browne had acquired the house which was still occupied by Margaret Fletcher. In about 1614 a new 'great house' called Fletcher's had been built on the site and Alderman Brown was a lessee of a malthouse on corporation land next to the river (this was later the White Hart Inn). Evidently, there was also a brewhouse here which he rented and this joint business was on a large scale. Joan Browne, who died in 1625, had malt and barley worth £126 and according to her will, she evidently grew hops. The Browne family held the property until 1625 when it passed to John Vernon, then it was owned by Dr Francis Gregory, who sold it in about 1662 to Sir Lyttleton Osbaldeston. He was a lawyer, MP and councillor, who had a brewhouse at the rear of Fletcher's House in 1685.

Harrison's Lane runs parallel to Park Street and gives access to a small stable coachhouse and brewhouse yard, to the rear of Fletcher's House. These outbuildings are all built of local stone. The brewhouse block was previously connected to the main house at right angles by a lengthy group of outbuildings, which may have formed the previously mentioned small malthouse. The more recent use of this yard and its cluster of buildings was by the county fire services. A stone extension projecting into the yard, with a metal staircase to the first floor, was built partially utilizing some of the stonework from the brewhouse. Inside the building, which has a modern mezzanine floor, is the still intact copper and its furnace set into the stone; its estimated capacity is about 200 gallons. Immediately above the rim of the copper is a wooden shutter, hung on handmade strap hinges which previously opened to the outside, thus allowing steam to be dissipated.

From the beginning of the eighteenth century, James Grove, a maltster, owned the house; he died in 1714 and his son, Joshua, continued the business until his death in 1740. The Duke of Marlborough bought the house in 1782 and either sold or gave it to his auditor, Thomas Walker. Five years later the house was let as a girls' school, but from 1794 to 1801 the house was unoccupied although the brewhouse was still listed in the property details and still in the ownership of Thomas Walker. In the 1790s, Thomas Walker was the duke's agent and town clerk. Although the Walker family still owned the house up until 1810, it would seem that brewing ceased in about 1801 as no further mention is made of the brewhouse in subsequent leases. Alderman William Margett acquired Fletcher's House in 1842 at which time he was the innkeeper of both the Marlborough Arms Hotel and the Bear Inn, Woodstock. Margett's son, William junior, who was clerk and later manager of Gillett's Bank, later to become part of Barclays Bank in 1919, sold Fletcher's House to Alderman R.B.B. Hawkins in 1867. In 1925 Captain E.W. Thring purchased the house who had sold it to Oxford County Council in 1949. The entire premises then became the fire brigade headquarters until 1965 when the County Leisure and Arts Department set up the excellent museum, as it is today.

In 1950 Kimbolton Castle, Huntingdonshire, was purchased by the governing body of Kimbolton School with the financial aid of the county council and grants from the Historic Buildings Council and Pilgrim Trust. Kimbolton School, which was founded in 1600 as a humble grammar school, had enjoyed rapid growth after the last war, and the purchase and renovation of Kimbolton Castle enabled this progress to proceed. The castle had been the home of the Duke of Manchester for over 300 years, when at the outbreak of war in 1939, the duke emigrated to Kenya. During the wartime period the premises were used by the Army Medical Corps who relinquished the buildings soon after the cessation of hostilities in 1945. The present 12th Duke now lives in Bedfordshire.

The first house on the site was built in the thirteenth century as a fortified manor-house for the De Mandevilles, and was completely rebuilt as a Tudor manor-house by Sir Richard Wingfield, friend of Henry VIII, in whose family it remained for the next 100 years. In the period 1534–6 it was the last place of confinement for Queen Katherine of Aragon. In 1615 the house was bought by Sir Henry Montagu, later to become the 1st Earl of Manchester. It remained the family home of the Earls and Dukes of Manchester until sold to the school in 1950. During the time of the 2nd Earl, who was a parliamentary general in the Civil War, extensive rebuilding took place. During the period 1690 to 1720 the 4th Earl undertook major rebuilding, once again supervised by Henry Bell of King's Lynn. He was responsible for the courtyard, great hall and part of the chapel and beautiful main staircase. The second stage of building works, commencing in 1707, included refacing the south range, the saloon

The brewhouse and laundry at Kimbolton Castle, designed by Robert Adam.

and several of the major rooms. These works were under the supervision of the eminent architects Vanburgh and Hawksmoor. The last major building work was the construction of the elongated gatehouse which was designed by Robert Adam in 1763. This imposing stone structure acted as a screen between the west front of the house and the broad street of the small town of Kimbolton. Adam's style of Doric severity includes a central arched entrance with wings on each side, terminating in triangular pedimented pavilions. Adam's original design shows saucer-shaped domes over the end pavilions and the ducal coat of arms above the central archway, also figures in the two end niches. However, these designs were not executed, the only Adamesque feature being two lion roundels to the archway. Adam's design for the north side was originally for the duchess's dairy, but in fact this was built as the brewhouse with the estate laundry to the south wing on the right-hand side. Both drew water from wells under the castle green, separating the brewhouse and gatehouse from the main range of buildings. The boiler to the brewhouse was mounted on brickwork to the front corner so that the hot liquor could flow to the wood mash-tun on an adjacent timber decking to the rear-end corner. Below the mash-tun was the underback, of the same diameter as the mash-tun but shallower in depth. Three shallow cooling trays were on an elevated timber stage so that the floor area was mainly clear, allowing for gravity flow of the beer from the coolers. At the join of the end pavilion section to the main wing, illuminated by three windows to front and rear, there is a brick arch which incorporates a brick flue which terminates in a cast-iron fire surround. This would have been to assist in controlling the temperature, particularly for the fermentation process. Tools included traditional wood shovels, a mash-tun rouser, several coopered buckets and a coopered keeler. As recently as the early 1960s there was a heavy perforated yeast tray and a delightful pair of patent shoes with built-up metal soles, thus enabling the brewer to keep his feet dry! Brewing ceased in about 1880, the previous large quantities of beer having been stored in at least three large tuns in the castle cellar. The beer may well have been transferred from the brewhouse to the basement cellar tuns by an underground pipeline. With the long period (at least eighty years) in which the plant and equipment had lain dormant, all the timber had become infested with woodworm and beetle so, sometime after 1961, it was removed. The brewhouse was then used as the school studio and is currently in use as offices.

Another example of Robert Adam devoting his superb artistic and architectural skills to the design of a brewhouse is to be found at Audley End, Saffron Walden, Essex. Sir John Vanburgh, also an eminent architect of the day, was consulted by the 8th Earl of Suffolk in 1721, having completed his commission at Kimbolton Castle. Audley End takes its name from Sir Thomas Audley who was speaker in the parliament of King Henry VIII which passed the Act of Suppression of the Monasteries. Sir Thomas Audley was rewarded by the king with the abbey of Walden which lay on the western side of the town of Saffron Walden. Nothing remains today of the Benedictine order abbey, nor of the first building which Sir Thomas built, having been created Lord Audley of Walden prior to his death in 1544. The property descended to Thomas

Kimbolton Castle interior with its keeler, rouser, shovels, mash-tun and fermenting vessel, all coopered timber. (Leigh)

Howard, son of the 4th Duke of Norfolk. Thomas Howard commanded a ship which was in action against the Spanish fleet at the Armada in 1588 and he was knighted, later being made Baron Howard of Walden by Queen Elizabeth I. He was later made lord chamberlain and lord high treasurer. The Earl of Suffolk built the great Audley End in 1603, taking thirteen years to complete it and at a cost of £200,000. The house is approached via a bridge over the River Cam from the west, but the original property had a grand entrance flanked by circular towers which led into a typical medieval large courtyard, with a small courtyard to the east, nearest the town. The outer base court and wings were demolished in 1721 but the great hall and range of rooms to the smaller courtyard remain today, as do the detached stables and coachhouse near the river. After the Civil War, Charles II found that many of the royal palaces had suffered damage and so, after several years of negotiations, the king acquired Audley End in 1669 for £50,000. It remained in royal use until 1701 when it returned to the former family, Henry, 5th Earl of Suffolk. Lady Portsmouth purchased the house and estate in 1747; she died in 1762 having bequeathed it to Sir John Griffin Whitwell who succeeded to the Barony of Howard de Walden. He was created Baron Braybrooke in 1788. It was he who created the fine building of Audley End as it is today. He died in 1797, having been responsible for many works including the employing of Robert Adam to redecorate the living suites.

In January 1763 Robert Adam submitted his account of twelve guineas to Sir John Griffin Griffin (he having taken the appendage of the second 'Griffin' in lieu of Whitwell, according to Lady Portsmouth's will): 'to a new design of brewhouse, offices, plans and elevations'. The total account was for £190 6s 6d. Most of the bricks used in the construction in 1763 were

Audley End brewhouse of 1763 with the former Royal Palace in the background.

manufactured on the estate, with pantiles for the roofs of farm buildings imported from Holland in four loads. Much of the ashlar and clunch stone used came from Ketton, Burwell and Eversden quarries. Westmorland slates amounting to 10 tons (at a cost of £3 per ton) were delivered on 6 October 1763; this cargo had been received at the Vine Inn, London, and was transhipped up the Lea Navigation by Ware barges. The brewhouse block is a single-storeyed building, constructed of light coloured bricks under a slate roof. The brewhouse range measures about 23 feet wide by 105 feet long, consisting of five basic rooms which are on the north side farthest from the main house. There is an 'L' shaped brewhouse yard with dimensions of 100 feet by 120 feet. Between the principal courtyard and the brewhouse is the great kitchen and wood yard, all situated to the west of the great pond.

Brewing was taking place in 1765, after the purchase on 2 April of various items of brewing plant, acquired by Thomas Pennystone:

3 casks, large at 3 hogshead each (162 gallons each)	£7	10	0
To firing & casks on butts	0	8	0
To working the head of a cask & barrel	0	1	6
To 8 iron hoops on butts	0	12	0
To setting on 6 iron hoops with pieces hogshead	0	2	6
To a stave in a couls tub	0	0	9
To 3 iron hoops hogsheads	0	3	9
To 8 bongs & sparge plugs	0	1	0
To 3 fast bongs	0	0	6
To fix fir, malt dust & corks & gronans of barrels	0	1	11
To time on sundry goings	0	2	0
	£9	3	11

On 30 April 1765 Thomas Pennystone received brewing tunning of 24 hogsheads, valued at £1 7s 0d. On the same date he purchased malt to the value of £17 4s 0d, having had previous malt deliveries as follows:

March 29th, to 4 qtrs of pale malt @ 28 per qtr	£5 12 0
To grinding	£0 2 0
April 3rd,	ditto
April 5th,	ditto

On 30 April 1765, from Thomas Day, he bought three consignments of fine hops at 2s6d with a total value of £10 10s 0d. In May a further setting-up cost of 5s was incurred for six iron hoops. Again on 30 April 1765, Mr Pennystone paid five guineas for eight barrels and butts for the cellar. Malt was supplied from one of the many local maltsters, a Mr Archer, and some of the hops – described as pale and brown – were supplied by Nicks and Nixon of London. The brewhouse possibly had some early teething problems in the first year of operation as Thomas Taylor of King Street, Golden Square, London, supplied four barrels of 'small beer' at a cost of £2, during February 1766.

A strong brew was authorized by Sir John to celebrate Admiral Howe's famous naval victory in 1794. Beer was supplied to twenty-eight domestic servants and some casual labour during the rebuilding of the house, as part of their remuneration. The wages of the under-butler (who assisted in the brewing) was £14 for the years from 1766 to 1784, rising to £16 per annum in 1791. Expenditure on beer amounted in the first year, 1765, to £97 13s 10½d. As previously mentioned, 1766 was a year of lower production, costing only £45 18s 8d. Up to the year 1780 the brewing costs averaged out at £100 per annum, rising to £160 from 1786. The highest expenditure for an individual year, 1794, was £227 16s 8½d. Audley End was lived in by the 7th Lord Braybrooke until his death in 1941 when it became the property of the nation, managed by the Ministry of Works, and now English Heritage.

In medieval castles and later in the great houses of the landed gentry, there was a strict hierarchy with the servants. The steward was in charge of the great hall, where important visitors were met and entertained; a chaplain or chancellor looked after the family chapel and the administration and finances of the estate. The chamberlain's responsibilities were to look after the great chamber, the main bedroom and also all the clothing of the owner and his family. The butler (or bottler) looked after the buttery where the beer was kept in butts or bottles, and organized the correct serving of a range of drinks. The usher was stationed in the hall and opened doors and announced visitors. The cook was, of course, totally in charge of the kitchen and its large staff, and she liaised with the head gardener to ensure that all produce necessary was available. The marshal looked after the stables and the carriages. Many of these titles have since been adopted as honorary titles but still with much the same areas of responsibility, and several of these are to be found in both the government and the royal household.

'A PINT OF YOUR BEST, LANDLORD'

The public house as it is known today has evolved and gone through many changes from its earliest days as a monastic guest-house. During the Roman occupation it was necessary to provide suitable lodging houses twenty miles apart along the main roads, both for the use of the troops and commercial travellers. Following the Saxon invasion, most of these posting houses were swept away, and so for the majority of wayfarers there were few places to stay overnight. The more wealthy traveller and the landed gentry would stay at manors and large estates and continued to do so for many hundreds of years. With the advent of the monasteries, travelling once more became commonplace. Each monastery throughout the country provided a guest-house or chambers. From these guest-houses, often with their own adjacent small chapel near the gatehouse, grew the inns of today.

Many of the travellers were pilgrims, particularly to such cities as Gloucester, York, Winchester and Canterbury. Provision was made for their stay over a number of days. Even the humble parish church had a small guest-house, often used by the parish councillors and bell-ringers. Some of these meeting places were the local inn, and many disclose their early origins in their religious names: The Bell, The Angel, The Golden Cross, The Fleece, The George and Pilgrims. It is fortunate today that many of these fine inns have survived and among these is the New Inn, Gloucester, which was built in about 1445 on the site of a small hospice, to accommodate pilgrims visiting the shrine of King Edward II murdered at Berkeley Castle in 1329. John Twyning, a monk of the abbey of St Peter, is credited with its construction. Today it is tucked behind shops and is approached by a covered archway. This opens out onto a cobbled courtyard with an open gallery at first floor, which gave access to the bedrooms and also permitted audiences to view Tudor plays in the yard below; today customers may still enjoy the character of this ancient hostelry.

At Battle in Sussex, the appropriately named Pilgrim's Rest was a hospice attached to Battle Abbey. Its existence is known to date back to the fourteenth century, its timber construction of cross-beams and spandrels, and a fine king-post, revealing its age. The Angel and Royal, Grantham, built of local mellow sandstone, is one of the few remaining medieval hostels. It is a building of high quality and was therefore provided for the more wealthy merchants and pilgrims. Some parts of the building, including the cellars, are believed to date back to the time of the Knights Templar who were dissolved in 1312. The central round-headed archway was built in the reign of Edward III and at its centre is a carved and gilded angel holding a crown below an oriel window which was built during the rebuilding of the front façade in the fifteenth century. Another religious inn, The Star at Alfriston,

Star Inn, Alfriston; one of many ancient inns that served the pilgrims. (Trust Houses Ltd)

One of the many superb art nouveau panels commemorating the monks at the Blackfriars Inn, City of London.

Sussex, was founded in the thirteenth century and known as The Star of Bethlehem. It was built by the abbey of Battle for its pilgrims and on an internal wall beam are carved the letters 'IHS'. Many of the beams have fine carvings probably so well preserved by the lath and plaster removed at the turn of the century. Among these carvings is depiction of a mitred abbot or bishop.

Two of the most popular pilgrim routes were from London and Winchester to Canterbury. The pilgrims would probably have started their trek from the Hospital of St Cross, Winchester, where they would have received their wayfarers' dole. Their journey to Canterbury was along the well-trodden South Downs route via Alton. The Cistercian pilgrims needed regular stopping-off places for victualling and one of these to survive is The Crown at Chiddingfold, Surrey. Its earliest history as an inn dates back to 1383 when Thomas Gofayre, a brewer, took the lease of the property then known as The Hall. The building is timber-framed with curved braces and wattle and daub infill panels. The top floor at one time had the local characteristic tile-hanging.

From London travellers would assemble together at numerous hostelries, the site of one of these on the north bank of the Thames where today stands the Black Friars. This is beside the bridge named after the monks. The pub is unique with its art nouveau decorative panels, murals and stained glass windows, depicting the Dominican priory monks going about their daily activities. Across the Thames on the south bank was the famous Tabard Inn, Southwark, demolished in 1874. This was a typical galleried inn made famous by Chaucer in his *Canterbury Tales*, the ebullient landlord being a friend of his. The Tabard was built as an ecclesiastical guest-house by the abbot of Hyde, Winchester, and survived several alterations and a fire in 1676 when it was rebuilt and renamed The Talbot. The pilgrims' route to Canterbury was via Dartford and thence through Kent where many smaller inns provided suitable quantities of their home-brewed ales to sustain the weary travellers.

Once the pilgrims arrived in Canterbury to pay their respects at the tomb of Saint Thomas à Becket, many guest-houses were required for the large numbers. One of the earliest lodges was the Canterbury Pilgrims' Hospital, the chapel and undercroft are open to visitors today; other rest houses were St Thomas's and the Poor Priests' Hospitals. The Falstaff stands close by the Westgate in St Dunstan's Street, and provided travellers with hospitality outside the gates after they were shut out at curfew. The top two floors project in the typical medieval style, the painted sign indicating that it was built in 1403. The pictorial swing sign on its elaborate and decorative carriage shows a hooded monk with what else but a foaming tankard of ale!

Provision for travellers was not confined solely to outside the priory walls; at Canterbury and most other monasteries a guest-house was provided within the precincts. At Glastonbury, Somerset, The George and Pilgrims, a stone-built and crenellated building, looks for all the world like a religious gatehouse with its strong vertical lines of stonework windows and coats of arms above its central door. It was built in 1475 by Abbot John de Selwood for pilgrims to the Benedictine abbey, where they received free board and lodging. The entire front façade remains unspoilt, one of the carved stone shields above the entrance door bearing the arms of the abbey. Inside a flagged hallway leads to a parlour where the abbot received his guests. From one of the upper bedrooms, Henry VIII is said to have watched the burning of Glastonbury Abbey in 1539.

In the same county of Somerset, another fine old hospice stands, the George at Norton St Philip. This was built by the Carthusian priory of Hinton, and dates from about 1397. It also served as a wool storehouse, the monks depending on their sheep for revenue to augment their meagre existence. A fire damaged the upper floors which were rebuilt with infilled timber framing on top of the earlier stone ground floor. These top two floors overhang and on the first floor, there are three oriel windows with a central pointed archway and single flue, stone chimney-stack. To the right of this entrance door are stone steps leading to a mezzanine platform, most likely a loading stage for the wool. While the Duke of Monmouth was staying at the inn, a shot was fired at him on 26 June 1685 but it missed, the assailant no doubt attempting to claim the £1,000 reward offered by King James for his death. Further into the West Country is the George at Hatherleigh, a 700-year-old inn in the heart of north Devon. The picturesque upper courtyard is approached under the archway, while the old brewhouse and lofts where the annual rent audit dinners were once held, are now converted into new rooms for the hotel. In a corner of the yard stands an old granite brewing trough. The thatched roof is so typical of Devon and, despite many modernizations, the ancient inn still retains much of its past. Sadly, brewing of home-brewed is not among its present attributes.

No records exist of the Saxon alehouses, but it is known that the Romans indicated their tabernae or tavern with a garland of vine leaves. Another symbol used by the Romans was the chequer design, of which examples were found at Pompeii. As far as is known, there is only one example in this country where the painted chequer design, on each side of an entrance door, is still perpetuated. This is at the Methuen Arms, Corsham, Wiltshire.

With the boom in the wool trade during the fourteenth century, the merchants became rich, particularly in both the West Country and East Anglia. Here they spent much of their riches on building beautiful churches. The masons and other craftsmen had to be housed and many public houses were built near to these religious building sites. After long and strenuous hours of work it was of course necessary to provide the men with beer. With the decline of the church's power and influence in the sixteenth century following the Reformation, these residential inns became the centre of village community life just as many are still today. It was not until the seventeenth century that some roads were improved to a condition which allowed wheeled coaches and carts to pass with more ease. Prior to these improvements on turnpike roads, only the king and his retinue and wealthy gentry could afford the vast heavy wagons drawn by many horses to carry them around the countryside.

From the eighteenth century the increase in travellers necessitated the alehouse keeper, who brewed his own beer, to become the publican brewer or brewing victualler. More often than not it was the wife who did the brewing. With the coming of the great age of the horse-drawn coaches in the latter half of the eighteenth century, new and enlarged premises were required for the many travellers and the frequent changes of horses. These coaching inns had to be at regular intervals or stages (hence stage coaches), along the major roads, linking the growing towns. Many of these roads had been built and repaired by private individuals and as turnpike roads they were permitted to erect a gate across and charge tolls. Many of these locations had a pub nearby and were suitably named, such as The Gate, or The Gate Hangs Well. Some of the older inns were converted and enlarged with stables and hay lofts being provided to the rear of the premises. There were also many new coaching inns built from 1780 onwards, and inevitably they had an archway leading off the street into a courtyard. Where these inns existed on land owned by the local squire, many such inns took the coat of arms of the owner as a sign. So it is that so many inns today portray heraldic devices in various forms. The inn courtyards assumed greater importance with the coming of the coaches, the yards became a hive of frenzied activity on the arrival of a coach, heralded by the coachman's horn. The ostler, warned by the horn, arranged a rapid change of horses while the passengers, particularly those riding on the outside, quickly repaired to the inn parlour for refreshments. From 1784 the faster mail coaches were to be seen on the turnpiked roads, taking much traffic from the slower stage coaches. The heyday of the English inn was surely during the hundred year period up to 1840, when the railways started spreading all over the country. Within only a few years, many of the once grand coaching inns were in decline, being replaced by the ubiquitous railway hotel at nearly every railway station. They in turn became less popular with the onset of the motor car in the 1920s and 1930s when many a coaching inn took on a renewed importance.

The George, Dorchester, Oxfordshire, is at the confluence of the Rivers Thame and Thames. Dorchester was therefore a most important Saxon town, the capital of the kingdom of Mercia. The many gabled and jettied front façade of the George Hotel was formerly a hospice to the abbey, whose church still stands opposite. The George has a cobbled courtyard and gallery once so typical of inns of this age. The monks' old brewhouse remains today; it is a high beamed dining-room with half-timbered walls and a large fireplace and is an excellent example of medieval construction. However, the George's heyday was in the coaching era as it is situated on the old London to Oxford route. A reminder of those days was the delightful original coach which was sited on the front forecourt. With the decline of the coaching trade in the nineteenth century, it fell on hard times. The yard was put to other uses including a coal yard and a wheelwright's shop, but today the mobility of the George's customers has ensured its popularity.

The Lansdowne Arms, Calne, Wiltshire, is a very elongated building situated on one side of the market square close to the town hall. As the Catherine Wheel it was founded in about 1582 when first mentioned in borough records, but during the reign of George II it was enlarged by incorporating neighbouring property. As part of the rebuilding the hotel was improved up to coaching standards, with an archway leading through to the cobbled yard. In this courtyard the old brewhouse remains, once bearing the painted legend, 'Welcome ye coming Speed ye parting Guest'. On the rendered front elevation there is an unusual circular barometer built into the wall. Today the name of the Lansdowne Strand is painted boldly on the parapet having been renamed in about 1826 after the Marquis of Lansdowne, whose estate is nearby and who owned the property in 1925. The 'Strand' area was used up until recent times as an animal market and the old coach and posting inn did a roaring trade from all the visiting farmers. In the coaching days, the previous stage was at the Castle and Ball, Marlborough, on the London to Bath route when it was diverted via Calne instead of through Devizes.

Brewing was last carried out at the Lansdowne Brewery in 1930 by Arthur Milton Portch, who not only brewed for the hotel but also had a considerable local trade and delivered to country houses. The brewhouse and adjacent offices are still extant, built of stone and brick,

The Lansdowne Arms, Calne, brewhouse.

to one side of the cobbled yard. Access is via a side road through an archway facing the brewhouse, with stables to one side and storerooms to the rear. The entire courtyard complex is built into the hillside so that there are three storeys in the yard and only one to the external elevations. All are built of stone with the rear section facing the hotel, once the cart sheds. It is supplied with water from a constant spring once used in the brewing process. Access may also be obtained to the brewhouse from the high-level road at the rear. Underneath the brewhouse there are cellars with a brick arched opening beneath a ramp. The stone chimney-stack still towers above the louvred brewhouse, with a later addition of a tall Victorian chimney-pot. The old office section is now in use as bedrooms to the hotel, its walls once resplendent with large letters reading 'Lansdowne Brewery'. In a 1907 advertisement the hotel refers to itself as a 'Family and Commercial and Posting House'. Charles Edward Fox sold the business in 1914 to S. Belsey, who passed it onto Albert C. Belsey, he retaining it until 1923. Arthur Milton Portch finally gave up brewing in 1930. Home-brewed beer was available in casks from 6 to 54 gallons, flagons and one and two gallon jars (the stoneware type with taps). Harvest ales were also supplied up until at least 1907, so the local farmers were wanting for nothing.

In Lancashire, at Ormskirk, the Buck-in-the-Vine is an old coaching inn dating from 1650. It still has the fabric of its brewhouse at the rear. The town of Macclesfield benefited from the southerly coaching route from Manchester and the importance of the town as a major market-place. There were numerous beerhouses and several coaching inns catering for the needs of the busy community, and the Bull's Head Hotel was probably the largest coaching inn in town. Of three storeys height and with four large windows to each storey, the building has an arch to the left which led to stables accommodating thirty horses. Henry Shore transferred to the Bull's Head from the Sun Inn on Chestergate in 1841 and decided to expand the brewing side of the business and advertised his wares to 'Farmers and Private Families'. However, brewing only lasted another twenty-six years as in 1867, John Keogh acquired the business and sold off the brewing plant which consisted of a 'two load copper brewpan'. Evidently after the death of Mr Keogh, his widow carried on the pub business as she advertised the fact that she was being assisted by her nephew Mr Samuel Lunt. Included in this advertisement she indicated that 'Stancliffe's Bitter' and 'Allsopps Burton Ales' were supplied in 9, 18 and 36 gallon sizes and that 'All orders promptly attended to', thereby indicating that the previous home-brewing trade of supplying farmers and families was being replaced. Around the turn of the century the property was sold to Ind Coope or Allsopp's prior to their amalgamation, and it remains today in the Carlsberg/Tetley estate, successors to Allied Breweries and Ind Coope.

Chelmsford is the county town of Essex where a property with its origins going back to the De Vere family prior to 1560 was known then as the Crown Inn. Later in the same century it was known as the New Inn. It was in 1642 that the site of the three-storeyed building became known as the Black Boy and as such it became renowned as a substantial coaching inn. It stood on the junction of the High Street and Springfield Road which was the coach road from London to Colchester and Harwich in the east. The brewery was in evidence in 1790, catering for the large trade in travellers. On 15 July 1793 a meeting was held in one of the many rooms in which it was resolved that a canal should be built between Chelmsford and the sea. In 1810 Rob Dixon was the owner of the Black Boy Inn and

Brewery and a detailed plan drawn up in 1817 indicates the commodious accommodation. This plan was made following the death of Mr Dixon and was arranged by his executors for the firm of Dixon and Carter. Included in the sale were eight public houses so, by this date, the brewery had become a common brewery. With the decline of the coaching business the Black Boy was auctioned in 1857 and most of the buildings demolished. A few years later a temperance hotel was built on the site, finally becoming retail shops but the area where the small brewhouse had once stood became W. Gray & Sons Brewery, founded in 1828. This business finally ceased to brew in 1974, although most of the brewery and malthouse buildings have been incorporated into a modern shopping precinct.

An Act of Parliament of 1552 fixed the number of alehouses in each town and district, this was followed on 10 July 1577 by an order to obtain the exact numbers of the different types of drinking establishments, with the purpose of levying a tax on them to raise money for the repair of Dover harbour. This survey showed that there were 14,202 alehouses, 329 taverns, 1,631 inns and another 3,597 not specified, but probably hotels, the total amounting to just under 20,000. The population at this time was under four million thereby giving each member of the fraternity a licence for every 187 people. By comparison today there is one licence for approximately every 600 people, with a population increased by more than tenfold. The above mentioned Acts of Parliament were by no means in isolation as the earliest forms of control on the licensed trade came about with the Assize of Bread and Ale in 1267, and subsequently there have been numerous taxes imposed since that date during the last 700 years.

During the early part of the sixteenth century the publican brewers met with competition from a newly developing brewer called a common brewer. These were brewers who started to expand their business beyond just supplying their own alehouse, by acquiring other outlets in which to sell their beer. The acquisition of these additional alehouses came about in a number of ways including the supply of a more consistent and better quality product. Initially many of these other alehouses who gave up brewing still retained the ownership of the property, but in order to improve or maintain their business they had to borrow capital in order to carry out these improvements. Here the entrepreneurial brewer was able to give the cash loan on the condition that he had exclusive rights to supply the beer; in this way the tied house system came about. Should the borrower default in any way the entrepreneurial brewer called in his loan and was able to purchase the freehold of the alehouse. The histories of nearly all the major present-day brewing companies can trace their early history back to just such a set of circumstances. The publican brewer, however, did not only have to contend with the rise of the common brewer: a much smaller but nevertheless important competitor came on the scene. This was the retail brewer.

The retail brewer did not own any retail outlets and brewed primarily for the family, farm and estate trade. Consequently he was very vulnerable to the whims of his customers and the growing competition of the common brewers who were introducing machinery and new technology into their professional business. He had no guaranteed outlet for his production and so there were comparatively very few retail brewers. In my own family's history, a George Peaty is listed in Pigot & Cos Directory of 1830 for Winchester as a retail brewer at 31 High Street, at the same address he also traded as baker and flour dealer, thereby diversifying his business. This joint business of baking and brewing can be traced back for many hundreds of

Little & Sons' delightful Wiltshire brewery.

years and was more often than not situated side by side in the great estates of the landed gentry. The reason for this was the common use of yeast, or barm, in both processes, the brewing production giving larger quantities that were used in the baking trade.

In the wooded folds of a valley in Wiltshire lies the small village of Slaughterford. Just across the road from the pinnacled church tower is an eighteenth-century stone building with a cluster of outbuildings and a brick-built chimney-stack dominating the landscape. This is the old brewing premises of Little and Son. The two-storeyed Cotswold stone building under a red pantiled roof and Cotswold stone slabs, still has its louvred windows to the upper section. Capping the roof is a louvred turret above the old copper, now fighting off the growth of a Russian vine. The Little family trace their history in the area back to Richard Little who was baptized in 1675 and buried on 18 July 1737 at nearby Biddestone. The family remained within the area for several generations, with marriages and burials taking place in Malmesbury, Kington St Michael and Castle Combe. The cluster of buildings around the family home show several stages of growth with the final ground plan forming a 'U' shape. On one end of a projecting wing from the house was a 'jug and bottle' department, the worn stone step showing how popular this must have been over many years. Across the rear yard is the other projecting wing which was the fermenting and cooling area. A part of the growth of the business was the building of the brick chimney-stack and single-storey extension of the boilerhouse, dating from the Victorian era. The smaller original stone brewhouse developed so much that, at the time of closure in 1939, the company had become a small common brewer, owning five public houses, one of which was in Weston-super-Mare, forty-five miles distant! With the steep hills around the brewery, delivering beer in winter must have been a nightmare.

A unique retail brewer, also of the West Country, was Combe's Brewery at Brockhampton, near Cheltenham, Gloucestershire. Down a short cul-de-sac in the quaint Cotswold village lies the small brewery and malthouse complex that was once renowned locally for its very early 'home-brew packs'. The malthouse, brewhouse and owner's house and outbuildings are on the southernmost tip of the village of Brockhampton, on the River Coln. This emanates from the manor-house grounds of Brockhampton Park. The buildings consist of an early eighteenth-century house built of coursed squared and dressed limestone under a stone slate roof, this house is adjacent to the similarly built three-storeyed malthouse. This has two gabled buildings adjacent to the cul-de-sac road; on one of the malthouses there is a dated and initialled stone plaque over a door which reads, 'I WOOD, 1769'. The other building has a door to each floor in the gable end, giving access to the storage and top growing floor. To the right, and between the malthouse and owner's house, is the former well, to the rear of this area is the kiln complete with perforated earthenware tiled floor. Sadly the roof cowl has been removed. Inside the ground-floor doorway is the still complete steep cistern, where the local barley was soaked before being hoisted up to the top floor where it was spread out and allowed to germinate. At the appropriate stage it was raked up and transferred to the slightly lower kiln floor; there the grains were roasted until germination was arrested. Then the malt was shovelled down through hatches to the lower floor where it was sacked, stored and when required, taken across the yard to the brewhouse opposite.

The small brewhouse is constructed of similar dressed limestone, the earliest part is of late seventeenth- or early eighteenth-century construction, with the top gabled floor dating from the eighteenth century. A centrally placed doorway on the ground floor has a heavy timber lintel. On the second floor are two small casement windows to the front elevation and to the rear are two louvred windows either side of a Victorian brick chimney-stack. On the top front elevation is a doorway which was evidently equipped with a hoist to draw up sacks of malt and hops. The brewhouse roof has red tiles which compliment the elaborate red brick chimney-stack at the rear which is a feature of the landscape. The head of the stack has an oversailing course of cream bricks while the top of the flue has cream and blue engineering bricks laid in a sawtooth design giving it a most pleasing aspect. Attached to the right-hand side of the rectangular brewhouse is a two-storeyed building of the nineteenth century which has internal stairs to the top floor where the fermenting vessels were previously housed.

Combes' Cotswold tower brewhouse.

The ground floor has engineering tiles and a drain, and this is evidently where the beer was racked and the drays were kept. To the left of the brewhouse, facing the house, were the previous stables, now demolished.

The malthouse and house were probably built for the Wood family, some of whose descendants still live in the village. George Combe, born in 1815, was recorded as being the village baker in 1870, while one of his sons, Thomas, was a tailor. Another son, Benjamin, owned the Grafton Brewery at Cheltenham which had ceased brewing by 1899 when it was taken over by the Nailsworth Brewery Co. Ltd. Family deeds indicate that the Brockhampton brewery, malthouse, bakehouse and cottage were purchased for £400 in 1840. George Combe died in 1871 aged fifty-six and so Thomas Combe inherited the family's new wealth and it was probably he who extended the original brewhouse by an additional floor and the brick chimney-stack. In 1885 Thomas was first recorded in *Kelly's Directory* as a brewer and baker. He continued in this joint role until about 1897 when his son, George Thomas, took over the business prior to 1906. He had two sons, the eldest, Reginald George Bradford born in 1896, inheriting the now flourishing concern. It was he who introduced the idea of packaging the home-brew kits in the 1920s. These contained 'Celebrated Cotswold Malt and Hops, with Yeast' which would make 3 gallons; the cost 10½d. A 'light' and 'dark' version were available, as was another style called Hopamalt which would make 2½ gallons of beer for the cost of 6d. Notes on the packaging included: 'If you possess a Brewer's Licence you may brew beer of any strength by reducing the quantity of water to this packet of Hopamalt'. Also on this package a box note said: 'This packet produces 1½ gallons of a nourishing and sustaining beverage similar in character to that which our forefathers drank and enjoyed and on which they thrived and lived happily together.' The brewing directions stated that the contents of the packet should be added to 1½ gallons of water and boiled for one hour, then strained with one pound of sugar added. When cooled one tablespoonful of yeast should be added. This was to ferment for 24 hours or until fermentation ceased, then it was to be placed in jars or bottles. A final sales blurb said that the products were 'prepared under the personal supervision of one whose forebears have for generations been handling similar ingredients'.

Brewing ceased in 1927 when the business was acquired by Showell's Brewery Co. Ltd of Oldbury but malting continued, so it is likely that it was the brewing goodwill which was acquired and not the premises. Besides the home-brew kits, R.G.B. Combe promoted the sales of yeast, supplied in quantities from one to twelve dozen bottles. Hops packed in ¼ and ½ lb packages could be purchased in quantities from 7 lbs to 112 lbs. Two qualities of malt were available, roasted was priced at 12s per bushel and pale malt cost 10s. A discount of 5 per cent on cash paid in seven days encouraged prompt payment and notice was required if the malt was to be ground ready for immediate brewing. Some unusually sized wooden casks could also be purchased with a 3-gallon size costing 10s 6d each, 4½-gallon at 11s, 6-gallon at 12s, 9-gallon at 14s and a 12-gallon for 16s.

At the outbreak of war in 1939, the home-brew packs had to be discontinued due to the shortage of sugar. The brewhouse and malthouse were taken over by the Ministry of Defence, and the Northumbrian Division were billeted there on their return from Dunkirk. The troops slept in the malthouse and the brewery side was converted into a kitchen; it may have been at this time when all the brewing plant was removed, the precious metals being in great demand. Several of the officers were billeted in the house and later one or two German POWs worked on the farm and malthouse, which was then used for drying corn. This had been salvaged from bombed or torpedoed ships which had been brought into Bristol Docks, the grain then brought to Brockhampton to be dried in the malt kiln. Before being re-sacked, it was passed through a winnower to separate each grain. Other spoilt items such as spices and ginger were also dried.

One of the few workers remembered was Bill Locke whose job was head drayman, he was one of eleven children in his family. He delivered beer to several local pubs including the Bell and the Plaisterers at Winchcombe, the Kemble Inn at Fairview, Cheltenham, and the Horse & Groom, St James Street,

DRINK —
COMBE'S
HOME BREWED BEER.

Cheltenham, now demolished. Evidently the pub adjacent to the old brewery, the Craven Arms, is of comparatively recent licensing and was never owned or supplied from the Combe's Brewery.

A third brewing branch of the very large Combe family is the best known part, this is the one which went to London and eventually amalgamated with Watney and Reid's breweries to form Watney, Combe & Reid. The Combe family trace their ancestry back to John da Cumba who owned property at Fitleton on the Hampshire and Wiltshire borders in the twelfth century. The farming family prospered with John's great-grandson being appointed as high sheriff of Wiltshire in 1289. During the sixteenth century, another John, the name persists throughout the ages, lived near Shaftesbury. One of the farm buildings was the ancient thatched tithe barn which still exists. Edward Combe, the youngest of four brothers, farmed in Somerset; his grandson, also named Edward, was called to the Bar at Lincoln's Inn, and his son practised law in Hampshire. His son, Harvey Christian Combe, acquired the Woodyard Brewery, Castle Street, Long Acre, London WC2, in June 1787. In addition to being a London MP he was also lord mayor of the city of London in 1799. Another branch continued farming in Wiltshire with John Combe at Tisbury Mill from 1757 to 1831, although today there are none farming there, only at Burcombe, Dinton and Barford St Martin. Sadly, the decline of this extensive family with its three varied brewing interests of the past reflects what has happened to the brewing industry over the past 150 years.

The humble surroundings of the early publican brewers would be hard to contemplate today, were it not for some beautiful paintings by George Morland (associated with a brewery of that name today in Abingdon) which show the conditions of country

alehouses. Most customers of the working classes would sup their ale in meagre and simply furnished rooms, or in better weather sit on wooden benches outside. The buildings would often be damp and quite inhospitable by today's standards, but the more well-to-do customer would be invited into the landlord's private parlour, where at least there would have been a fire burning. The brewing of the home-brew would have taken place in the kitchen or its annexe, in most cases where the household's laundry was also washed. From these humble beginnings the publican brewer slowly evolved in the nineteenth century, in which time the previous privately owned alehouse became an area for improvement and some professionalism. The brewery architect had arrived – or at least his forerunner had!

In the early 1830s, as with so much else at this time, the growth in the population expanded in pace with developments in new technology and industry. Drinking establishments were now being specifically designed and the private parlour had given way to the designed bar room. The word 'bar' referred originally to the hatchway separating the kitchen from a room in which the drinks were consumed, more commonly called the taproom, inferring that the cask of beer had been tapped ready to serve the home-brewed beer from. Sometimes the storage cellar was adjacent to the bar with the wooden casks sitting on a stillage, this form of dispensing still being in fairly common usage up to the 1960s and later.

The Beerhouse Act of 1830 permitted householders to sell beer from their private houses, although a separate licence to brew was required. This Act was introduced to encourage the greater consumption of beer as opposed to spirits, especially gin. For several decades the importation from Holland and the cheap production of gin in London had had disastrous effects on the drinking public; drunkenness and poverty were rife, as depicted in one of Hogarth's paintings of Gin Street. The effect on the now respectable publican brewer was equally devastating as he saw much of this business slipping away to the huge proliferation of beer-drinking dens. It took another thirty-nine years for another Act of Parliament, the Wine & Beerhouse Act, to take effect in which a Justice's Certificate was required to obtain an excise licence. Publican brewers had of course been required to pay beer duty, whereas the private brewer remained exempt. Duty was paid on two strengths of beer, small or strong, and this had been the case for some 200 years. It was therefore easy for the publican to mix the two beers after they had been assessed and duty paid, and to sell this half-and-half

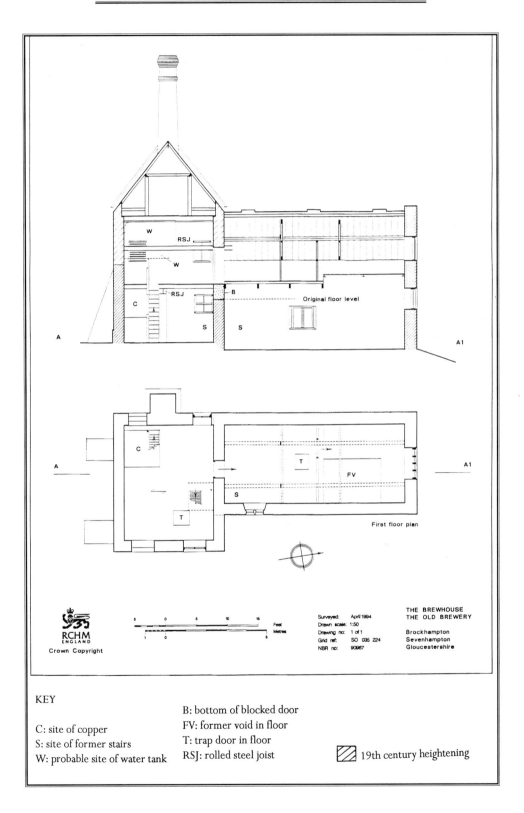

KEY

C: site of copper
S: site of former stairs
W: probable site of water tank

B: bottom of blocked door
FV: former void in floor
T: trap door in floor
RSJ: rolled steel joist

19th century heightening

as the stronger beer, a clear case of fraud to his customers and the excise duty. In order to overcome this deceit the method of duty payable was altered from the beer onto the malt and hops used. Later in 1847 this levy also applied to sugar.

To illustrate the relative numbers of common and publican brewers the table below clearly shows the decline of the publican brewer.

YEAR	COMMON	PUBLICAN	RETAIL
1690	780	47,500	—
1790	1,300	27,000	—
1890	2,330	6,350	—
1914	1,335	1,477	880

The last year in which statistics were published for the publican brewers was 1914 although despite the continued decline, two strongholds in the Midlands held out where several home-brewers continued. The Black Country and the town of Derby were the bastions, with only four home-brew pubs in the country surviving into the 1980s. They were the All Nations Inn, Madeley, Shropshire, the Blue Anchor Inn, Helston, Cornwall, Old Swan (Ma Pardoe's) Netherton and the Three Tuns, Bishop's Castle, also in Shropshire. The brief history of each of these shall be recalled, as they stood alone among the great tide which swept all the others away.

In 1789 Mr Christopher Bagley built his stone and brick public house, with its small brewhouse behind, into the steep hill across the wooded valley from the Blist Hill open-air museum of today at Madeley. When built, the pub was situated beside a narrow gauge tramway which crossed the valley by a metal girder bridge, called the Lee Dingle Bridge, from the pit head and dock area serving a branch of the Shropshire Canal. Here were sited the small colliery and furnaces served by the renowned Hay Incline, linking the high level with the River Severn. From the tramway beside the All Nations Inn, a further incline surmounted the hilltop where the Meadow Pitt Colliery was situated. No doubt this busy scene, with its many thirsty workers on the site of the early Industrial Revolution, prompted Mr Bagley to set up his home-brewing business. In 1934 Bill and Eliza Lewis purchased the property from a descendant of Mr Bagley and ran it for forty years. They sold it to their son-in-law, Keith Hardman, the present licensee and brewer, in 1975, the year that William Henry Lewis died and Eliza felt that it was time to pass the mash paddle on to her daughter Jean and husband Keith. Eliza recalled how, when she was ten, 'I used to scrub out the bar floor of the Bird in Hand in Ironbridge for me dad before I went to school, then when I came home there'd be a basketful of ironing because me mam was helping in the pub.' Only one draught beer has been produced, this is a light mild of only 1032° OG 3% ABV, made using the town water supply. For the seventy years from the turn of the century, the water had been obtained from bore holes near Beckbury. Malt and yeast are obtained from Holden's Brewery, Dudley, and hops from Charles Faram, Malvern, Worcestershire. The original coal-fired copper was replaced in 1971 by a propane-fired one obtained from the Druid's Head Inn, Croseley, West Midlands, on the death of the owner Jack Flavell. Also from this home-brew pub was obtained the mash-tun, lined with polypropylene.

This has perforated base plates of a similar material but, because of their light weight they have to be held down by the original copper ones. The wooden fermenting vessel is of 10-barrel capacity and is used every ten to fourteen days. This vessel was manufactured by E. Potterton & Son, brewers' engineers, Villa Street, Birmingham, which is engraved on the brass excise gauge plate. The volume of beer brewed averages 200 gallons a week. In 1977 Mrs Lewis confessed that she had six successive bad brews that had to be poured away, due to lack of fermentation, which she incorrectly put down to the hops. 'I nearly gave up then, I said that if it didn't work the seventh time then I'd pack it in for good'; fortunately the seventh brew proved satisfactory. During the late 1970s the old coal-fired boiler blew up and this was converted to propane firing, at the same time an electric pump was installed to alleviate Mrs Lewis's task of ladling, by hand, up to 350 gallons into the copper!

Today the cottage-style pub, with its spartan bar, continues the evocative simplicity that was so familar all those years ago to the men working on the railway and in the collieries. Outside, the garden patio is set off by the white painted walls of this 200-year-old building. The steep gravel drive leads up to a car park beside the old railway bridge and its massively ornate iron abutments. Brewing today is carried out by Keith Hardman, still using an ancient wooden paddle for rousing the wort in the mash-tun, just as this type of tool has been used for centuries. The single hand-pump with its 'clip' on the bar counter shows two crossed flags, one is the Union Jack, the other anonymous; perhaps it's Keith's own flag!

Keith Hardman rouses the mash-tun at the All Nations brew-pub, Madeley.

Down in the deepest West Country in the Duchy of Cornwall lies the town of Helston, famous for its annual Floral Dance. It is equally renowned for its ancient home-brew pub, the Blue Anchor Inn. At the beginning of the seventeenth century the Blue Anchor was one of thirty alehouses that brewed for a population of only 300. The early history of the property was as a resting house for monks in about 1400, who were working among the poor, and they no doubt brewed their own beer. The building became a beerhouse in about 1550 and a skittle alley was built which attracted the local landowners and so gave the Blue Anchor an edge on its competitors. The local tin-mining industry flourished in the middle of the last century and the inn again encouraged the miners to quaff their ale, by allowing their weekly wages to be paid in the public bar. The clerks of the mining companies collected the money from the court house and distributed the cash in the bar. The court house was known as the Coinagehall which later gave its name to the street in which the Blue Anchor stands.

Today the inn has blue-painted windows and doors set into the warm coloured stone under a thatched roof. The central doorway leads to the rear yard where the brewhouse is approached by a flight of nine granite steps to its unusual location on the first floor. Befitting its great age and local character, the two bars on either side have stone chimney-breast walls and darkened beams, the locals' bar is at the front and the visitors, known locally as 'emmets', tend to go to the rear. More recent history recalls that about 120 years ago a customer entered the empty bar and, on enquiring why there were no customers, was told that they were all upstairs as the pub was being auctioned that day. Whereupon he went upstairs and by the end of that day had purchased the pub and its brewery. The inn has been in the Richards's family since Thomas Richards first acquired it, with his grandson, Geoffrey, continuing the brewing. His father was born in one of the upstairs rooms and was the originator of the pub's renowned Spingo beers, produced after the end of the First World War. Geoffrey Richards was brewing from 1940 and included the bottling of Guinness, Bass and Worthington beers. More recently, in 1973, the long history of the Richards's connection with the Blue Anchor came to an end when they sold out to Mrs F.S. Jones who remained there until 1978 when she sold it to Patricia and Sidney Cannon. The present owners are licensee Kim Corbett, assisted by Simon Stone, who purchased the business on 23 July 1993.

The beers have a just reputation for their excellence and strength, the most popular, Mild, has an original gravity of 1050, normally associated with other brewers' premium strength beers. The Best Bitter is at 1053, a Special at 1070 and an Extra Special is 1076, the latter is brewed for one month only at Easter and Christmas. The brewer for the past seventeen years has been Tim Sears, who works in his brewhouse at the rear. Underneath is the cellar and behind this is the fermenting room. In this room are five fibreglass vessels each of a capacity of 150 gallons, lagged with timber staves. Upstairs the 100-year-old mash-tun of 80-gallon capacity is close to the open copper cooling tray and the copper of 150-gallon capacity, installed earlier this century. Kent Golding hops are used, and malt and yeast from the Redruth Brewery have been used. Water is obtained from the pub's own 25-feet-deep well which has maintained a constant flow, even in the dryest of summers. Several years ago a beermat was produced depicting the anchor sign with the words 'Spingo home-brewed Ales'; the word Spingo is a northern term used to denote a strong beer. In 1981 a bottled beer called Prince of Ales was produced to commemorate the marriage of the Prince of Wales, the owner of the Duchy of Cornwall.

Inside the ancient Blue Anchor, Helston, Cornwall.

There can be few pubs, if any, that are better known by their licensee's name than the correct name of the house – such is the case with the Old Swan Inn, of Halesowen Road, Netherton, West Midlands. It is affectionately known to customers and beer enthusiasts everywhere as 'Ma Pardoe's'. Netherton is two miles south of Dudley town centre, itself some eight miles west of Birmingham Bull Ring. The area is hilly and was described as 'abounding with numerous coal and iron mines'. At the turn of the century Dudley had thirty-nine home-brew pubs and thirteen common brewers, while Netherton was also well accommodated with several home-brew pubs. Of all of these once numerous pubs who brewed for themselves, Ma Pardoe's is the only one that survived well into the 1990s; alas, for the past few years it has failed to produce a drop of its own beer.

The Old Swan was first mentioned in a *History of Dudley* in 1840 with the census in the following year indicating that a Joseph Turner, carter and his family of five, was the licensed victualler. However, it was not until the earliest deeds of 22 April 1863 that a brewhouse and other ancillary outbuildings were indicated, when the property was bought by John Young. By 1872 the business had changed hands again with Thomas Hartshorne, from Gloucestershire, taking on the role of landlord and brewer. This family retained the Old Swan for ninety-three years with Thomas senior passing it on to his son Thomas, who retired at the age of seventy-three. The Jones family had held the licence at the Britannia at Wednesbury, Staffs before the First World War, then moved to the Angel, Castle Street, Dudley, then their daughter Doris married Frederick Pardoe when he was twenty-five and she a slip of a girl of nineteen. Doris's parents moved to The Bush in Dudley for only a few months and again moved to the Old Station Hotel, also in Dudley, leaving Fred and Doris Pardoe as the landlords. Fred and Doris held the licence at the British Oak, Sweet Turf, for one year and moved to the Old Swan in 1931. The British Oak was one of the many home-brew pubs in the area, having been built in 1861. The last brewer was Edward Prince in 1930, the house being sold to Hanson's Brewery of Dudley in 1932. The couple's time at the British Oak was their introduction to the brewing world and stood them in good stead for the future.

Brewing at this time was carried out by Ben Cole and briefly for the Pardoes by Henry Brown. Fred was satisfied that he could do the job and continued up to the time of his death in 1952 at the age of fifty-nine. Doris took over the reins immediately and so a legend was born. She finally passed away at the ripe old age of eighty-four in April 1984. Fred and Doris had a daughter, Brenda, and she followed in their footsteps. She ran the White Swan, also in Dudley, with her husband Sid Allport. George Cooksey was the brewer since the last war succeeding his father, Solomon Cooksey, in the same job. George recalled that in the past several pubs also sold his beers, with the family wine and spirit business taking a back seat.

A typical brewing day started at around 6 a.m., the liquor having been brought to boiling point the previous day. The mash-tun held 15 barrels with mashing taking about 1½ hours before the first of two run-offs were set into the copper. The gas-heated copper was then on

The Old Swan, better known as Ma Pardoes, a typical West Midlands home-brew pub.

for 1¼ hours boiling before being drained off through the hop-back and paraflow, and then finally into one of two 14-barrel fermenting vessels. The hop-back was destroyed in a fire but was renovated, utilizing the original segmental filter plates. The fermenting vessels are a legacy of the past as they are entirely made of unlined timber, no doubt quite a problem when it came to cleaning. A mobile heating coil was used to provide a controlled temperature, so that racking off into casks was carried out after maturation of six days duration. The total capacity of the brewhouse was 28 barrels per week, but had been producing only 10 barrels towards the end in the early 1990s. The Old Swan was moving into a difficult trading time and so Hoskin's Brewery of Leicester came to the rescue. George Cooksey the brewer left and this job was taken over by Nigel Burdett, Hoskin's brewer, in October 1988, who also continued to brew at the Beaumanor Brewery, Leicester. The previous Old Swan Bitter had been brewed at a low OG of 1032, and on Nigel taking over, it was increased to 1034. Prior to Hoskin's acquiring the business, a Public Limited Company was formed in 1985, with the name changing on 20 March to Netherton Ales PLC. Accounts for 1986 showed that the turnover was £133,588 with an operating loss of £24,737, sad times indeed. The fixed assets were valued at £125,062. From the period of October 1988 to December 1990, the Old Swan faced much buffeting with threats of legal battles and share wrangles. The Netherton Ales company had CAMRA investing £10,500 from their headquarters, and another £50,000 came from regional branches, all of this to keep a legend alive. All was still not well and the concern was sold to the Wiltshire Brewery, Tisbury, Wilts. Today, this renowned pub continues to retail beer in its terrace house location, its famous signed frontage proclaiming in bold letters 'Pure Home-Brewed Ales'. The small Victorian brewhouse behind the kitchen stands silent, awaiting the day when some good knight charges in and relights the copper – may this not be too long.

The Three Tuns brewhouse is the classic Victorian tower brewery serving a home-brew public house of the same name. Everything about the brewhouse, its equipment and the public house, bear testimony to home-brewing as it used to be. The public house, with its three bars decorated in an unassuming but congenial manner, was built in 1897, as a terracotta plaque of Queen Victoria proclaims high up on a chimney-breast facing into the brewery yard. On two other sides of this small yard is the old stable block, now used as a cellar on the ground floor with a snooker room and function room upstairs.

Projecting partly into the yard by its entrance is the three-storey brewhouse, with a small projecting lucarne for hoisting malt to the loft on the top floor; on the side facing into the yard a shoot projects on the front corner for spent grains discharge. At the ridge of the Welsh slated roof there is a small vented cowl and to the left of the red-brick tower is a black and white timber, two-storey building. This is the original brewhouse first licensed in 1642, now the store for malt and hops, its heavy timber roof rafters and tie beams and floor proof of its ancient past. From the yard an archway leads through to another courtyard with the stable and cartshed block all built of red bricks in about 1880. Above the cartshed with its double doors is a small pedimented roof dormer with projecting timber-beam and tackle to lift hay bales into the first floor loft. Now no horses tread the steep streets of Bishop's Castle with beer from the Three Tuns to be delivered to local private houses. In the 1920s the Three Tuns had competition from three other home-brew public houses, two in Church Street. They were probably the King's Head and the Boar's Head Inn; the other was The Hit-or-Miss, in Union Street, owned by Richard James.

Shropshire's renowned Three Tuns, Bishop's Castle, its seventeenth-century brewhouse to the left beside the Victorian tower brewhouse.

The brewhouse is entered from the front beneath three louvred windows on the first floor with 'Three Tuns Brewery' written above them in Victorian ornate lettering. One of the renowned previous owners was John Roberts who, with his son, owned the business until 1976 when they sold it to Peter Milner. He in turn sold it in June 1981 to James Wood, the father of the present proprietor and brewer, Dominic Wood. Dominic Wood has run the business on his own since 1990 when his two brothers, Jack and Robert, handed over to him after ten years in order that they could follow separate interests. When John Roberts owned the brewery he also had his own malthouse in Welsh Street, but malt is now obtained from the Beeston Maltings, Nottingham, with hops being purchased in the traditional 6-feet long pockets from Charles Faram of Malvern. These hops are locally grown in Worcestershire and Herefordshire. The town supply of water is utilized but Dominic treats it with crystals to Burtonize it; yeast is obtained from the Highgate Brewery, Walsall.

On entering the ground floor, immediately to the left is the doorway connecting to the original Tudor brewhouse. Here is situated the vertical boiler installed by Mr Milner which was coal fired, consuming £1,300 worth of the best steam coal in a year, until it was converted to oil burning in 1992. Dominic Wood and his brewer Jeremy Blundell brew every Wednesday, devoting between 12 to 18 hours to produce 12 barrels per week, with Tuesdays set aside for preparation, such as cask-cleaning. Also on the ground floor are the three fermenting vessels: one copper one is an original from the 1880s, another of plastic was installed in 1976 replacing a worn-out copper pattern, the third is a strange galvanized one with a tubular steel frame installed in 1986 and used only for the strongest beer.

Ascending wooden stairs to the first floor, with its three sets of wooden louvred windows to the front and one to the side, one notices the very simple but effective method of opening and closing the louvres by means of a central thick dowel with smaller pointed ones protruding at right angles, one under each louvre. An up or down movement of the central dowel opens or closes the vents. On this floor is an almost unique piece of this once traditional plant – the open copper cooling tray. This extends the full width of the building, about 17 feet long by 6 feet wide and 12 inches deep, the window louvres being to assist in the cooling process, as is the copper coil which can be dropped in and cold water passed through. To the rear corner is situated the copper of 7-barrel capacity, made entirely of cast iron. Ascending once again by wooden stairs to the second floor, here is situated the mash-tun with its removable fibreglass cover. Beside this and above the copper is the hot liquor tank and the base of the grist case with discharge into the mash-tun. On the top floor there is the door opening and platform, with lifting tackle and two opening flaps on the balcony for hoisting the malt sacks. These are discharged into the top of the grist case situated above the mash-tun. In the back corner is the top of the hot liquor tank. A hand-operated ratchet winch controls the steel hawser to the lucarne hoist. Before racking into the wooden casks on the ground floor, the beer passes via a copper paraflow cooler. There are some 100 oak wood coopered casks from pin size to hogshead, supplemented by a few metal casks. The current range of beers includes a strong beer called Jim Woods, named after Dominic's father, a bitter, the most popular in the range and a light mild; the total weekly production is about 12 barrels. In the time of John Roberts, when the beers were supplied to other local pubs and private houses, production was as much as 640 gallons a week. John Roberts's

Three Tuns copper cooling tray and associated wood louvred shutters.

range included X, XX, XXX and XXXX in draught. Bottled beers have been Charter Ale in 1973, Salutation, a special brew for Charles and Diana's wedding, Jubilation, produced in 1977 to commemorate the silver jubilee of Queen Elizabeth II, and A Very Special Brew for the 21st Anniversary of the Committee of Salop Steam Engine Society. Another special brew of only 6 barrels was Old Scrooge, an oatmeal stout. John Roberts also had his own blend of Scotch whisky which he bottled, known as Special Scotch – all of these labels recording the past history of this superb home-brew establishment are on display in the bar of the Three Tuns public house. More recently Dominic Wood has introduced a 'Home-Brew Bitter, 5 Gallon Dry Kit', packaged in a red, black and white carton replica of the tower brewery. The pack contains malt extract of fine Yorkshire pale ale malt, crushed crystal malt, Fuggles hops, dried brewing yeast and finings. All that is required is to add sugar and water; a case of a home-brew house producing the necessary ingredients for domestic home-brewing.

The earliest directory record of the Three Tuns is in 1885 for Richard Hughes, so it is probable that it was he who was responsible for the building of the tower brewhouse, outbuildings and the Three Tuns public house. This is the finest surviving 'publican brewer's' tower brewhouse.

There were two areas in which home-brewing survived the longest, the Black Country and the town of Derby. However, there were at least two other enclaves where small-time brewing held out for some time. Local directories for Preston indicate that, in 1935, there were thirty-five home-brew pubs still operating. In Leeds several of the very small 'back-street' breweries were still in existence until quite recently. In these four areas there are two common factors shared between two towns which have influenced the retention of home-brewing. Firstly, the very close-knit community and secondly, the high level of the densely populated areas who were engaged in a demanding type of manual work.

Three small breweries in the Armley district of Leeds appear to have been built at about the same time, and either designed or built by the same builder. They are the Barleycorn Hotel, 114 Town Street, The White Horse, 87 Town Street, and the Union Cross Brewery, 17 Stocks Hill, Armley. Each was distinguished by the white bricks set into the top of their chimney-stacks on all four sides. The Barleycorn had a 'T', the White Horse an 'H' and the Union Cross a '+'. The brewhouse at the Barleycorn was largely demolished in the mid-1980s and the area is now the beer garden. The White Horse brewhouse was demolished in 1993, however, 'Home-Brewed Ales' may still be discerned in one of the windows. A photograph indicates that the Albion Brewery received a gold medal and also that the house previously advertised, 'Spencer's Fine Sparkling Ales brewed on the premises'. The brewer in 1926 was Ralph Rowak, and it is likely that he was the last to be brewing. Nothing remains of the Union Cross Brewery, the chimney-stack being demolished in March 1992. Stephen Wood was recorded as the last brewer here in 1902.

One of the first bus companies in the Leeds area was formed by Sam Ledgard, who built up a fleet of 100 buses which served Bradford, Otley, Ilkley, Pudsey, Horsforth and of course Leeds. The bus company had the reputation 'for getting thru'. Sam's father owned the Nelson Inn in Armley Road, Armley, and he recalled that they found themselves alone at Christmas 1896. Sam cooked the dinner of bacon and potatoes and his father told him that if he did not get married and take over the business, the place would be sold and he would have to fend for himself. Sam did marry and take over, and he also developed the business by supplying race meetings and agricultural shows. This extension of his victualling brought him into the transport business, even to purchasing several charabancs in 1913. Sam Ledgard died in April 1952 leaving an estate valued at £129,491 most of which went to his son Tom and daughter Ruth, but also to some of his workers. Brewing ceased at this time.

Of the once very numerous home-brew pubs that were in Leeds, the Tetley Brewery-owned Cardigan Arms in Kirkstall Road remains a classic, now listed Grade II. The public house is in a most ornate Victorian style, with yellow stone ornamentations, flying gables and finials. In contrast, immediately to the rear, is the three-storey red-brick tower brewhouse and outbuildings. Plans indicate that 'rebuilding of the pub, including the brewhouse and stables', was to be carried out in 1894 for Benjamin Greaves. A William Mitchell Charlton was recorded at an unknown date as a brewer at the Cardigan Arms. It is interesting to note the decline of Leeds home-brew pubs; from the turn of the century up to 1920 there were 13 closures, during the 1920s there were 105, in the 1930s only 10 and in the early 1940s, only 8. By comparison Preston only had one closure in the decade up to the 1920s, 45 up to 1930, 42 up to 1940, and 54 during the 1940s and 1950s.

In the case of the two regions previously referred to, the Black Country and the town of Derby, the major factor for the survival of several houses into the 1970s was the heavy manual work carried out in the area, making for great thirsts. In the Black Country, coal and iron mining and associated furnace industries, such as chain-making, nails, locks, etc., made for strenuous work from an early date. Derby became prominent as early as 1844, when the North Midland, Midland Counties and Birmingham and Derby Junction Railway Company amalgamated to form the Midland Railway Company with their headquarters in Derby. Here were located the railway locomotive and wagon- and carriage-building workshops and the large offices to run a major railway company. In 1923 a further amalgamation of railway companies formed the London Midland and Scottish Railway Company which was the largest railway company in the country. Derby had a population of about 100,000, of whom a large percentage worked on the railway. In Derby there were several common brewers but strangely, even after having acquired several home-brew pubs, brewing continued in them for a number of years. One such was the Crystal Palace in Rosehill Street, where Fred Shreeve sold out to Offilers in 1924 but, despite being subsequently taken over by Charrington, brewing was still taking place in 1966. In 1960, Derby still had twelve home-brew houses.

Offilers Brewery Ltd in Ambrose Street, Derby, was by far the largest purchaser of Derby home-brew pubs, acquiring at least seventeen, and allowing several to continue brewing, including the Barleycorn in Canal Street. The Seven Stars in King Street was one of the

Tower brewhouse behind the Nelson Inn, Armley, Leeds.

oldest to brew, tracing its foundation back to 1680 and only finally succumbing to purchase by the major brewery company of Scottish & Newcastle in 1962. William Beckett brewed at his White Bear in Derwent Row for over forty years and was the doyen of Derby's home-brewers, finally giving up in 1962. A year later Annie Winter retired at the Copeland Arms, Copeland Street, while well into her eighties. The Exeter Arms was the last home-brew pub in Derby. Highly densely populated towns such as Dudley and Derby, both with a tradition of small family-run pubs, managed to survive, the cult of the local 'Mild' and a strong community feeling holding neighbours together. Working for one firm for most of one's life bred loyalties now often ignored, but each local pub had its regulars who would swear that their home-brew was the best! So, until redevelopment came in these areas, home-brewing continued. The many reasons why there was a decline in home-brewing shall be looked at in detail later.

Not only does Ye Olde Trip to Jerusalem in Nottingham claim to be the oldest public house but it also claims to be the oldest 'home-brewed inn'. An old painting in the Rock Lounge shows the inn, then called the 'Trip to Jerusalem Inn', in 1189 with, beneath this sign, 'The Oldest Home Brewed Inn in England'. A further sign on a lean-to outbuilding reads, 'Free House for Wines, Spirits and All Ales Brewed on the Premises'. Situated at the base of the sandstone rock on which Nottingham Castle was erected in 1068 by William Peverill for William the Conqueror, the brewhouse was evidently built into the caves soon after the construction of the castle as the beer was soon required for the king and his estate. The caves, with their regular, mild temperature, were ideal locations for all-year-round brewing. There are two vertical shafts through the rock from the caves at the base which emerge outside the castle walls, thereby not hindering the castle's security. One emerges in what is now known as Brewhouse Yard Museum, the other in the top lounge of the inn. It is believed that these were used as a malthouse in the past, the controlled and even temperature ideal for growing the barley, and one of the shafts was used as the malt kiln flue. The name of the inn is evidently based on the connection with the Knights Templar and hospitaller and the crusade. Part of the land in close proximity to the castle had been awarded for favours by the king to the priory of Lenton in about 1213, at which time they passed between the priory, the Knights Templar and the Knights of Saint John of Jerusalem. Many of the early records of this time have not lasted, and it is in the city records of 19 January 1618 that first documentary evidence states: 'Brewhouse – the matter touching the purchase of the brewe-house here spoken by Maister Recorder is required to deal in ytt this tearme thatt answere may againe sent upp either to conclude ytt or to breat ytt.' This statement suggests that the brewhouse was for sale to the council, but they evidently declined the offer, it being eventually sold in 1621. King James I granted under his seal the separation of the brewhouse from the castle which was a royal residence. The present appearance of the inn is as a result of it being purchased by William Stanford, who was also responsible for other fine buildings in the period of 1751. Earlier ownership was in the hands of Edward Ferres and Francis Phillips, but there is no clear evidence that it was a public house at that time. The earliest reference as an inn was as The Pilgrim, having been named after a group of religious people who called themselves by this name and who resided in the brewhouse. The first recording of its present name appears in local directories of 1799. As befits an historic house, it had at least one character and this was George Henry Ward, known as 'Yorkey', the licensee in 1894 who had his nickname painted on the house wall. Three years earlier he had been licensee at the Meadow Inn on Arkwright Street, and then for one year at the Fox and Owl, Parliament Street; he died in 1914.

Today this renowned inn is a Hardy & Hanson's house, the local independent brewer, who has retained many of the characteristic aspects of the pub, including the natural sandstone bar, complete with one of England's oldest games. This is 'Ringing' or 'Baiting the Bull' which consists of a bull's horn on which one has to hook a bull's nose-ring, the ring being suspended on a cord. A rear bar is almost as it was in 1660, with a massive timber beam and spartan decor except for a collection of old photographs. Going upstairs one enters the Rock Lounge, this is the room where malting once took place with its 60-foot chimney-shaft. The inn's own cellars, although not available for viewing by the public, extend some 100 feet under the castle rock, and there is an old cock-fighting pit. Smaller caves to one side were evidently dungeons for the castle, now used for the storage of the local brewers' fine traditional ales. At the opposite end to the two dungeons is the site of the old brewhouse, underneath the Rock Lounge, where brewing for the inn only ceased some forty years ago. A necessary form of communication between the brewhouse in the depths of the rock and the inhabitants of the castle is an old speaking tube, the top end having been destroyed when the Duke of Newcastle's mansion was built above. A visit to this fascinating inn is highly recommended, not least for quaffing an ale or two in the most unique of English bars.

Cyril Wilkinson was the last brewer and owner of the Cricketers' Arms in Brown's Croft, Old Basford, in 1930 when he ceased brewing. The home-brew house was established in 1853, possibly by Cyril's father, and was a small pub

Ye Olde Trip to Jerusalem, Nottingham claims the be the oldest inn and brewery.

consisting of two ground-floor bay windows to the bars. To the right-hand flank wall signwriting indicated, 'An old home-brewed house, established 1853, matured in deep rock cellars'. Across a cartway on the right was the single-storeyed brick-built brewhouse with pantiled roof, the overall length about 18 feet long. Double doors on the front led into the brewhouse, which had its small copper on the right-hand side and to the rear.

In the 1920s Cyril Wilkinson had a small brochure produced, clearly with the intent of promoting his beers to the trade. 'In issuing this circular I wish to bring to your notice that my Original Brewing Plant can meet my own demands and also supply a limited quantity to the Trade.' He further went on to say that, 'All my Beer is Brewed in the old English way "More Malt – Less Chemicals" and therefore guarantee my Beer to be of absolutely the Very Best Quality, only Best Kentish Hops and English Malt used.' A claim which may have been challenged was his claim that his beer was 'the cheapest in the country'. Cyril was the sole proprietor and, judging by the size of the brewhouse, he was probably the only brewhouse worker, although he would have hired a labourer/general hand to do the cleaning jobs. He no doubt did the delivering and collecting orders and cash himself.

Cyril Wilkinson's son related many years ago that his father had two prices in his pub, depending on whether beer was filtered back into the barrel from the drip trays, or not. The price difference was about a penny per pint. Across the road in front of the Cricketers' Arms was a garden with rustic wood benches and tables. The reference and emphasis on the use of the 'deep rock cellars' enhanced the all important control of quality, as they would remain at a constant temperature of about 50° all year round. Other prominent home-brew pubs in Nottingham were The Gate Hangs Well, on Castlegate, where Nathan S. Woodward was still brewing in 1908. The Postern Gate which stood on the corner of Drury Hill also 'brewed ales on the premises' until 1911 when it was demolished. Both pubs advertised their wares in very large lettering and they both used the abbreviated spelling of 'BREW'D', a style apparently more common in the Midlands.

The father-to-son tradition is strong within the licensed trade, both at breweries and inns, and possibly nowhere was that stronger than at the Crown Inn and Brewery, near Walsall, north of Birmingham. The family connections are long and varied, and to look at the history it is as well to start with the last brewer and licensee, Mr Norman Bird, who was the fourth generation up to 1960. His two sons, John and Jim, are the fifth generation to have been born in the same bedroom in the Crown Inn. Norman's parents were Mr and Mrs James Bird who ran

A trade advertisement of the 1930s from the Cricketer's Arms, Nottingham.

the business for 40 years. Mrs Bird's grandparents were Mr and Mrs Samuel Birch who founded the family interest at the Crown. Their daughter became Mrs Josiah Brookes and with her husband she inherited the inn and brewery and she passed it on to her daughter, Mrs James Bird and her husband.

Mr Bird's parents took the Butts Inn, Walsall, in about 1885 and he himself was born there, with his mother carrying on a similar business of home-brewing and running a public house. The concern was at 46 Butts Street, Walsall, and was registered in 1920 to acquire the Butts Inn with brewery and two other public houses; it went into voluntary liquidation in October 1929. One of these two pubs would have been another Crown, at Long Acre, Walsall, which was run by Mr Bird's grandparents. At the time when Mrs Bird's parents ran the Crown, the business also included a large grocer's shop, and the business card of Mr J.J. Brookes indicated some of the other wares which he dealt with: 'dealer in hay, corn flour meal, pig feeds, blasting powder, compressed cartridge, hickory halves, tape oil, candle and general stores'. The inn and stores served numerous local coal and ironstone pits, and it was recalled that miners' wages were once paid by 'butty' colliers and foremen in the Crown clubroom. A warm coal fire had to be ablaze by six in the morning ready for the men coming off the night shifts, and if the landlord didn't open on time the workmen would soon make their presence known.

Mr James Bird was quite a local character, excelling first at Queen Mary's Grammar School, Walsall, where he was a proficient athlete. He was destined for the Civil Service and was at the college in Edinburgh when his father died, so he returned home to look after the brewery. He had several positions within the local licensed trade bodies and he and his wife both took an active part in their local church. Norman Bird took over the Crown Brewery and Inn just after the end of the Second World War. A fitting tribute was paid to James Bird on his eightieth birthday when the Walsall and District Licensed Victuallers' Association raised their glasses in a toast to him at the Butts Inn, Walsall, accompanied by his son Norman.

John Jukes, a nailmaker by trade, was living in a terraced house when, in 1832, he opened his small property as the Britannia Inn, Upper Gornal, Staffs. John was born in 1796 and had married Hannah who was three years older than himself; they had a son, Richard, who was born in 1816. John died in 1858, aged sixty-two, and so his widow and son William continued the business for a further six years. In 1864 Henry Perry, a butcher, took over the licence, being recorded in the census of 1871 as being aged twenty-nine with a wife, Rebecca, of the same age and their two children James aged two and Nellie, eight months. Two years later Rose was born and

A classic diminutive West Midlands home-brew house at the Britannia Inn.

another son, Louis Peacock, in 1875. Evidently this young couple decided to continue the butchering trade and moved the beershop from the front rooms to the rear and had the butcher's shop in the front. The rear beershop was probably found to be easier to run with the small brewhouse nearby in the backyard. Henry Perry had bought the Britannia Inn on 19 June 1874 from Joseph Round Cartwright and his son Louis bought an additional acre of land to the rear in 1910. After Louis's death the property passed to his widow Sarah and their daughter, who inherited it in 1942, shortly after she had married Frederick Walter Williams. Frederick, better known as Wally, came from Sedgley and became the brewer, producing the typical Black Country dark and heavy mild – he is best remembered, however, for his Gornal Old Ale, nicknamed by locals as 'Cow and Gate'. At this time, the mild ales of the area were strong, dark and sweet, with an average strength of 1060 OG Regrettably brewing ceased as recently as 1959. Over the years the original small 'local' had developed into the neighbouring house in the terrace but the early visions of John Jukes for his convivial beerhouse remains much as he would have wished. Sallie Williams died in 1991, thus ending 127 years of a continuous family involvement in this Black Country region. John Burrows was the licensee for only a year, passing the ownership to Philip Bellfield, the present licensee, on 2 November 1992.

The Puzzle Hall Inn and Brewery, Sowerby Bridge, Yorkshire, lives up to its enigmatic name, as the true reason for such an unusual name is now lost in folklore. There are three schools of thought as to the origin of this name: one says that there was a 'puzzle' or maze garden belonging to the pub; another theory suggests that it once had a monkey puzzle tree and the third suggestion, and the most likely, is that the name refers to the assortment of buildings, roof elevations and chimney-stacks that make up the inn. The pub is squeezed in between a canal and the River Calder, with only a narrow road and the tow-path for access. There is precious little room for a maze garden or for a monkey puzzle tree!

The pub clearly was never a hall as it started life as a two-roomed cottage in about 1650. At that time it stood on a minor packhorse trail which linked Sowerby Bridge with the Burnley Road. The pub is situated down the narrow Hollins Mill Lane, and the yard and lane are still paved with cobblestones. The previous single-horse stable which backed onto the river has been demolished and there is now a small drinks patio in its place. The original buildings are built of the local honey-coloured stone which with age takes on a blackened discolouration; these areas are roofed with local stone slabs. In the single-storey building facing the canal and the roadside,

The Puzzle Hall ex-home-brew pub and its squat tower brewery behind.

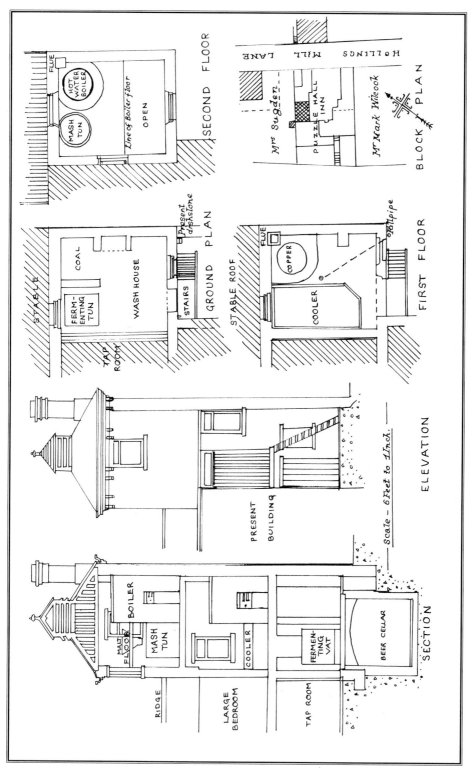

Plan and elevations of the Puzzle Hall development of 1905.

with its several chimney-stacks, was originally the small brewhouse, now the kitchen. Walker's *Halifax Directory* of 1845 makes reference to John Arthington, a brass founder, at Puzzle Hall, also Thomas Willey, a whiting manufacturer and coal merchant, of Lower Puzzle Hall. It is therefore evident that by this date the area had taken on the name of the pub and that the area was becoming heavily industrialized in the valley. It is probable that brewing had been taking place at the Puzzle Hall Inn since the early 1700s.

A Mr Schofield Hainsworth was the landlord of the Puzzle Hall Inn until his death at the age of forty on 31 January 1894. His parents, John and Ann Hainsworth, had previously brewed and run the inn, possibly with the assistance of a James Bowes Robson. He died on 2 November 1867 at the early age of twenty-six, and is commemorated on a headstone with the Hainsworth family at Sowerby Bridge cemetery. There is no obvious link with the family; he may have become a family friend or brewing servant. The grave was purchased by Ann Hainsworth who outlived her husband John by twenty-two years. Lydia Heavysedge Hainsworth was born in 1857, but it is not clear as to whether she was the daughter of John and Ann and therefore sister of Schofield Hainsworth or she could have been Schofield's wife. Either way, she married John Platt who suffered a tragic accident. The *Evening Courier* of 24 October 1912 reported that, while John Platt was repairing the roof of one of the outbuildings, his ladder slipped and he rolled down the roof, first alighting on a porch and then slipping off, with his head hitting against the pavement kerb, fracturing his skull. He was rendered immediate medical attention but died within ten minutes. Evidently he had been at the Puzzle Hall Inn for about fifteen years and had come into possession through marriage to Lydia. Mr Platt had only been married a few years when the Boer War broke out and he at once enlisted; after the war he returned to the inn. He left his widow Lydia but no children. He was aged thirty-eight.

It would seem that Lydia was the driving force behind the business as another curious aspect of the inn is highlighted by a set of drawings for a new tower brewhouse, addressed to 'Mrs Lydia H. Platt'. These were produced by T. Lister Patchett, architect and surveyor, Halifax, Yorkshire, in February 1905. The three-storey tower brewery was built of yellow bricks relieved with local stone sills, lintels and oversailing capping to the short chimney-stack. The roof is slate with hipped ridges which terminate with a small louvred vent, capped with a pagoda lead roof and ball finial. There is an underground cellar built into the hillside, with the ground-floor plan consisting of the washhouse, coal storage area and beside that a single fermentation vat, measuring 4 feet square. On the first floor there was a cooler measuring 10 feet long by 5 feet wide with one corner splayed. Above the ground floor coal storage area was the copper of 3 feet 6 inches in diameter. Access to this floor was made via an external open-tread staircase opening onto double doors. The second floor was partly open with the hot-water boiler above the copper, both using the one single flue in the corner to the chimney-stack. Beside the boiler was the mash-tun, also of about 3 feet 6 inches in diameter. Above the mash-tun was the malt grist case suspended on a small mezzanine floor, giving access to allow the discharge of sacks of malt into the hopper grist case. The overall height of the tower to the eaves was 30 feet and in the plan almost a square, measuring 13 feet 6 inches by 12 feet.

Despite his early demise, John Platt made the Puzzle Hall Inn well renowned locally for home-brewed stout. The label appropriately depicted a view of the new brewhouse, as does the present-day swing sign. Lydia H. Platt, then a widow, sold the business in 1919 to Mr Arthur Culpan and he in turn sold it for £1,500 to a Mr John Hesselden. He sold it in 1936 to Ward's Sheaf Brewery, Sheffield. It is not clear as to why Ward's purchased it, being some 40 miles from Sheffield and 10 from their nearest pub. Evidently the beer came by rail and on being informed that it had arrived, some of the regulars were dispatched to collect it in a hand cart.

An uneven and patterned cobblestone yard surrounded by staddle stones and ancient stone troughs filled with flowers, outbuildings also showing their age, all testify that the Fleece, at Bretforton, Evesham, Worcestershire, was once a medieval yeoman's farmstead. The timber-framed building with white painted brick noggings under a graduated local stone tiled roof, sits in one corner of the village green known as The Cross, opposite the squat mellow stone parish church. Towards the end of the fifteenth century the living quarters at one end were rebuilt to make what was then the popular open hall and solar. The farm animals occupied the thatched end farthest from the village green and during the seventeenth century a kitchen extension was built, forming a 'T' shaped ground plan. Today, close by this extension, now grows a venerable walnut tree, protruding through the rough cobblestone yard. The building is situated end on to the main village, with a narrow passageway facing the front of the building and a row of quaint domestic houses. Entering the pub via a porch from the rear yard, one is immediately faced by the bar servery, where today a good range of small local brewers' beers are available. To the left one enters the 'T' section extension, originally built as a kitchen, but used from the mid-nineteenth century as a brewhouse for both beer and cider, also probably for cheese-making, the cheese molds and press still in situ. Off this room is a step down into a spartan area known as the dugout. Turning right on entering the pub one enters a magnificent room dominated by a dark oak dresser full of a pewter plate collection. This is said to have been given by Oliver Cromwell to a previous yeoman owner in exchange for gold and silver plate taken to pay the parliamentary army. The eight large chargers were made in Worcester and have been dated from the Cromwellian period, the remainder were mostly made at Bewdley. The three separate bar and servery areas are all heavily timbered with beams and full of antique furniture and bric-a-brac. In the area that was the brewhouse is to be found a timber malt shovel and copper mulling funnel near the fireplace, and hanging from the heavy central ceiling beam are five small coopered 'harvest ale' casks. These were used by farmworkers to collect their ale or cider in and to take back with them to the fields. On the top shelf of a wall dresser are Victorian china loving cups and quart tankards.

The Byrd family had occupied the farmhouse for some 400 years but, in 1848, Henry Byrd sold the farmland and purchased an excise licence for two guineas and turned his home into a beerhouse. The Ale or Beer Act, introduced on 10 October 1830 by the Duke of Wellington to discourage the excessive gin drinking by encouraging people to sell beer, resulted in some 25,000 licences throughout the country in just a few months. Henry Byrd evidently realized that there was a better and easier living to be made from brewing and selling beer and cider. Brewing continued well into this century, with the great-grand-daughter of Henry Byrd, Lola Taplin, carrying on the fine family tradition for thirty years until she died at the age of eighty-three in 1977. It is recalled that she ruled her house with a rod of iron and any customer not complying with her standards was asked to leave. On her death, she willed this unique public house to the National Trust on the understanding that nothing was changed. All the artefacts and furniture are as she left them and it is run as an unspoilt country pub, just as she would have wished, a truly unique house fortunately preserved for all to enjoy.

A coal quay on the north bank of the River Severn served the small village of Ashleworth, as did several other quays along the length of the river during the nineteenth and early twentieth centuries. The village is noted for its fine fifteenth-century manor-house and ancient stone-built tithe barn beside the parish church and just behind the Boat Inn. Beside the coal wharf was situated the Wheatsheaf Inn which served cider only; this was demolished in the 1960s. Between the Wheatsheaf and the Boat Inn a passenger ferry operated to the south bank, and it was claimed that this had been in operation for several centuries, the original licence having been granted by King Charles II to a former licensee of the Boat Inn. The ferry ceased operating several years ago, Edward Jelf operating it in 1939.

The current licensee of the Boat Inn is Miss Irene Jelf who is assisted by Mrs Jacquie Nicholls, the present-day owners who are carrying on a long line of family ownership. Mrs Nicholls's aunt, Sybil Mary Jelf, was the licensee from 1966 until December 1991, when Irene Jelf took the licence. Mrs Nicholls's father held the licence before that, following her grandfather, Edward John Jelf, from 1903 to 1966. Prior to 1903 the licence was held by David Jelf, whose wife Sarah died in 1895. It was Sarah's father Thomas Jelf, born in 1791, who owned the inn. Before Thomas it was Walter Jelf who had two brothers, William and John. Thomas was married twice, his first wife was Rebecca, his second was Sarah. David and Sarah Jelf bought the Boat Inn in 1887, maintaining and perpetuating the long Jelf family tradition.

In front of the inn is a small detached part-stone, part-brick structure facing the river; this is the brewhouse. Until a few years ago it had two chimney-stacks, but the one which served the brewing copper was demolished a few years ago due to its deterioration. At this time the cast-iron copper was also removed and this now lies in the rear garden; it would appear to have a capacity of some 100 gallons. The oldest part of the brewhouse is the curved stone section which was probably built around a circular tun, and may well be several hundred years old, the brickwork being of Victorian construction. Brewing is believed to have ceased at the beginning of the First World War when the local farming population would have been much depleted with the men going to war.

The once busy wharf which received coal for the local community and loaded out hay for transhipment to Gloucester docks, would have generated many thirsty workmen. The dusty and arduous work of wheelbarrowing the coal up planks to the dock by the Severn trow boatmen would have also added to the trade of the Boat Inn. Home-brewing for all these customers kept the Jelfs in business for a long time and fortunately for us today this small delightfully unspoilt single-bar pub remains much as it must have been for a very long time – long may it be so.

The Boat Inn, Ashleworth Quay, with its small brewhouse near the River Severn.

Ashleworth was one of several places on the River Severn where fishermen placed their nets across to catch salmon, the first from Gloucester was Parting, the next after Ashleworth was Apperley. When motorized tugs were approaching, the crew gave a blast on the hooter to warn the fishermen to remove their nets. Canal traffic on the Severn dates back to an Act of 1532 in which the riverfolk were permitted a tow-path on both banks of 4 feet 6 inches width. Behind the Boat Inn were, until recently, two cottages, there is also a small brick building across the approach road, which was where the making of osier baskets took place.

David Jelf was described in *Kelly's Directories* from 1870 to 1897 as a farmer, with William Jelf working as a hay and coal dealer during the same period. The basket-making business was carried out in the small building opposite the pub by Samuel Jelf in 1870 to be followed in 1885 by Jeremiah Jelf, with Thomas Jelf's occupation given as a fisherman. The passenger ferry was in use up until at least 1963, but subsequently in recent years the banks have been considerably raised to restrict river flooding, consequently the old coal wharf and quay have also disappeared. Besides salmon fishing, the other delicacy caught on the Severn is elvers. Thomas Jelf also plied his fishing craft to collect these elvers when they were in season and running up the river. He used a home-made withy framework with a fine net fixed to a long pole. Sadly even this old craft has died with the older generation, just as home-brewing has at the Boat Inn.

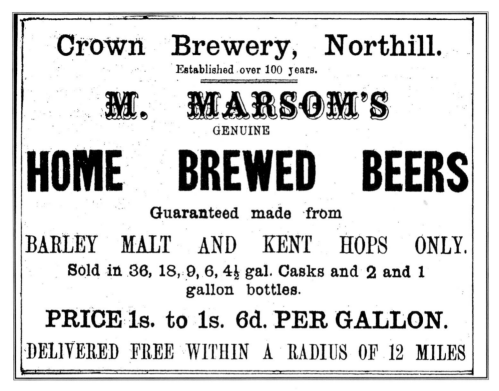

Trade advertisement placed in July 1901.

Born in 1833, Martha Marsom was destined to be the last brewer of home-brewed ales at the Crown Inn, Northill, Bedfordshire. The *Biggleswade Chronicle* reported her death on 2 May 1916; she was the daughter of a Mr Sabey of nearby Biggleswade and married Fred Marsom who was landlord at the Horse & Jockey, Biggleswade. They moved to Northill in about 1885 and succeeded Mr Fuller at the Crown; Mrs Fuller was née Marsom, so evidently family connections led to the Marsom family involvement. Their son John lived with his parents and after their death he carried on the licence. Prior to the Fullers, Charles Nicholas was recorded in *Pigot's Directory* for 1847. The Crown was originally part of the Harvey estate and was purchased by Martha Marsom on 1 September 1913 for £1,350. The conveyance was dated 16 June 1914 and on the same day she conveyed it to Newland & Nash Ltd of Bedford. At this date brewing ceased, but from at least the turn of the century mineral waters had been manufactured in a building opposite. Advertisements placed in the local newspaper in 1900 indicated that the Crown Brewery had been established over 100 years. The Crown is a timber-framed building at least 250 years old, which backs onto the parish church graveyard with the large vicarage behind. The brewhouse measures 12 feet by 15 feet and is raised up from the remainder of the bar areas by some 2 feet 6 inches and is evidently a later addition. The bare brick walls show indications of a timber mezzanine floor, an old cast-iron furnace hatch remains as do the small floor tiles. To the rear of the premises are two wells with the water table remaining constant at a depth of about 2 feet; clearly there was an abundant water supply.

Somewhat unusually for a home-brew public house, a range of three beers was produced in 1904, these were H.A. at 1s per gallon, P.A. at 1s 2d per gallon and S.P.A. at 1s 4d to 1s 6d per gallon. These were available in one and two gallon jars and cask sizes from pin to barrel (4½ to 36 gallons). Delivery was free within a 12-mile radius of Biggleswade, the effective distance that a single horse and two-wheeled trap could manage. A further unusual aspect of the Crown Brewery was the bottling of beer; this was in operation from about 1900 with several varieties of green bottles in use, some bearing the sandblasted name of 'M. Marsom, Brewer, Northill', others were embossed with the 'Crown Brewery' and an ornate crown. This bottling would have been done by hand and carried out in the mineral water factory which had all the necessary bottling machines and the beer bottles were all corked. Martha Marsom was also an agent for Phipps & Cos, Northampton, and Whitbread & Co. of London Ales and Stouts. This small village of Northill had one other pub besides the Crown, The Queen's Head, which has been closed now for some time. The mineral water business was not included in the sale when it was acquired by Newland & Nash Ltd in 1914, and continued for a number of years in the ownership of the Marsom family. The Crown public house and its attached brewhouse were acquired by Wells & Winch, brewers of Biggleswade, and subsequently became the property of Greene King, Bury St Edmunds, Suffolk, the large regional brewers.

The Fox Brewery, Dunmow Road, Bishop's Stortford, Herts, was probably a development of a much older malting business of which there were a great number in the town. A conveyance in 1877 referred to the property as 'commonly called Hall Croft', with a frontage of 51 feet and containing 25 perches. Part of the sale included two spring carts, one van and three sets of harness. The first mention of a brewery was in a sale poster dated 16 September 1890 which stated that the brewery was situated in Hockerill near the Union House, Dunmow Road, with a 51-foot frontage; this was sold by the local auctioneers Sworders at the George Hotel, Bishop's Stortford. The details included a beerhouse, large enclosed yard, four stall stables and sheds, and that the capacity of the brewery was two quarters. The strong copper (of 144 gallons capacity), mash-tun with staging, three coolers, two squares and a capital force pump with pipes indicates the small size of the business which was acquired by Joseph Flinn for £660. The inventory was valued at £100 and included the small stock of 6 barrel-sized casks, 36 kilderkins, and 30 each of firkins and pins, a stock of 180 gallons of 'Old Beer' was also included.

The letterhead used by Frank Flinn in 1905 indicated that Flinn & Sons were maltsters at Bishop's Stortford, Newmarket, Dullingham and Saffron Walden. Frank Flinn was in partnership with Thomas Coates Charnley, both of Bishop's Stortford and both maltsters, who agreed to sell the business on 8 April 1902 to William Radwin Stanton, a brewer of Cambridge, for the sum of £2,300. A 10 per cent deposit was given with the balance of £2,070 to be paid on completion on 24 April 1902. Evidently there was some considerable dispute in the sale finances as Frank Flinn wrote on 19 January 1905 to W.R. Stanton, offering £25 'for any claim you may think you have against me'. The brewery manager at that time was a Mr Holloway who assessed 'good or bad debts or doubtful'. Mr Flinn claimed £350 while Mr Stanton offered £250. Flinn eventually 'to close the matter agreed to accept £275', notifying Mr Wootten, his solicitor, accordingly. However, this was not the end of the dispute, as Stanton wrote to his solicitor on 1 March regarding Flinn's 'bad management' regarding a cheque. The matter was sent to arbitration. Flinn indicated that he required the 'bad debts' to be included in the sale so that he could clear his father's estate.

On 9 March 1905 Stanton's solicitor was endeavouring to serve a writ on Flinn's partner Mr Charnley, but stated that he believed that Mr Charnley had severed his connection with Flinn and had left his lodgings in Bishop's Stortford. The long drawn-out dispute was eventually resolved and finally the business was sold to Bailey Brothers, who engaged the brewing architects and engineers, Messrs William Bradford & Sons of London, to build a new brewery on the same site. Bailey Brothers were the patentees and manufacturers of hollow concrete blocks of which the new brewery was built in 1906 and it seems likely that they built their new brewery to the designs of one of the most renowned brewery architects, with the view to publicizing their new patent product. In 1915 the brewery was finally acquired by Benskin's Watford Brewery Co., who had also previously acquired the local Hawkes's Brewery in Bishop's Stortford in 1898. The brewery buildings were still standing in 1921 but nothing now remains of them, a modern garage occupying the site.

In 1778 Robert Perks, pig butcher of Monkton Combe, sold a large area of fields in the valley called 'Hopyard' to the Somerset Coal Canal Co. Ltd. Twenty years later Charles Perks the eldest son of Robert had an indenture made on his forthcoming marriage to Betty Howell. In this document the property, the Viaduct Inn & Brewery, is described as 'newly erected'. On 18 May 1840 an auction of the premises was made but there was no purchaser and two months later Joseph Willis acquired the property for £435 from the county court, acting as the liquidator on Robert Howell Perks being declared bankrupt in May 1840.

In the sale document the inn is referred to as lately called the Queen Adelaide, now the Viaduct Inn. The first mention of a brewhouse with stables, outbuildings and blacksmith's shop and the public house is on 13 January 1841 on a lease between Dr J. Carpenter and others to Mr J. Willis. The tenant at this time was William Ralph who was followed by Robert Haunam until at least 1871. Several mortgages were made for the purchase by Frank Oxley at this time with the requirement that a fire insurance premium of £500 per annum was paid. The purchase price paid by Frank Oxley to Joseph Deans Willis on 25 March 1871 was now £720. On 1 November 1892 Joseph Richard West sold the Viaduct Inn & Brewery, stables and outbuildings to the Bath Brewery Co. Ltd at 16, Milsom Street, Bath for £2,000. This included an acre of grounds on Motley Hill which had a large combined bowling saloon, dining and concert hall, situated as it still is behind the small tower brewery, overlooking the valley southward towards Warminster and the now filled-in Somerset Coal Canal which forms the boundary. In 1898 the Bath Brewery Co. acquired a further strip of land bordering the canal for £10 from William Jeffery, the approved liquidator of the proprietors of the Somerset Coal Canal, whose winding up was done on 2 August 1893.

In a letter from the Great Western Railway Co. to the Viaduct Inn, the tenant mentioned is Mr Bodman, and in the following two years strips of land on the boundary of the old canal were sold to the GWR for £300 and £36 for one acre. This was to enable a branch line to be built from the junction on the main line in the River Avon valley. On 1 October 1923 the Bath Brewery Co. sold the entire premises, including public house, stables, brewhouse, and the former blacksmith's shop situated on a triangular plot of land opposite the pub, to Bristol Brewery Georges Co. Ltd, for £150,391. At this time Herbert Phillip Hoffer was in occupation and would most likely have been the last brewer, if the Bath Brewery Co. had not already ceased brewing when they acquired the premises in 1898. A conveyance was made on 1 September 1962 between Bristol Brewery Georges Co. Ltd to Courage Barclay &

Simonds Ltd, subsequently Courage (Western) Ltd in 1973. Currently the Viaduct Inn and its adjacent redundant, but very fine brewhouse, complete with local stone-built chimney-stack, trades under the sign of Ushers of Trowbridge, Wiltshire.

It would appear from the available records that there were no other public houses supplied from the Viaduct Inn Brewery on a tied house basis, but due to its comparative size to the public house, it may well have supplied local country houses and farms and possibly several local free houses. The Viaduct Inn no doubt enjoyed quite a large trade in its heyday of the mid-nineteenth century, not only from the canal traffic but also the Black Dog turnpike road; hence the large stables and blacksmith's shop. While owners of horses were having them shod, they no doubt popped in to the Viaduct for a pint or two of home-brew.

Neat ashlar limestone blocks used in the construction of the Viaduct Inn, Monkton Combe.

An unusual later use of an old brewhouse is that at Staplecross Brewery on the high ground overlooking the River Rother valley and Bodiam Castle in East Sussex. Today it takes the form of a hop oast with a ridge cowl to the kiln. Due to its last use as a joiner's shop the ground floor has had a large glazed window inserted and several smaller ones put in on the top floor. The mellow red-brick building with its top floor front elevation clad in weatherboarding has two doors to the top floor, one situated beneath a gabled dormer hoist complete with pulley wheels. The roof, including the small circular ridge cowl, is clad in handmade peg tiles. The building would appear to be of late eighteenth-century construction. A sale catalogue of 7 March 1878 throws light on the extent of the business carried on which included, by this date, the hop drying oast and cooper's tools and casks included in the sale, 24 100-gallon cleansing or tunning casks used in brewing, 40 36-gallon casks, 120 kilderkins, 100 firkins, 50 6-gallon casks, 70 pins and 20 half-hogsheads. Only one 'young and useful black mare' and two four-wheel spring drays formed the necessary transport so it is possible that at this time brewing had made up a very secondary part of the business.

The extent of the previous brewing capacity is indicated by the inclusion of a Thompson's 4-quarter masher, two rousers and two mashing oars. Included in items in the stables and yard were the usual chaff-cutters, brushes, pails, forks and shovels but also a quantity of staves and cask-hooping. Specifically not mentioned in the brewing plant was a copper, hop-back or cooler, so brewing most probably had ceased some time previously. The hop oast kiln would almost certainly have been installed in the area of the brewhouse, thereby

A Sussex brewhouse was converted to a hop-oast in its latter days.

dispensing with some of the missing items of brewing plant from the sale in 1878. It is possible that the conversion to oast house took place in about 1848 and as the sale catalogue also included a hop press, hop pocket strainer, sacks, etc., evidently the use of the building for hop drying also ceased at this time. On the demise of William Beck as a brewer, he took new occupations as an overseer, surveyor and schoolmaster. For many years now the building has been empty, with no activity from the last joiner and is now falling into decline and decrepitude.

The name used by this house does not indicate its ancient past, but The Ostrich, at Colnbrook, near Windsor, is a corruption of 'hospice', its name at one time being the Ospridge. As a hospice to Abingdon Abbey, it has had many a dignatory staying under its roof. King John is said to have enjoyed its hospitality on his way to nearby Runnymede to place his seal on the Magna Carta. Many foreign ambassadors and their retinues have also taken refreshments on their way to Windsor Castle to see the monarch.

The Ostrich is, however, notorious for the bizarre activities of one of its landlords, a Mr Jarman. In order to enrich himself beyond his normal profits from the food and ale of the inn, he selected wealthy customers and placed them in a special bedroom above his brewhouse. The bed was fixed upon a hinged flap and when the 'guest' was asleep, the flap was released, thereby precipitating the unfortunate individual into the boiling copper of the brewhouse beneath. As with many murderers he became careless and when, on the third occasion that Jarman had tried to manoeuvre a wealthy clothier, Thomas Cole, to take this bedroom, despite his own trepidations, his wife insisted that they proceed with their villainous deed. Cole was duly killed and his badly burned body thrown into a nearby brook. The inn was soon searched and several of Cole's possessions were found, thus incriminating both Mr and Mrs Jarman who were duly hanged. The original inn was later destroyed by fire, but an Elizabethan-rebuilt inn showed its guests the very room above the brewhouse and this was enhanced by a working wooden model of the murderous system. The building has a jettied first floor flanked by a gable at each end, the front façade built of exposed timbers and painted plaster.

The Georgian façade of the Methuen Arms, Corsham, Wiltshire, with its pillared main entrance porch, belies the true age of this fine inn. The Georgian facelift was carried out in about 1805 to a Tudor building that had been the Red Lion Inn some 200 years previously. The original medieval house was known as Winter's Court and was the home of the Nott family from the fifteenth century until 1732, during which time it became an inn. The initials of the Nott family, 'N.N.N. 1650' are carved on the wall of the old wing facing the Laycock Road. Beneath these initials is 'C. 1749', which refer to alterations carried out by a relative of the Notts, Christine Webber. On her death the inn passed to the Methuen family of nearby Corsham Hall, and it was at this time, in about 1805, when the Red Lion changed its name to the Methuen Arms.

On entering the inn yard from the Laycock Road, one immediately notices the attractive stone-built barn with pierced holes for the ancient dovecote, which backs onto the Corsham Hall estate. On the left is the stone-built Tudor wing which was once the brewhouse and malting, later used as a skittle alley and now a conference room. Within this building there are two stone arched fireplaces and facing onto the Laycock Road are several very small windows. An entrance from the road to the public bar retains a unique feature once commonplace to all ancient inns. Painted on the stone columns in the doorway is a blue and white chequered design, denoting that this was an inn. The origins of this sign go back to Roman times, a similar design having been found in ruined Pompeii on a tavernae. Facing into the yard the old brewhouse has a flight of stone stairs which lead to an upstairs door, probably previously the germinating floor of the old malthouse. The mansard roof has been retiled in Victorian times as has the main building with Welsh slates, but the mellow stone walls and two external doors divulge the considerable age of this building.

Approaching Much Wenlock from the delightful Wenlock Edge, as one enters the town on the crossroads on one's right is the old coaching house, the Gaskell Arms Hotel. On the old stables to the right is a blue and white enamel sign which proclaims 'The Motor House (certified) Posting & Livery Stables', this sets the tone for the entry into the lovely high street of Much Wenlock. On the left is an old malthouse and next door the rambling Wheatland Fox. Close by is the fifteenth-century Ashfield Hall, previously the Blew Bridge Inn, in which Charles I stayed on his way to the Battle of Edgehill.

Just as the High Street is reached, on the right is a white painted terrace building. This has a small swing sign featuring a rather strange picture of George and the dragon. This is a pub

Much of the George & Dragon home-brew pub's history is to be seen carved on its bar fireplace beam.

worthy of the best accolades for it has excellent beer and a unique collection of bar decorations. The front bar walls are entirely covered with old trade advertisements, many from defunct breweries. Hanging from the low ceiling beams are water jugs and tankards, but all attention and interest is centred on the central fireplace. Over the fire is a shield depicting George and the dragon with old wooden harvest ale casks on either side, and above these is a large blackened heavy beam. Carved along its length is a catalogue of some of the pub's history over the last 160 years. In the centre there is a cross with G. Yates to the left of it and to the right, the date 1834. On the extreme left is carved AY 1850 and below this, JY 1892. To the right-hand end of the beam is carved GY 1857, below that FWY 1900 then on the extreme end, GY 1944 and below that, IAY 1948. These are the records of the Yates family and their association with the inn.

To the right of the pub a passageway leads from the High Street to a small yard and rear access lane. On the right-hand side, situated behind an adjacent shop, is a single-storeyed stone structure – this is the old brewhouse. All that betrays its past function as the Yates family brewery is the now deteriorating corrugated iron ridge roof cowl and adjacent brick chimney-stack. In this brewhouse the successive Yateses brewed their ale from at least 1834 until the 1950s, when the George & Dragon was the last home-brew pub in the town. Mr F.W. Yates, known as 'Gaffer', who evidently took over in 1900 had Charlie Jones as his brewer and barman to help in his old age. He also had an assistant on brewing days who also helped in the brewing of cider and perry which continued after beer-brewing ceased.

The Excise man pays a visit to the George & Dragon, Much Wenlock, assessing the beer strength, watched by brewer Charlie Jones.

According to the *Kelly's Directory* of 1885, a George Yates was the licensee of the George in Hospital Street. This would appear to tie in with the GY 1857 inscription carved on the fireplace beam. Hearsay has it that George Yates was responsible for several plaster pargetting relief designs to the rear bar walls, also the unusual design repeated on the external swing sign, and so it would appear that he also changed the name of the pub to the George & Dragon. His artistic talents have been carefully retained, a reminder of days gone by when the locals supped his home-brewed ale.

From these potted histories of a few home-brew establishments from around the country, the reasons why all but the few gradually ceased to brew can now be examined. Probably the most damaging factor to the existence of all home-brew pubs was the depredations of the common brewers who, from their early but slow establishment in the sixteenth century, made inroads into the trade – this was particularly the case in towns. Common brewers, because of their size, were producing 50 and 60 barrels or more, compared to the publican brewers' level of only up to 5 barrels a week. Their bigger size gave the common brewer many technical advantages which allowed him to produce a more consistent quality of beer, something that nearly all home-brewers were unable to do. The common brewer was also able to experiment with new brewing recipes and produce a range of beers all very much to the customers' liking. In London in the latter part of the sixteenth century there were twenty-six common brewers, although the vast bulk of beer was brewed by the retailers and 100 years later, by about 1690, the numbers of common brewers had increased to nearly 200. The large scale of the common brewers, particularly in London, led to the introduction of a strong and dark beer that became known as Porter in 1720. Its popularity lasted for about 100 years and changed the working man's style of drinking. The beer was originally called 'Entire' as it was a combination of several beers, but to the larger brewery companies, the large-scale brewing of this type of beer made it very profitable, something that no home-brewer could emulate. As an eloquent example of the scale to which the large London brewers went, several, such as Whitbread's, had vast storage vats with the enormous quantity of 20,000 barrels. In 1814 one of these gigantic vats burst its many iron hoops at the Horseshoe Brewery of Meux's in Tottenham Court Road, killing eight people and causing much damage to nearby property.

The strength of these growing brewery companies was based on their acquisition of public houses, thereby giving them a guaranteed outlet for their products. This pattern of increasing the tied estate of breweries has continued right up to the end of the 1980s. Another major factor which assisted the common brewer was his ability to set up local depots from which he could supply his growing tied estate of pubs. With the growth of the canal system, particularly in the Midlands and the north, the transport of beer became easier in the early eighteenth century. Towns and villages along the tow-paths were able to be supplied at short notice and the navvies needed vast quantities of ale when building the canals, just as the railway navvies did 100 years later. At most points along the canals, where horses had to be changed or the barges went through locks, one could find a pub. These canals allowed beers to be shipped from towns such as Burton-on-Trent, Newark, Sheffield, Nottingham, Derby and many others. With the coming of the railways in about 1840 the speed and distribution became complete. No home-brewer could compete in this new mechanical age. In more recent times other factors have come into play to dog the home-brewer, and some potted histories of pubs which illustrate a number of these points shall also be considered.

Established in 1801 by Samuel Bradford, the Moulton Chapel Brewery situated behind the Wheatsheaf pub, near Spalding, Lincs, finally ceased brewing in the first week of August 1927. During all this time it had been in the hands of the same family with Samuel passing it on to his son George Henry Bradford in 1892. George continued until June of 1920 at which time his son Alfred Bradford took over until its closure in 1927. Mr A. Bradford stated to *The Lincolnshire and Boston Press* on 16 August 1927, 'the last brew was in progress a week last Monday, when the mash tub gave up and operations had to cease. I always said I should never leave off in my time, if others did after me, but it is too expensive to bring the brewery up-to-date, and the barrel trade having dwindled away for the bottling trade. I have to close it, much as I regret it. . . . In harvest time,' Mr Bradford said, 'we brewed as many as four times a week, and in normal times once or twice. We supplied three public houses, The White Lion at Spalding, The Mermaid at Holbeach Fen, and our own house the Wheatsheaf at Moulton Chapel.' He further stated that 'the war' (First World War) took a large amount of trade away from them. Before the war, he said, 'beer was only 2d per pint, and we could not brew it fast enough to supply the people. With large outputs it paid. Now and since the war price of beer has been increased to 5d and 6d per pint and the people can't afford it. During the war we were limited and could only brew in small quantities.'

Alfred Bradford died in 1971, the beer since home-brewing ceased having been supplied by Soames & Co. of nearby Spalding, when they were taken over by Steward and Patterson of Norwich. A sad misfortune took place in the brewhouse when one of Alfred's two sons was tragically drowned in the mash-tub when only a little boy. The old brewhouse was in what is now referred to as the top bar. Malt and hops were stored in the first floor of an outbuilding, now used as the free house's cellar and bottle store.

The *Stanford Mercury* newspaper of 31 December 1971 reported that Mr Harold Pawlett and his wife were soon to retire, and that their Cross Keys Inn, at Oakham in Rutland, was to be demolished to make way for the Oakham Bridge relief road scheme. The Cross Keys was believed to be 300 years old and was owned by G. Ruddle & Co. Ltd, the Oakham brewery; the Pawletts were the company's oldest tenants. Mr Pawlett had formerly worked for the Oakham Gas & Electric Co. for twenty-seven years. He courted the niece of former licensee, Mr Tom King, and married her just before the war. Mrs Pawlett was living with her aunt and uncle when they moved to the Cross Keys from the Windmill, Redmile, in 1932. Her aunt died ten years later and her uncle continued until his death in 1949 when Mr Pawlett took over. The Cross Keys was one of the last public houses in Oakham to brew its own beer and some evidence of the brewhouse remains at the rear.

The stringent postwar restrictions on brewing due to continued shortage of raw materials prompted many a response from brewers to the quantities allowed to be brewed. These levels of production were sent out by the Brewers' Society under the auspices of the government scheme, whereby production in 1945, 1946 and 1947 would be based on pre-war figures. Consequently many requests were received by the Brewers' Society for increased allowances, one of these was from A.E. Jew & Son of the Fox Hunt Brewery, High Street, Old Hill, Staffs.

In his letter of 29 October 1946, Mr Jew indicated that the excise officer had told him that his brewings for October 1946 were to be based on those of the previous year. He pointed out that his copper had begun to leak badly and that it had to be replaced during October and November 1945. He had great difficulty in securing the services of a tradesman who was skilled enough to do this, and this was why the replacement took such a long time. He was unable to brew between 9 October and 6 November 1945 and as a consequence his production was 124 gross standard gallons. His production for the two following months were 408 and 508 gallons. He therefore requested an average figure of the two, namely 458 gross standard gallons. He went on to make his point that, during the first four months of 1946, he had had trouble with his plant, producing only 324, 285, 286 and 284 gallons, totalling 1,179 gallons. The comparative gallons for the same four months in the previous year was 1,474 gallons. It is not clear as to what the outcome of this request was, but as there were a number of similar well-founded claims, it is probable that the Brewers' Society acceded to Mr Jew's request.

Another home-brew pub also in difficulties in the postwar years was the Bowling Green Inn, on Ribbleton Avenue, Ribbleton, near Preston, Lancashire. Here Sam Valentine complained again to the Brewers' Society and requested 'a favourable reply', following the excise officer advising him that he was to reduce his production by 251 standard gallons for the period ended 30 April 1947. He commented that the reduction was 'hitting me badly, and I am unable to offer for sale on Mondays and Wednesdays'. To strengthen his claim he drew attention to a considerable potential increase in his demand for beer by 100 new houses being erected, most of these were prefabricated and many were already occupied. He had previously applied to the board of Customs & Excise for an increase which they had turned down, with their recommendation that he should apply to the Brewers' Society to have a share of their 'reserve pool for cases of special hardship'.

An auction sale at Uttoxeter in the late 1950s, conducted by Messrs W.S. Bagshaw and Sons of High Street, Uttoxeter, sold the well-known country public house, The Bird-in-Hand, at Hilderstone, Stone, Staffs for £3,000; 'it was a shocking price for such a place', said the auctioneer. For more than 200 years the inn had been occupied by the Shelley family and Mrs E.M. Nash recalled in the 1970s that, 'my great grandmother brewed the first ale for sale (in a copper I believe) only in a small way, this was carried on by my grandfather during his lifetime and he built the brewery etc. into a thriving business. There were at least three pubs belonging to the Bird-in-Hand, and beer was also supplied to free houses in the area of Stone, Stafford and Cheadle. Brewing ceased after the take-over by my uncle soon after the estate was divided up; the last brew being put in on 20 December 1927. No beer was bottled but spirits were bottled and sold.'

The property came onto the market and was acquired by Mr G. Saxton of The Bear Inn, Wirksworth, Derbyshire, following the death of Mr T.H. Shelley and through the poor health of Mrs Shelley, his widow. The property included the house, public bar, serving bar, smoke room, two beer cellars, office, spirit stockroom, four bedrooms and a bathroom. Outbuildings included a stable, garage, the brewhouse, 500- and 1,000-gallon tanks, store places and a range of farm buildings.

Evidently some bottling was carried out in pre-war days at the Queen's Arms, Wolverhampton, by the then owner Charles Hilton who also designed the labels. On his death he left the business to Mr Shelton who had been his manager and brewer for many years. Mr Shelton's son, J.H.G. Shelton, said, 'I assisted in the brewing from the age of fourteen. The bottling side of the business was only a sideline as producing draught beer for the pub entailed many long and hard working hours. We finished brewing in December 1959. This was due to a number of circumstances. The whole of the houses in our area came under the Compulsory Order for Demolition, apart from the Queen's Arms, and the district was scheduled for industry. We lost our well which supplied our cooling water for brewing, and a little while later our steam boiler was condemned as unsafe by the Insurance Company's inspector. So my father decided it would cost too much to get back to brewing so we carried on as a free house buying in beer. My father died in 1964, leaving the business to me which my wife and myself carried on very successfully until my health began to fail and we sold out to Ansell's Brewery in 1964.'

Of all the disused home-brew brewhouses that remain, the one in the yard at the Golden Lion, Southwick, Hants, is the most complete. Brewing ceased here in 1956 when the last brewer, Mr W.J. Hunt had to give up because of his advancing years. Beer was brewed primarily for the Golden Lion public house, but a considerable trade was done in supplying other public houses and an off-licence trade. The public house is very much older than the brewhouse which is set at right angles to the pub, in the rear yard. The brewhouse was built in the 1850s and measures 19 feet 6 ins wide by 52 feet long. It is of red brick with two storeys and a loft, which has a louvred housing to the roof ridge. Attached to the brewhouse and of the same width was the two-stall stable with hay loft above, and attached to the stable is a storeroom. Facing the yard/car park there are two double doors and two small windows between to the ground floor. The right-hand set of doors lead into the engine room with its vertical coal-fired boiler, water pump and cranked engine which drives a lay shaft and belts. In the centre is the base of the two timber stave fermenting vats which extend up into the

The detached brewery behind the Golden Lion, Southwick, Hants.

first floor. A wooden staircase opposite the other doors leads up to the first floor, where the small sugar room is housed. Close to this storeroom are the two coolers and hop-back in a room which has large windows with wood louvres. Beside one set of louvres is the mash-tun with its spent grains shoot passing through the louvred window. The belt drive from below comes up beside the timber mash-tun and drives the cast-iron paddles within. To the rear of this first floor is the open top to the two fermenting vats, and beside them is the brick-built copper, with wooden steps between the copper and mash-tun; there narrow steps lead up to the loft. At the end of this floor is the malt store, above and to the same size as the engine room on the ground floor. The chimney flue is in the rear corner and serves the boiler; it terminates externally with a rectangular brick stack with one oversailing brick course at the top. In the loft there is the cold liquor tank in the centre with the smaller hot liquor tank beside the grist case in the eaves. The grist mill is also tucked under the eaves in the area above the malt store.

Mr Hunt is known to have bottled at least one type of beer, namely Sparkling Pale Ale. Its label indicates that he was also a wine and spirit merchant, and that he had premises at Kingston, facing Lake Road, Portsmouth. This was an off-licence which was sold to the Courage brewery in 1972. In 1971 the existence of the redundant brewhouse came to the attention of Mr Michael Tighe and under his auspices, meetings were arranged with two members of the management from Courage's Alton Brewery, who were the tenants of the Golden Lion and its brewhouse, the freehold being owned by the Southwick Estate. The objective was to ensure the preservation of this unique brewhouse with a secondary scheme to turn it into a museum. Meetings were arranged with a number of interested people and organizations, including the then Brewers' Society and The Incorporated Brewers Guild. Sadly, due to lack of financial support, the museum project was never fulfilled; however, the prime object of preserving the brewhouse intact has been achieved, thanks to Michael Tighe and Pam Stephens, both subsequently to become members of the Brewery History Society founded in 1972.

The earliest reference to a brewer at Southwick was in 1847, when a C. Foster is known, but there is no evidence to show that he was brewing at the Golden Lion. James Hunt is shown in directories as a brewer at the Golden Lion in 1852 to be followed in 1891 by William James Hunt, presumably the first James's son. The Hunt family also owned the Egremont Brewery and beerhouse, Craswell Street, Portsmouth, from 1846 to 1878, purchasing it when it was only a year old. William died in 1859 aged eighty-three and it passed to his son, also named William. On the latter's death in 1878 the detached brewhouse was sold to a corset manufacturers. The Egremont beerhouse remained in the hands of the grandson, William Fabian Hunt, until his death in 1890 when it was sold to the Beehive Brewery, later to become a part of Portsmouth United Breweries. This trend was repeated almost everywhere.

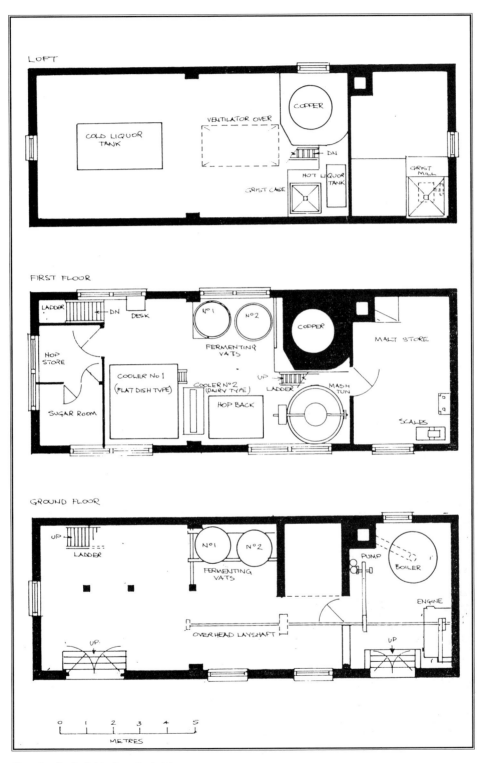

LOFT

COLD LIQUOR TANK

VENTILATOR OVER

COPPER

DN

GRIST MILL

GRIST CASE

HOT LIQUOR TANK

FIRST FLOOR

LADDER — DN   DESK

N°1   N°2

FERMENTING VATS

COPPER

MALT STORE

HOP STORE

COOLER N°1 (FLAT DISH TYPE)

COOLER N°2 (DAIRY TYPE)

HOP BACK

UP
LADDER

MASH TUN

SUGAR ROOM

SCALES

GROUND FLOOR

UP
LADDER

N°1   N°2

FERMENTING VATS

PUMP

BOILER

ENGINE

UP.

OVERHEAD LAYSHAFT

UP

0 1 2 3 4 5
METRES

Floor plans for the Golden Lion, Southwick.

The approach to Badminton House, the seat of the Duke and Duchess of Beaufort, is through the delightful village of estate houses, built of lovely warm Cotswold stone. Each of these houses is resplendent with the 'Portcullis' crest of the ducal family, as is the long building facing the small greensward near the entrance to the park. This was formerly the Portcullis Inn and Brewery.

The symmetrical building has a central archway with a pediment and on either end a raised parapet. The windows and doors are framed in stone and each corner has a castellated stone quoin. The roof is of local stone, as are most of the village houses, although there are several *cottages ornée*, with overhanging thatched roofs supported by rustic wooden posts. A map held at Badminton House muniment room dated 1708 indicates a large building on the same site, although there is no reference as to its use. The first record of the Portcullis Inn is an inventory dated 1780, although the first Duchess of Beaufort was responsible for the village almshouses and school built in 1714. The archway, with its Portcullis keystone, led into a double courtyard with a brewery adjacent at right angles to the rear of the alehouse. This range of stone-built buildings continued at various heights, serving several purposes connected with horses. Forming a line parallel to the alehouse are a large number of stables, with a smaller tackhouse protruding into the yard. The two-storey brewhouse has two wooden louvred windows to the top floor, with access to this level previously via an external stone staircase. Overlooking the stairs is a stone mullioned window above the lean-to single- storeyed cellar. Besides the ground-floor entrance door there is a stone wall enclosure, the site of the original water supply to the brewhouse, replaced in 1898 by the West Gloucestershire Water Company.

The Duke of Beaufort's Badminton Estate brewery.

Joseph Davies was the last brewer when, in 1902, an inventory was made prior to the plant being disposed of. This shows that there was a vertical 4 h.p. steam engine with feed pump and all the necessary iron shafting, belts and cogs to drive the plant. There were two coppers, one of 60-gallon capacity with two brass cocks, the other 300-gallon capacity, both with timber staging. There was a galvanized portable hop-back, two coolers measuring 13 feet by 6 feet, a vertical refrigerator built by Llewellyn and James, a mash-tun with a copper-slotted, false iron bottom, and a mashing machine fixed to the grist case. The underback was made of oak and held 220 gallons, and the movement of the wort was assisted by several gun-metal pumps. There were seven vats in the cellar ranging in size from 1,800 gallons to 2,560, a total capacity of 14,660 gallons. On the day the inventory was carried out there was 4,656 gallons of 'Old Beer' and 4,085 of 'Mild' in these vats. On tap in the cellar were 3 hogsheads and 80 dozen of small Bass bottles and 6 dozen and 8 small bottles of Coomb Valley Brewery Stout.

In this inventory there is no listing of any malt, although one pocket each of Farnham and Worcester hops are mentioned in addition to two Bavarians. It would therefore seem apparent that brewing had just ceased prior to the inventory being carried out. In the office there was a 4 Motion Bottling Machine, scales and weights, a brewer's saccharometer in its case, a new copper thermometer and two wood rousers. It is evident from these brewing plant details that the Portcullis Inn was a busy establishment, primarily serving Badminton estate workers. During the period 1899–1903, quite large quantities of beer were supplied to Badminton House. These purchases were for harvesters, haymaking, carpet beating and special occasions such as the visit of the Prince and Princess of Wales from 3–5 March 1902. In 1903 the following meals were supplied to estate workers: '1st July – 46 rent audit dinners; 8th July – 132 earth stoppers feast dinners; 1st August – 150 Puppy Show luncheons'. At these occasions beer was of course supplied, and this came from the Portcullis brewery, as the brewhouse at Badminton House had closed many years previously.

An establishment of estate workers was made in 1836 for his Grace, the 8th Duke of Beaufort, totalling 271 persons. Of these, 67 were in the house and, besides, a steward, butler, grooms, ushers, footmen, lady's maid, housemaids, charwomen, nurses, brewers, bakers, two men for sundry work, butcher, knife boy and many others. In the stables there were 119 horses for carriages, hunting, hacks and ponies with 39 staff to look after them. The extensive gardens had 29 staff and a further 14 looking after the game, particularly the 400 red deer and 1,400 fallow deer. The house and its many outbuildings were maintained by 28 tradesmen, including a timber sawmill. Timber was, and still is, an important source of revenue and in 1836 there were 18 woodmen and cutters. To maintain the considerable roads, fences and walls, 20 boys were superintended by one man who also had a further 20 men to carry out stone quarrying.

The 7th Duke of Beaufort marked his eldest son's coming of age in great style, reported in the *London Gazette* of 8 February 1845: 'The carcasses of no less than six oxen were given away, besides an immense quantity of other viands, and twenty hogsheads of strong ale', this is 1,080 gallons or 8,640 pints. Next day 200 tenants (all men) sat down to dinner in the servants' hall to celebrate Henry Somerset's birthday. For such occasions, the brewhouse at Badminton House most likely called upon the neighbouring Portcullis Inn for additional supplies of beer, both Mild and Old Ale. In the late nineteenth century, the Beaufort estate included lands in the counties of Gloucestershire, Wiltshire, Brecon, Glamorganshire and Monmouthshire, totalling some 51,000 acres. During this century large tracts of the former considerable estate have been disposed of, including Raglan Castle, Tintern Abbey and Troy House. Consequently the large number of estate employees has dwindled with these cutbacks. Badminton House is so well known today for its Whitbread Brewery-sponsored three-day eventing horse trials, which continue the legendary equine interests of the dukes and their Beaufort Hunt.

From the end of the last war, for three years or so, materials of all descriptions were in very short supply, consequently causing many small businesses to cease trading. As part of these shortages was the lack of skilled tradesmen to carry out repairs to worn out brewing plant. Availability of copper to make the repairs or to provide new plant was scarce. During the war years, much of the brewing had been done by men too old to see military service and they were assisted by women. Many women were employed on the bottling lines in larger firms. With the continued scarcities up until late 1947 many decided to throw in the towel. Because so many young men never returned from the war, in the case of family-run businesses there was no one else in the family to hand the home-brewing down to. Following the massive bomb damage to most of the towns and cities, vast rebuilding and redevelopment programmes were started in the 1950s. Many pubs were swept away in road-widening and house-building projects which continued apace into the late 1970s. The final blow to many a home-brew pub that had survived all of this was the introduction by the large brewery companies in the 1960s of 'keg' beers – this was pasteurised and filtered but essentially dead beer.

Lager was to be the one major growth product from its early beginnings in the 1880s, to such an extent that by the 1990s, it now represents 50 per cent of all beer production. Keg beers are a product requiring considerable capital investment and are way beyond the means of the home-brewer. In the two decades of the 1960s and 1970s cask-conditioned beers brewed by the publican and domestic brewer were almost totally engulfed by the keg revolution. Fortunately, a few far-sighted people saw these dangers looming and formed the Campaign for Real Ale (CAMRA) on 16 March 1971 – the decline of the traditional British beer was halted. With a growing band of like-minded enthusiasts who only accept cask-conditioned beer served either direct from a cask, or by an unassisted hand pump, the membership of CAMRA has swollen to 50,000 in the mid-1990s. They are a power force who regularly lobby parliament in the interests of the 'real ale' drinker. Brewery companies have responded, with major companies reintroducing a large range of cask-conditioned beers. During this renaissance of all that is best in British beer has been the establishment of around 220 home-brew pubs and micro-breweries. Currently available are some 1,100 different real ales! From the four steadfast home-brew pubs who survived has grown a whole tide of new entrepreneurs with fifty new pubs setting up in business during 1994–5. The growing awareness and appreciation of the true British beer flavours has created a demand, now being responded to. With the current trend towards retirement at the early age of fifty, many companies closing down, and large corporations still acquiring smaller companies, a large pool of people looking for a new way of life has been created.

By 1986, there were at least thirty-two new micro-brewing companies that had an ex-major brewing company employee involved in their business. From a trickle of new breweries setting up in the latter half of the 1970s and the first two years of 1980, came a swell of more than ten a year during the remainder of the decade. The swell has increased further during the first five years of the 1990s.

Two ex-Romford Brewery Company employees, Bruce Wilkinson and Geoff Mumford, decided to step into the lion's den by opening their home-brew pub, the Burton Bridge Brewery, in Burton-on-Trent, right under the noses of the greatest in the land. While working together in 1979 they realized that they had a mutual interest in starting their own brewery. An advertisement in the trade newspaper, *The Morning Advertiser*, had the old Fox and Goose pub in Bridge Street, Burton, up for sale, and so a visit was made during the May bank holiday of 1980. The pub's freehold had been purchased in the early nineteenth century by Mr Bass from the Marquis of Anglesea and had remained a licensed house until closed and sold off in 1980. Bruce and Geoff gave notice to leave the Ind Coope brewery in October 1980 and set about purchasing the necessary brewing plant. After six months of hard work, assisted by two YOPs, brewing commenced on 25 May

A sign not seen in Burton for a very long time.

1981. The front bar, consisting of a very small servery and two rooms, opened on 1 August 1981. It had been appreciated that, despite many so-called free houses in and around Burton, all were tied via loans to major brewery companies. It was therefore essential to have their own pub, thereby ensuring that their beer was sold in the best of condition and the reduction of delivery and cask costs was minimized. Trade has developed considerably since those early days, as the transport fleet consists of a 35 cwt truck and a 10-ton Dodge with a tail lift. Outlets are now supplied on a weekly basis at Stoke, Leicester, Birmingham and the Black Country. Further afield areas such as Norfolk, Kent, Yorkshire and the West Country are visited.

Maris Otter and Pipkin malt is crushed on a two-roller Bentall mill and then manually lifted and roused into the mash-tun; the town's main water supply is used for this. Mashing the 420 kg of malt is strenuous work which takes about three-quarters of an hour. A 14-barrel copper is heated by natural gas using 450,000 BTU per hour via a tubular burner. There are nine fermenting vessels of various types and sizes, including one 7-barrel capacity plastic one from the Cotleigh brewery in Somerset. Fermenting takes five days, after which time the yeast is skimmed off. The yeast is selected from the National Yeast catalogue, based in Norwich, and the strain selected gives quick fining and slow fermenting qualities with an inbuilt wild yeast killer factor. Twelve hours after fermentation the beer is chilled to 12°C and then the beer is pumped to an outside racking tank. From this tank in the narrow right-hand yard racking into the steam-sterilized casks is carried out. The brewery owns some 20 barrels, 350 kilderkins and 980 firkins, indicating the diverse accounts supplied. Hand bottling of special one-off lines for commemorative purposes is a speciality. Of special interest is the Burton Bridge Brewery's Burton Porter at 4.5% ABV, bottled without a conventional label, but with all the details rubber-stamped into a patch of yellow paint. There are at least four excellent draught beers, a Bitter being awarded CAMRA Bitter of the Year 1983. The Good Pub Guide voted the premises the 1990 Brew Pub of the Year. The pub situated in front of the small brewhouse is now run as a tenancy by Penny and Kevin McDonald, so that Bruce and Geoff can concentrate on developing their brewery still further.

Many of the new wave of micro-breweries have been set up in small units on modern industrial sites. However, one or two of the more recent brewhouses have taken on an appeal of their own. At the Farmer's Arms, Apperley, Glos, which was extensively refurbished in 1992, real ale and local wine is now served. The real ale is Odda's Light at 3.8% ABV, named after the hermit who founded the chapel at Deerhurst in 1056. A stronger beer at 4.5% ABV is called Sundowner Heavy, named after the hobo who arrives too late to labour but in time to imbibe. Both beers are brewed in the new detached brewhouse on the edge of the car park. To look at it one would be forgiven for thinking that the brick and timber stud building was quite old. Below its thatched roof for all the world it looks as though it has been there for years. This is a skillful and most welcome progression of design into new and attractive brewhouses. One hopes that this sort of sympathetic lead encourages more to follow. The brewhouse is open for viewing to the public, and once the Mayhems Ales have been tried in the lovely pub, one is sure to return for another visit.

Unfortunately during the last twenty years there have been many casualties. As has been related at the Burton Bridge Brewery, it was soon found that many of the potential free trade outlets were in fact closed doors. The guest beer policy encouraged by the government has largely been thwarted by the undercutting of beer prices supplied by the major brewers. They have also introduced a guest beer from within their own portfolio of associated companies. Many of the new wave pioneers underestimated the market-place and the pricing structures, despite their producing some excellent beers. Another aspect of the major brewers' response to the increased real ale demand was to build their own brewhouses attached to some of their existing houses. In the period up to the mid-1980s, the two companies who were most active in this respect were Whitbread, with about ten home-brew pubs, and the Allied Breweries group with eleven. Whitbread's led the way with the Alford Arms, Frithesden, Herts, opening its brewhouse production in August 1981. Within the Allied Breweries group, Joshua Tetley opened the Station, at Guiseley, near Leeds, West Yorkshire, in September 1982. Clifton Inns, a subsidiary of Grand Metropolitan (Watneys) opened in February 1983, the first of their group of London home-brew pubs, with the Orange Brewery in Pimlico Road, SW1, a further four opened in the following year.

Mayhem's thatched brewery at the Farmer's Arms, Apperley, a modern micro-brewery that should be emulated.

Halls (Oxford & West) a subsidiary of Allied Breweries, had several interesting micro-brewery operations in the West Country and Midlands. The Plympton Brewery in Valley Road, Plympton, Devon, was founded in November 1984, with a 100-barrel brewing capacity to supply forty tied houses and the free trade accounts in the area. The Nailsea Brewery was founded in April 1980 by Dennis Jacobs, an ex-Courage employee, who sold his 50-barrel business to Halls (Oxford & West) in 1984. Halls moved the plant to the Southfield Industrial Estate where the company's delivery depot was and retained Dennis Jacobs as brewer. Dennis retired in October 1985 and brewing ceased. In Oxford city, Halls reopened the former Red Lion after extensive rebuilding in November 1984, which incorporated a bakery and a brewhouse from which the pub took its new name. Brewing ceased at the end of 1989 and all the brewing plant was sold to the Kelham Island Brewery, Sheffield. This new home-brew operation was opened in 1990 in the former Fat Cat pub, just around the corner from the recently closed down giant Exchange Brewery of Tennant Brothers Ltd.

In the West Midlands at Langley, near Oldbury, a new company was formed in 1984, Holt, Plant & Deakin Ltd which brewed for fifteen pubs within the pub chain. An acquisition which is proving to be of considerable success to the Allied-Domecq group of companies, is the Firkin Brewery. This was founded by David Bruce with the support of his wife, Louise, in July 1979, who borrowed £10,000 and opened a cellar brewhouse at the Goose and Firkin,

Borough Road, London, SE1. This was the first free house in London for decades to revive the old home-brewing craft. It was an immediate run-away success and the company rapidly acquired run-down and dilapidated pubs and converted them to the Firkin formula. David Bruce sold the business in 1988 to Midsummer Leisure (later to be called European Leisure) who then sold the pubs to Stakis Leisure in September 1990. The Taylor Walker London division of Allied Domecq purchased the company, and since then many of the company's own pubs have been converted to the Firkin image. There are now twenty-two in London, six in Birmingham and others in towns stretching from Edinburgh, Newcastle, Manchester, Leeds, Bristol, Oxford and Exeter. In total there are over 100 Firkin pubs, of which thirty-one have their own full mash brewhouses, often sited in cellars where customers are able to see the brewing being carried out. The largest of the chain is the Falcon and Firkin, looking across Victoria Park, Hackney, East London, and this supplies a range of six beers to at least six non-brewing pubs in the chain. Most of the brewing pubs have their own range, but all brew the excellent Dogboulter at OG 1059. This chain of revived home-brew pubs is a most welcome present-day development.

Of the many Whitbread home-brew pubs to be founded, the Frog & Parrot Brewhouse Company in Sheffield was probably the most renowned. A suitably named Stingo beer called Roger and Out was at its time the world's strongest beer at 16.9% ABV. Founded also in the same year, 1982, was Whitbread's Newcastle Brewhouse Company at the renamed Dog & Parrot, formerly the Golden Fleece Inn, in Clayton Street, Newcastle.

Scotland and Wales received scant attention from the major breweries, although the Alloa Brewery Company (Allied) did set up, in August 1983, the Rose Street Brewery at the former Cockade Inn, Edinburgh. Both Allied (Lloyd & Trouncer) and Whitbread set up small brewing concerns in Wales, the former set up the Minera Brewing Co. in Wrexham, and the latter the Heritage Brewery Co. in Cardiff. The Cardiff business was formed in December 1983, but had ceased brewing by January 1986.

As sure as the phoenix will rise, so did many a new micro-brewing operation set up business in previous old brewhouses. Perhaps the grandest setting of all of these is the Stanway House Brewery, at Stanway, near Cheltenham, Gloucestershire, founded on 17 March 1993, by ex-Davenport's brewer, Alexander Pennycook. Stanway House is one of the county's loveliest manor-houses which dates from the time of Elizabeth I. Built of golden limestone, the house has only changed hands once during the last 1,200 years.

Four monks originally lived at Stanway House and were supported by Sir William Tracy of neighbouring Toddington, on condition that they prayed for his soul. He died in 1530, declaring that he relied on salvation and not upon the monks' prayers for him. His body was exhumed and burnt on the instructions of Chancellor Parker of Worcester much to the revulsion of Richard Tracy, his son. He used his influence with Thomas Cromwell to obtain a lease on Stanway. The last of the Tracys was Susan, who married Francis Charteris, Lord Elcho, son of the 7th Earl of Weymss, East Lothian, in 1771. Ever since, the house has remained in the ownership of the Earls of Weymss. The house is currently occupied by Lord Neidpath and his family.

In the grounds of the house, close to the road and beside the village parish church, is a tithe barn built by the abbots of Tewkesbury in 1370. A magnificent gatehouse between the church and the south front of the house was built in about 1630 and is adjacent to the superb

The Jacobean manor of Stanway has its service courtyard through the archway. The brewery is on the left.

stone-mullioned oriel window. On the extreme left of the house a range of lower buildings were constructed in 1859–60, designed by William Burn. These consist of the kitchen, with separate rooms for the butler and housekeeper, still room, laundry, dairy, lamp room, servants' hall and fuel store. A covered archway, paved with cobblestones, leads through to the rear service wing. Inside this archway is a door on the left, stepping down into the brewhouse.

Last used before the First World War, a local lady called each autumn on her bicycle to brew for the house. She would no doubt have had some assistance, as still inside this brewhouse are the two original coppers. Immediately on entering, to the right-hand side are a stone-built platform and steps to the full width of about 14 feet. This serves a stone enclosed copper of 100-gallon capacity with a massive stone chimney-breast to the centre, and on the left side curved stonework housing a copper of 250 gallons. Both have large bronze drain-off cocks. Above the larger copper is a small 'L' shaped shallow tray which previously would have housed the second 'small beer' wort. At some time in the past the top few feet have been built up of brick, and a section of the stonework below has been chiselled out to allow a circular vat or cask to be pushed under the cock. The flues from the furnaces both discharge into the central chimney-stack between the coppers.

Access to the smaller of the two coppers is by an open-tread stair to a staging which covers the front half of the building. A further short flight of stairs leads up to a small platform which gives access to the smaller copper rim. On the staging to the front is the original shallow unlined wooden cooler. This measures 7 feet 8 inches by 18 feet and is now in an unusable condition. Above this is a higher level of narrow flooring which clearly had previously covered the entire width. At this level there is one wooden louvred window in the front gabled wall. At a lower level, and facing the old stable block, are two similar sized louvred windows, all with internal solid oak shutters.

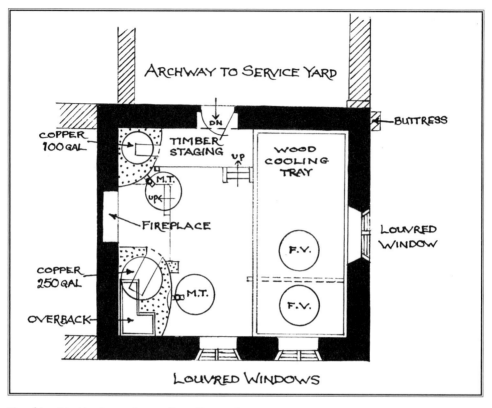

Plan of the original brewhouse at Stanway House, Gloucestershire.

Mains water supply has only been installed during the last three years, the supply having come from the Lidcombe Hills behind the house for generations. These hills are well wooded and provide timber, as they must have done for hundreds of years, for the copper furnaces of the brewhouse. In the heyday of the estate, which has 5,000 acres, there were eighty-six staff; in 1949 when most of the barn wing was demolished, there were only nine servants.

On the 17 March 1993, Alex Pennycook, who had worked for Davenport's Brewery, Birmingham, for fourteen years – the last two at the end of the 1980s as head brewer – recommenced brewing at Stanway. A unique feature of his modern micro-brewing is that he still uses the original large copper fired by logs from the estate. Each brew gyle is about four barrels and he produces in total about 6 barrels a week. Two draught beers are brewed, Stanney Bitter at 4.5% ABV (Stanney is the local name for the village) and the darker Old Eccentric at 5.5% ABV. The Stanney Bitter is true to its name giving a memorable aftertaste. It is racked in both kilderkin and pin-sized metal casks. Where the original equipment was removed in 1914, Alex Pennycook has obtained modern stainless-steel tanks, purchased from Vaux Brewery, Sunderland. A one-off beer of 4.5% ABV appropriately called Lords-a-Leaping was brewed in December 1994. A bottle-conditioned Stanney Bitter has also been produced. Besides Traquair House in Scotland owned by Lord Neidpath, Stanway House brewery is the only estate brewhouse to have been revived utilizing some of the original brewing equipment.

Also in Gloucestershire is Charles Wright's Uley Brewery Ltd which operates from the delightful group of stone buildings previously Samuel Price's Brewery. This was established in the eighteenth century, the present outbuildings in which the brewhouse is housed being rebuilt in 1833; an arched and carved stone window lintel bears testimony to this. Situated in the centre of Uley, itself deep in one of the typical Cotswold wooded valleys, what more pleasant a setting could there be for a brewery? On the front of the old cart shed, above the double entrance doors, can still be discerned the old Victorian elegant lettering which reads, 'Genuine Steam Brewery'. Sadly, the old stone chimney-stack has long been demolished.

In the late 1940s while passing the old brewery on my way to Sunday church from school, I well recall hearing the bark of hounds. At that time the grand house and outbuildings were the kennels and stables of the Kingscote Hunt. Appropriately today the Uley Brewery produces a most excellent range of beers, all relating in name to the Cotswold Old Spot pig. One of that name won first prize at Bristol in the 1985 beer festival, and justly so. A one-off beer produced in May 1994 was named the Dursley Donkey, after the now closed railway branch line to the nearby town. The capacity of Uley Brewery is 10 barrels, utilizing all modern stainless-steel plant.

Many of the revived breweries have been housed in old brewery premises, including the Canterbury Brewery set up in the old sample room of Flint's Brewery, Canterbury, Kent. David Cobb, of the old Cobb's Brewery, Margate, gave technical assistance from the founding in February 1979. In Somerset, Arnold & Hancocks Brewery at Wiveliscombe is used by the Golden Hill Brewery, and the Cotleigh Brewery also moved into the large premises which dominate the landscape.

Mr Price's original Uley Brewery, now resurrected and producing superb Cotswold ales.

First Glenny's brewery, and then followed by the Wychwood Brewery, occupy the old offices and malthouse of the former Clinch's Brewery, Witney, Oxfordshire. Two recent micro-breweries have also occupied former maltings and office/storerooms at Oakhill, Somerset. The Oakhill brewery was gutted by fire in 1925 and closed, although the extensive maltings were in use by Courage up to recent times. George Watts, ex-Higson's Brewery employee founded the Beacon Brewery in April 1981, but this had ceased trading by March 1983. A new company, the Old Brewery, was formed by George Watts in 1984, a case of the phoenix rising in the same brewery premises – twice! Two more recent breweries to set up business in former brewery premises are the Black Sheep Brewery PLC, at Masham, near Ripon, Yorkshire, where Paul Theakston, of the well-known small common brewery of that name in Masham, has set up in the former Wellgarth maltings. His output is capable of 300 barrels a week and is currently producing two draught beers. The Lincolnshire Steam Brewery Company has, since the summer of 1994, been operating its Maltings Brewery plant of 120 barrels on the site of the old Bourne Brewery. Four beers are available. Several new brewing operations have been set up in public houses where home-brewing had previously been carried out. The Camden Arms, Brecon, Powys, Wales, last brewed in 1942, but a revived company, the Brecon Brewery Ltd, was formed in 1979, only to cease brewing again in 1982.

The Linfit Brewery, at the Sair Inn, Lane Top, Linthwaite, near Huddersfield, West Yorkshire, has been brewing a large range of twelve beers since January 1983. Ron Crabtree, another employee from a brewery company, the West Riding Brewery, set up his original one-barrel plant in the Sair Inn, which was a nineteenth-century home-brew pub. Production was doubled in 1993 and again new plant increased capacity in 1994. Ron's range of beers extend from a Mild at 3% ABV, with a Summer Ale and Bitter both at 3.7%, a Special and Lee Porter at 4.3%, also two at 5.3%, English Guinea Stout (a nice pun on Guinness Stout) and Old Eli. At the top of the strength range is Enoch's Hammer and Xmas Ale, both at a massive 8.6%. The television producer and personality, Janet Street Porter, had a one-off Porter of 4.6% ABV named after her in November 1994.

The Beacon Hotel in Bilston Street is much better known as Sarah Hughes, and is one of previously many home-brew public houses in the town of Dudley. The three-storeyed red-brick brewhouse attached to the cream-painted walls of the pub is graced by a painted wall sign at one end reading 'Brewery'. Over the double doors into the brewhouse lower block is a small sign 'Sarah Hughes, 1921, Home Brewed Ales' and this is the clue to its popular name.

The first owner was Abraham Carter who probably erected the premises in about 1865. Abraham died in 1882 and so his wife Nancy carried on the running of the brewing and retailing business until she died in 1890. A Joseph Richards held the licence as a 'Tenant in possession' until 1902, then John Baker who was followed by James Fellows who purchased the freehold with Sarah Hughes in 1921; she was aged fifty-four. Sarah died at the grand age of eighty-four in 1951, having stamped her personality and name on this home-brew operation and so her son, Alfred, carried on after her demise. Brewing ceased in 1958 although the public house continued trading. All the brewing plant was left intact until Sarah's grandson John Hughes decided to recommence brewing after a lapse of twenty-nine years.

A phoenix arose, with all the brewing plant being renovated – the sunken copper in its white glazed bull-nosed brick surround intact, the wood grist case now discharging into a

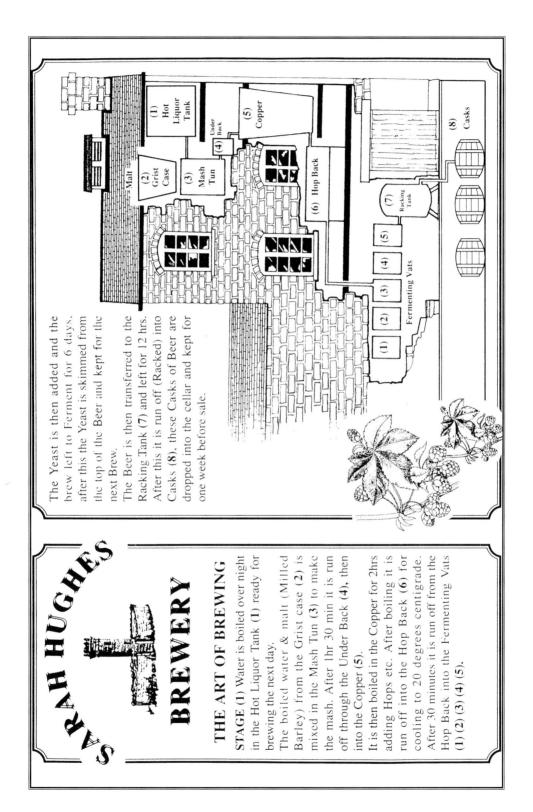

SARAH HUGHES
BREWERY

THE ART OF BREWING

STAGE (1) Water is boiled over night in the Hot Liquor Tank **(1)** ready for brewing the next day.

The boiled water & malt (Milled Barley) from the Grist case **(2)** is mixed in the Mash Tun **(3)** to make the mash. After 1hr 30 min it is run off through the Under Back **(4)**, then into the Copper **(5)**.

It is then boiled in the Copper for 2hrs adding Hops etc. After boiling it is run off into the Hop Back **(6)** for cooling to 20 degrees centigrade. After 30 minutes it is run off from the Hop Back into the Fermenting Vats **(1) (2) (3) (4) (5)**.

The Yeast is then added and the brew left to Ferment for 6 days, after this the Yeast is skimmed from the top of the Beer and kept for the next Brew.

The Beer is then transferred to the Racking Tank **(7)** and left for 12 hrs. After this it is run off (Racked) into Casks **(8)**, these Casks of Beer are dropped into the cellar and kept for one week before sale.

In the diagram:
- **(1)** Hot Liquor Tank
- **(2)** Grist Case
- **(3)** Mash Tun
- **(4)** Under Back
- **(5)** Copper
- **(6)** Hop Back
- **(7)** Racking Tank
- **(8)** Casks
- Malt
- Fermenting Vats **(1) (2) (3) (4) (5)**

stainless steel mash-tun encased in timber cladding, five stainless-steel-enclosed fermenting vessels in the basement area. As part of the renovations an additional floor was built on top of the tower brewhouse and this has been executed most sympathetically. Round-headed cast-iron windows maintain the old character as does the Welsh blue-slate roof with its small wooden louvred housing on the ridge. A stubby chimney-stack at one gable end and another on a flank wall are both relieved by oversailing brick courses. John Hughes, the third generation of the Hughes family, has done an excellent job in maintaining the old character of the brewhouse which he has inherited from Sarah. John was assisted in his renovation task by Peter Hickman who was also the first brewer on reopening. Technical brewing assistance was given by Chris Marchbanks and this led up to the first brew, which was formally pulled by Mr Adrian Hyde, the local CAMRA branch chairman, on 30 May 1987. The draught beer is Sedgley Surprise Bitter of 1048 OG and a limited edition of only eighty bottles of a Dark Ruby Mild, of 1058 OG in 275-ml bottles was produced for the opening day, based on an original 100-year-old recipe. This bottle label featured a picture of Sarah Hughes and a new similar bottled beer was produced in 1995 at 6% ABV.

A rear view of Sarah Hughes's tower brewhouse in the West Midlands.

The current brewer is Lee Cox who took over from Peter Hickman on his retirement. The average brew length is 5 barrels with a maximum capacity of 9 barrels with up to three brews per week, depending on demand. The mash-tun and paraflow are ex-Bartletts, Wenham Bridge, and the five fermenting vessels came from Savilles. Mains water is used and the malt is Crystal and White Malt. Two varieties of hops are used, one from Kent and the other from Hereford. A little sugar is used and a special yeast strain – the entire recipe remains secret!

Several farms have been selected as suitable venues for new brewing operations during the past few years. The Black Bull Brewery was founded in April 1994 at Ashes Farm, Ashbourne, Derby, by Michael Peach, where he produces a rich dark ruby-coloured Bitter of 1040 OG In Devon, two former dairy workers set up the Branscombe Vale Brewery in two cowsheds on the National Trust, Great Seaside Farm. From July 1992 they have been brewing two beers of 1040 and 1055 OG

Up in North Yorkshire on the banks of the River Swale at Thirsk, Hambledon Ales have been brewing since March 1991. The owner's original target output of 20 barrels a week has been considerably exceeded, with their range of eight beers being sold to over 100 free trade accounts. Their brewhouse is a Victorian barn. The licensee of the Dipton Mill Inn, Hexham, Northumberland has been brewing his four beers for his own pub and other accounts. The Hexhamshire Brewery was founded in November 1992. The Hog's Back Brewery, situated in restored farm buildings dating from 1768, at Tongham, Surrey, has promoted their range of eight beers. Success has been theirs due to aggressive marketing, which includes tours of the brewery, and a retail off-licence. This sells both English and Continental bottled beers and items advertising the business. The company was formed in August 1992, at the Manor Farm, The Street, Tongham, Surrey.

Richard and Lesley Jenkinson formed the Chiltern Brewery in 1980 producing four draught beers. The first was Chiltern Ale, a light ale of 1038 OG, followed two years later by Beechwood Bitter, at 1043 OG Three Hundreds Old Ale (OG 1050) was supplemented at the brewery's tenth anniversary with Bodgers Barley Wine (OG 1080). Three Hundred Old Ale is available in imperial pint bottles, and the barley wine is bottle-conditioned in imperial half pints. Water for the brewery is obtained from bore holes in the Chiltern Hills bordering the brewery.

A more recent formation of an exclusive micro-brewery is the Enville Ales, in April 1993. Owner Will Constantine-Cort, in partnership with Mark Hill of Brewers' Wholesale, share the site on the Enville estate. Initial production was 5 barrels a week which has now increased to 30 or more. The head brewer is Richard Wintle who was formerly at another brewery, Moorhouses in Blackburn. Richard won a silver medal for creating Pendle Witches Brew. He is now responsible for using honey as priming in all the Enville Ales, the recipe based on one over 120 years old. The honey is obtained from the brewery's own 250 bee-hives, the blending a closely guarded secret. Water here is obtained from the estate's own spring. The beers made in the converted farm barn are Enville Ale (4.5% ABV), Gothic Ale (5.2% ABV) which is a black old-fashioned style dinner ale and Enville White at 4.2% ABV which is a dry wheat beer, containing 30 per cent wheat. This too replicates an old style beer. Enville Bitter, 3.8% ABV is a quaffing session beer. It is most encouraging to find such new micro-breweries bringing back old-style beers. With more of these entrepreneurs professionally running their businesses, the long-term future looks very bright indeed.

The convivial surroundings in the bar of the Beacon Hotel.

These and many other micro-breweries are meeting the demand from the more discriminating drinkers. Until the last two decades it had been very difficult for the landlord to brew his own beer. The smallest plant then available was 5-barrel (1,440 pint) brew, often too large for most pubs to handle, particularly if they had a brewery tie. The cost of the plant was at least £10,000. During the last few years equipment taking no more space than 10 square feet of floor space, is now available priced at around £1,000. The major benefit to the publican brewer of today is that he has little or no transport charges, and he takes all the profit from his own production. Increasingly the new micro-brewers are finding that initially it is essential that they have one pub of their own. This gives them immediate cash flow and a suitable venue to display their wares. From these small beginnings development into the tough world of the free trade can begin. Soon several of these more successful home-brew pubs and micro-breweries will be joining the Independent Family of Brewers of Britain and the brewing circle will become complete as they join the ever-popular group of common brewers.

'Blessings of Your Heart, You Brew Good Ale'

Two types of brewing shall be examined in this final chapter: mini-scale – that carried out for domestic use in farms and cottages – and that carried out by the retail and publican brewer and on large estates. Domestic brewing was the earliest form and from it developed the progressively larger brewing operations, from that on the aristocratic estates, through the publican and retail brewers, to the regional and national brewery companies.

As we have seen with the early alehouses, women took an early role in domestic brewing, as this craft was closely allied to baking and washing. These activities more often than not were carried out in the same outbuilding or kitchen scullery. Sometimes even the same copper was used for washing the household's laundry. From medieval times, the women of the house became known as the alewife or brewster. The latter name is the feminine form of brewer and it is significant of the ancient position that women held in brewing. This particular word nowadays is used for the annual licensing sessions, where each landlord is required to obtain a licence to trade. Probably the best known alewife was Elynor Rammynge of Leatherhead who learnt her trade from a Jew in the early sixteenth century. An old Durham rhyme makes a nice point on an alewife's behalf:

> *I'll no more be a nun, nun, nun,*
> *I'll be no more a nun!*
> *But I'll be a wife,*
> *And lead a merry life,*
> *And brew good ale by the tun, tun, tun.*

The equipment used for brewing in cottages and farms would vary in capacity from only a few gallons to up to about 100 gallons a brew. The smallest volumes would utilize a cast-iron cauldron, set into brickwork above a fire, and fuelled by gleanings from the hedgerows. In place of a mash-tun, the malt would be stirred in any suitably sized kitchen cooking pot. For the final stage of converting the sweet wort into beer, a glazed earthenware pot was used, containing up to 3 gallons. This had a wide mouth and lip, and on the wide shoulders there were two built-in carrying handles. Also at the widest point of the pot was a small 'vent' hole, which allowed the carbon dioxide produced in the fermentation to escape. This probably had a piece of straw tucked into it to prevent flies getting onto the head of yeast. The wide mouth would be sealed by a damp rag or sacking wrapped around a wood or cork bung. This type of pottery fermentation vessel has been in use from at least the seventeenth century and almost certainly dates back to Roman times. There were understandably regional variations, particularly in regard to forms of glazed decoration. Some types would also have a hole near the base, from which a wooden tap would allow the drawing off of the fermented beer. For slightly larger quantities of domestic brewing, coopered barrels have been used up until recent times in Wales. At least one example in the late 1960s, at Hafod Las Uchof Farm, Llanboidy, Dyfed, used a coopered butter-making churn, which stood on a wooden trestle. Widow Wood of Beckenham Alms House was said to have 'brewed with her ordinary cooking utensils, and the fireplace of her little room; a tin kettle served her for a boiler, she mashed in a common butter-firkin, ran off the liquor in a "crock", and tunned it in a small beer barrel', so described by Hone in *Table Book*.

In 1610 the justices of Rutland, in setting the rate of wages for domestic servants, decided that a woman who could bake and brew and make malt should be paid the sum of 24*s* 8*d* a year. Those who could not make malt received 1*s* 4*d* a year less. The very rudimentary skills and kitchen equipment available to the domestic brewer meant that the quality of beer varied considerably. This variable quality was also affected by the malt used and even the weather conditions. The lack of any method, other than by rule of thumb, to judge water temperature and possibly even time spent in the various operations, must have often produced inferior tasting beers. Those who were more careful in the cleaning of their plant and took more care and detail with their brewings inevitably became successful brewers. These were the early forerunners of our entrepreneurial brewers of today. From the few successful domestic brewers it was a logical progression for them to sell their beer, and so their cottages became the early alehouses. The servants who could make malt in the early seventeenth century were able to produce it in very small quantities at home. All that was required was for them to purchase a sufficient quantity of the best available barley from the farmer. The grain was then soaked in a coopered vat or washing tub, and when it was just beginning to sprout, it would be spread out on a flat dry surface. This may have been in a barn or outhouse and when the sprouting grain had reached the right stage, it was collected up. The grains would then be rubbed between the hands to remove the shootlets, and then put into a cast-iron pan and 'cooked' over the open fire. Again their knowledge and judgement was critical to obtain roasted malt suitable to their requirements.

Water quality, which is very important to the brewing flavours, varied considerably around the country. Cottages and farms usually drew their supply from wells or springs and even from rainwater collected in butts. Because of the large variation in the mineral contents of the water, this too affected the success and flavour of the brews. Water was always needed in abundance, not only for brewing but also for cleansing the tools and plant. More recent and sophisticated requirements for water are its organic purity and that it should hold certain saline ingredients, carbonates and sulphates of lime, magnesia, and chlorides of sodium and potassium. This may be naturally occurring or it is added artificially. Many of the medieval and later watercourses had lead pipes, also pottery and wood channels. It has only been in recent times that the detrimental effect of water in lead pipes has been appreciated. In stone districts, mainly in the north, slabs of local stone were commonly used by the monks to form leats and water channels for their supplies. In the bursar's accounts of Durham in 1338–9 the following entry illustrates that even the best of engineered water supplies could not always be relied upon: 'to women carrying water from the Wear to the abbey for the bakehouse, brewhouse and kitchen at divers times when the pipe was frozen', and 'in drawing water from the draw-well in the cloister and for work about the pipe'.'

On 25 August 1883 *The Wiltshire Telegraph* reported on: ' "Beer versus Water." At 7 o'clock, at Beacon Hill, farm of George Melsome, near Amesbury, Wilts; a bet for £5 lasting all day in hot weather. The bet at Salisbury between Mr Turrell, corn dealer, challenged Mr Abbey, from Oxfordshire, a farmer and lecturer for the Church of England Temperance Society. The issue, who would do most work in the harvest field, the former on beer or the latter on water alone. 15 acres to each pitcher were allowed. Mr Turrell from the first held large lead, at 4pm he had cleared 15 acres, 3 roods, 16 poles and by Mr Abbey, 14 acres, 3 roods. There was great interest.' Several weeks later Mr Turrell was presented with a medal, a silver tankard and a good sum of money! On one side of the medal was a sheaf of wheat and a prong, on the reverse side it bore a laurel wreath and an inscription.

Besides water, known as liquor in the brewing industry, malt is the material used in bulk. Malt is produced from barley in malthouses and a description by William Cobbett in his *Cottage Economy*, published in 1821, gives a clear indication of the process involved: 'Nothing is so easy as to make your own malt, if you were permitted. You soak the barley about three days (according to the state of the weather) and then you put it upon stones or bricks and keep it turned till the root shoot out; and then, to know when to stop, and to put it to dry, take up a corn (which you will find nearly transparent) and look through the skin of it. You will see the spear that is to say, the shoot that would come out of the ground, pushing on towards the point of the barley-corn. It starts from the bottom, where the root comes out; and it goes on towards the other end; and would, if kept moist, come out at that other end when the root was about an inch long. So that when you have got the root to start, by soaking and turning in heap, the spear is on its way. If you look through the skin you will see it; and now observe, when the point of the spear has got along as far as the middle of the barley corn, you should take your barley and dry it. How easy would every family and especially every farmer do this if it were not for the punishment attached to it. The persons in the "unkempt places" before mentioned dry the malt in their oven! But let us hope that the labourer will soon be able to get malt without exposing himself to punishment as a violator of the law.' In his time Cobbett was a constant scourge of the government regarding its burdensome taxes, and took every opportunity to promote his cause for reduced taxation.

The early barley strains in the eighteenth century were of the two-row variety known as Spratt, but by the 1750s the narrow-eared barleys had been developed into three strains. In certain areas a few unselected sorts of barley such as Old Wiltshire, Nottingham Long Ear, Early Welsh, Scotch Common, Old Irish and Old Cornish, were grown. 'About the year of 1820 John Andrews, a labourer of Mr Edward Dove of Ulverston Hall, Debenham had been threshing barley, and on his return at night complained of his feet being very uneasy, and on taking off his shoes he found in one of them part of a very fine ear of barley – it struck him as being particularly so – and he was careful to have it preserved. He afterwards planted the

A small Kentish hop oasthouse with its original square kiln, supplemented by a nineteenth-century roundel kiln.

few grains from it in his garden, and the following year Dr Charles Chevallier coming to Andrew's dwelling to inspect some repairs going on (the cottage belonging to the Doctor) saw three or four of the ears growing. He requested they might be kept for him when ripe. The Doctor sowed a small ridge with the produce thus obtained, and kept it by itself, until he grew sufficient to plant an acre, and from this acre the produce was 11½ coombes (in about 1825 to 1826). This was again planted, and from the increase thus arising, he began to dispose of it, and from that time it has been gradually getting into repute. It is now well known in most of the corn markets in the Kingdom and also in many parts of the Continent, America etc. and is called the Chevallier barley.'

Chevallier was further developed, with each grain becoming rounder and more plump, into three further varieties in this country and two additional ones in Denmark. The other noticeable difference between Chevallier barley and the earlier types was its propensity to bend, or droop, when ripe. Chevallier barley marked a considerable advance in both yield and quality on the earlier narrow-eared forms. Archer quickly took the place of Chevallier and other strains, it being at least 10 per cent higher in yield, but its defect was that it was late in ripening, particularly in wet seasons and reduced sunshine. Further hybridization took place in about 1914 and Spratt-Archer appeared, giving a still heavier yield of 10 per cent on the original Archer strain. Plumage-Archer with Spratt-Archer were dominant varieties for nearly forty years. The renowned maltster, the late Dr E.S. Beaven, introduced English-Archer. Today Maris Otter is the most popular variety grown since its introduction in the 1960s. Its claim to fame is its winter hardiness with malting ability. All previous malting varieties were only able to be sown in spring. In today's advanced strains, barley is required to be thin-skinned and low in nitrogen. The finest barleys are grown on light loaming and drift soils overlying chalk formations, and so the eastern counties have been dominant for barley growing, just as Kent has been for hops.

Malt is produced in variations ranging from a very light colour to near black, Crystal, Brown, Chocolate, Black, Cara and Amber. The darker heavily-roasted varieties are used to make Porter and Stouts, imparting the natural dark colour and strong malt flavour to the beers. With home-brewing often dependent on variable colours, quality of the barley and dry storage, the infinite range of beers is considerable.

Hops impart a stringent taste and preservative qualities to beer. Before hops were introduced to this country from the Flemish area of the Continent in about 1520, the product produced by fermentation of wort was called ale. In about 1550 the government of the day brought in hop farmers to develop the hop in Kent. Only twenty years previously King Henry VIII had forbidden his brewer at Eltham to put hops or brimstone into his ale. Thomas Tusser, a farmer from Rivenhall, Essex, wrote his *Good points of Husbandry* in 1557 and he had this to say on 'The Hop-yard – A digression':

Whom fancy perswadeth, among other crops
To have for this spending sufficient of hops
Must willingly follow, of choices to chuse
Such lessons approved as skillful do use.

Ground gravelly, sandy, and mixed with clay.
Is naughty for hops, any manner of way.
Or if it be mingled with rubbish and stone
For dryness and barrenness let it alone.

Chuse soil for the hop of the rottenest mould
Well dunged and wrought as a garden plot should:
Not far from the water (but not over flown)
This lesson well noted, is meet to be known.

The sun in the south, or else southly and west,
Is joy to the hop as a welcomed guest.
But wind in the North, or else Northerly east,
To hop is as ill as a fray in a feast.

Meet plot for a hop-yard, once found as is told,
Make thereof account, as a jewel of gold.
Now dig it, and leave it the sun for to burn,
And afterward fence it, to serve for that turn.

The hop for his profit, I thus do exalt
It strengtheneth drink and it flavoureth malt;
And being well brewed long kept it will last,
And drawing abide if ye draw not too fast.

Many additives were imparted to beer before and after the introduction of hops. In medieval times rosemary was used for its tonic properties, and the monks also used bog myrtle to make Gale Ale. Both nettles and common burnet were used as flavourings to make Tonic Beer. In the sixteenth century, alecost, a common herb, was used to make ale spicy. Herb bennet or clove root, placed in a bag and suspended in the brewing vat or cask of beer, was used for some 200 years from the mid-1600s. Mint, tansy and wormwood came into use in the seventeenth century, the latter, with broom, were the only herbs allowed by law in addition to hops. During the nineteenth century there was some limited use of these as hop substitutes. Scurby grass and burdock was utilized during the nineteenth century, burdock being a popular flavouring in Botanic Beers. Probably illegally used during the nineteenth century was yew, which made beer more intoxicating. For bottled beer, cloves were added with sugar to give an alternative flavour. Alternatives or additions to hops in the eighteenth and nineteenth centuries also included gentian, orange, quassia, sweet flag, chamomile, bitter bean, centaury and several others. Some of these were poisonous and were usually used to increase the intoxicating effect of beer; these included laurel and deadly nightshade.

The Brewer's Assistant, written in 1815, gave the following advice regarding yeast: 'If flatulant or acid state from heat or long standing, may be revived with some malt or bean flower, burnt or calcined allum, or un-slacked lime, reduced to a fine powder together with a handful or two of salt. 2 or 3 ounces of the allum or lime or together to a gallon, may be sufficient, but more when quite old and solid. A gallon of yeast will weigh from 3 to 4 and from that to 10 or 12 pounds and upwards.' A Suffolk countryman's brewing instructions from the turn of the century stated: 'Start day previously malt in tub being steeped in water. Next morning, malt mixed by hand and then put into the Keeler a tap at base projected inside keeler where the wilsh – a sheath of wickerwork was fitted to prevent grains being lost. Malt then covered with water and third pail of boiling water from copper laddled in with the wooden hand cup, usually made from willow, sometimes with a groove in the handle so a sample could be taken. Keeler was then covered with a sack. Then 10 gallons of boiling water added and thoroughly mixed with a masher. Mash tub below keeler so that liquid could run in to stand for four hours, this is the first wort. Further water added to the keeler for second wort, which is called Small Beer. First then poured into the copper with three-quarters of hops added, then boiled for four hours, then drained through sieve into mash tub. Second wort then boiled in copper with remaining quarter of hops. Sometimes the two worts are then mixed. When cool, one pint of yeast is added for the fermentation. When fermentation complete, pour into wooden casks using a funnel.'

Similar but much more detailed notes were written by Mr Stanley James King, a small brewer of Coggeshall, Essex, in January 1885, he referred to the brewing instructions as 'Mr Sarvard's System': 'Let the liquor over the plates then let the malt in with the liquor 168° shaking it with the oar, put qr of 16 of Gypsum to the quarter when all the malt is in, cover the mash tub over, raise the liquor to 186° then turn on and work with the oars till all is well mixed, cover the tub over again, after 1½ hours set tap, heat should be 145° to 150°. Sparge on enough liquor to fill the Copper for boiling, then let the wort drain out of the Mash Tub. Close the taps and sparge on the rest required which will be about 10lbs, let it stand 1½, convey the wort into the Copper and get it to boil as fast as you can, when 196 to 190, skimmed the duty malt flour off when she commence to boil, put the hops in and areate, boil steadily 2 hours, let it out into hop back and cool down to 60° in Gyle pitch with 1 to 2lbs per barrel and rouse up well, when ready to skim take the top off and take it off continually until all is taken off, just leaving the surface covered. [This last sentence refers to the removal of the surplus yeast.] Skimmed first about 36 hours after setting to work. If the wort is good it should run down bright and clear into the Tun. If the beer refused to attenuate, the cause of it is that the wort is not conveyed quickly enough from the Under Back to the copper.' In a Scotch brewer's instructions for Scotch Ale, dated 1793, may be found a strange note: 'I throw a little dry malt, which is left on purpose, on the top of the mash, with a handful of salt, to keep the witches from it, and then cover it up.'

As early as 1587 a Mr Harrison described home-brewing which was, 'once in a month practised by my wife'. He went on to mention, 'Having therefore grooned eight bushels of good malt upon our querne, where the toll is saved, she addeth unto it half a bushel of wheat meale, and so much of otes small groond, and so tempereth or mixeth them with the malt that you cannot easily discerne the one from the other, otherwise these later would clunter, fall into lumps, and thereby become unprofitable'. Harrison calculated the cost of home-brewed beer and this worked out at a little over a penny a gallon.

Brewing was carried out during every month of the year for the common households, although March and October were the favoured months for making strong ale. In the accounts for brewings rendered by a John Killane to the Honorable Sir Richard Atkins of Hertfordshire, in the year 1696, the days of brewings were:

May 20	Sept 9	July 1	Nov 4	Aug 26	Dec 2	June 3
Sept 30	June 17	Oct 21	July 15	Nov 18	Aug 5	Nov 25

Each brewing was charged at 5s, the cost for the whole year being £3 10s.

Harrison further commented that at 'noblemen's tables, is commonly of a yeare olde, (or peradventure of twoo yeres tunning or more, but this is not general) it is also brued in Marche and is therefore called Marche Bere but for the household it is usually not under a monthes age, eache one coveting to have the same as stale as he might so that it was not soure'.

Trouble was often encountered with sour beer and there were a number of methods of 'recovering' the ale or beer. One such direction to the housewife was to put a handful or two of ground malt into the beer and stir it well. Another recipe to the brewer was to put a handful of oatmeal into the barrel, another idea used was to calcine oyster shells, beat them to a powder with a similar quantity of chalk, then put this concoction in a bag and put into the beer, hanging it almost to the bottom, and within twenty-four hours the beer should be palatable. The flag iris was an effective cure for sour beer, particularly in warm weather. It was also used as a flavouring. Cinnamon was also used to overcome a poor quality flavour, the pods probably imparting an entirely different taste. Ginger acted in much the same way, but it also increased the fermentation.

An instruction from the *Brewer's Assistant* said the following: 'Wash coolers and utensils in lime water, particularly in warm weather, to prevent foxing, bad smell and flavours etc, bay salt with hot liquor. Infections from dirty liquor backs, utensils etc, filthy reservoirs, wells or poor quality malt (mustiness) also taking liquors at improper heats, over liquoring the goods upon a second or third mash, letting it remain too long and running it off too fast. Also the worts, particularly the last lying too thick and long in the coolers or underback [when a white frothy matter on the top of the wort in the cooler appears] is a sure sign of this infection.' Not mentioned, because it was not appreciated at that time, was the ravages caused by wild yeast strains. In the year that the *Brewer's Assistant* was written, three items were in use that assisted in the improvement of brewing beer. Both the thermometer and saccarometer were tools which the more advanced brewer could fully make use of, while the introduction of isinglass as a fining agent to clear beer superseded many previous ingredients.

Ale cost, or ground ivy, was used in the sixteenth and seventeenth centuries for 'dispatching the maturation'. Wood sage, lemon balm, verbena and oak galls, were all used to clear beer. The concoction made using oak galls required 3 lbs of galls mixed with 4 oz of potash, and these were boiled together for three hours and then 12 lb of water was added. When cooled, 2 pints of wine spirit were added and then it was bottled ready for use. Sugar, honey and molasses, liquorice root, ginger, hartshorn, multam, all these have been used in beer-making. The first three were to be used for only ten or fifteen minutes before striking off or turning the wort out of the copper.

Draught beers of a darkish hue were the normal type available for centuries, and over time developed from a mild type into several variations. Mild was generally low in alcohol with, in more recent times, a 'cloth-cap' image. But there are always exceptions to the general rule, as stronger milds were and are produced in the West Midlands. The revived Sarah Hughes Beacon brewery produces a dark ruby mild which is fruity at 4.8 ABV. The world's most famous brown ale is the bottled Newcastle Brown Ale which was launched in 1927. This is reddish brown and has a nutty dryness and fruitiness, with malt flavours. A close contender is Mann's Brown Ale which was brewed at the Albion Brewery, Whitechapel, East London; this style of beer was produced by nearly all English breweries.

Old Ale is usually dark, rich, sweet and strong. For the smaller brewer this style was brewed in the spring for consumption during the summer, its strength ensuring that sometimes after a year's maturation it would still be in good condition in the hot weather. Even stronger in strength is barley wine which is always bottled and usually in 'nip' sized bottles. This was brewed and bottled from the late 1800s, although a similar strong draught version now called Winter Warmer was produced. The style is rich, malty and dark and has an 'estery' or winey flavour, and is matured for eighteen months. In draught form the casks were awarded the highest number of Xs. The most famous dark draught beer style was Porter, first brewed at the Bell Brewhouse, Shoreditch, London, in 1722. It was at first called Entire and this word is often to be seen on old photographs of pubs. Entire meant that the beer was a mixture of several draught beers, but as it gained popularity with the large number of porters at the London food markets, it took on their name. The first mention of Porter was in the 1740s. The world famous Guinness Brewery in Dublin produced the style in vast quantities and made Porter up until 1974. The beer is a very dark mahogany colour, fruity with strong roasted malt flavours. In recent years several new micro-brewery companies have introduced a similar brew, with the Burton Bridge Brewery at Burton leading the field. Their bottled version is true to the style.

Dry Stout, a roasty, hoppy, fruity, acidy beer is produced by Guinness with top fermenting yeasts. In the 1820s the Guinness casks were marked with X and XX. The double X was renamed Guinness Extra Stout Porter and was exported originally to the Caribbean, where it proved very popular. In turn this was renamed Foreign Extra Stout and it varies from ABV of 7.5% to 8.0% and is brewed in several of the warmer continents. There are only a few breweries who imitate their style, two in Ireland where it is the national form of beer. A Porter recipe from the 1820s reads: 'A quarter of malt, with these ingredients will make five barrels of good Porter. Take one quarter of high coloured malt, 8 lbs of hops, 9 lbs of treacle, 8 lbs of colour, 8 lbs of sliced liquorice root, 2 drachums of salt of tartar, 2 ozs of Spanish liquorice and half of capsicum. From a more recent book on brewing, 8 bushels of malt for 180 gallons, that is 25 gallons to a bushel. The cost of malt at 8s a bushel and 8 lbs of best hops at 1s a pound, therefore malt and hops cost 72s or 4s per gallon, retailed at 16 pence per gallon.' Imperial Stout was exported to the Baltic regions from Thrale's Southwark Brewery, London, from at least 1781. This very strong bottled beer with roasty burnt and smokey flavours, is still produced today by one company only.

Oatmeal Stout, which includes anything up to 15 per cent of oats, has hints of nuttiness, coffee and perhaps chocolate flavours and is generally around the lower range of strengths at 3.6% ABV. Sweet stout, however, is always low in alcohol, around the 2.7% ABV mark. As its name implies, it is sweet, with sugars being added before bottling. Variations on this common style are Milk and Cream stouts, made famous by Mackeson at their Hythe brewery in Kent, from their test brew in 1907. It became a national drink and remains so today, having recently retained the milk churn depicted on the bottle label. Many small brewers emulated their style.

Bitter is the traditional draught beer of the British Isles, although the word 'bitter' was only first mentioned in the 1850s. It has a dryness and aftertaste of hops so typical, each brewer varying the quantity of hops in the brew and dry hopping the cask just before delivery to the pub. The variety of hops used also produce the wonderful range of flavours available today. A fascinating variation of dispensing draught bitter is to be seen between roughly the north and south of the country. The variation is a preference in the south for 'flat' beer served with little or no head, while in the north, and most certainly in Yorkshire, the demand is for a full head. Guinness is also required to have a similar large smooth head.

Pale Ale, or India Pale Ale (IPA), was popularized by Burton, the brewing capital of the UK. This beer style was formed in a teapot in 1822 by the Allsopp brewery and became one of this country's most renowned types of bottled beer. In 1882 Manet's painting of the 'Bar of the Folies Bergère', showed a barmaid flanked on either side by a bottle of Bass Pale Ale, with its distinctive, and first trademark, of a red triangle. The beer type was formulated with a light nuttiness and malt character to an OG of 1040–50 for export to India. When, as part of the Commonwealth, there were large numbers of civil servants and troops requiring an English beer, it needed to be of a reasonable strength to withstand the long sea voyage. It became so popular abroad that the style was and is reproduced by nearly every brewery. Today, IPAs are sold as premium beers, and those brewed outside the Burton catchment area treat their water to simulate that of the gypsum salts of Burton water.

Stingo is a term chiefly used in Yorkshire for an old strong ale, although the term was used more widely. In particular the Blue Anchor, Helston, has for a number of years referred to all their beers as 'Spingo'. John White of York wrote 'The praise of York - shire Ale' in 1684 and had this to say:

If it be like the Ale we drink this day:
Call in my Land-Lady let her Appear,
Famous she is for brewing Ale, I swear;
And I a badge of Honour will bestow
Upon her without fail, before I go;
And so a Clerke was call'd to Exemplifie,
The letters Pattents following daintily:
Bachus Prince of good Fellowes; To all to whom
These our brave Letters Pattents shall now come,
Whereas we've bin Informed now of late,
That Nanny Driffield our great Court and State,
For many years last post hath much advanced,
By her strong humming Ale and as it chanc'd,
We having ample Proofe thereof, so now
We our Princely grace, would have you know
This Land-Lady unto the Noble State
And Honour of a Countess, we Create:
Any by our merry Fudling Subjects, She
Countess of Stingo henceforth call'd shall be.

In earlier times the Englishman's preference was undoubtedly for strong ale, and many a town up and down the country made claims for the excellence of their strong beers. In the Black Country, where the preference is still for Mild, this was 'small beer' formed from the second extract from the malt. This was sometimes referred to as 'pit beer' because it was so popular with colliers. The All Nations home-brew pub in Shropshire produces one beer, a mild of only 1032 OG, which is typical of this beer style and locational demand.

Many beers brewed locally took on generic terms, such as Brides Ales, brewed for the special wedding feast and Church Ales, which were an early method of raising funds for the church and would have been brewed by the churchwardens from malt donated by parishioners. Just as the bride had her Wedding Ale, so she also had a Christening Ale. For the churchwardens, who brewed in the Church House, adjacent to the church, they also had Clerk Ale, to pay for their parochial duties! A Whitsun Ale, an Easter Ale and Help Ale, also known as a Bid Ale and made to raise money for the poor, were also brewed. Most of these were popular before the Reformation and so gradually gave way to other styles in the seventeenth century.

Audit Ale is another strong beer, more commonly brewed only once a year, and this has remained a bottled beer by at least one East Anglian regional brewer. Audit Ale was brewed on landed estates as well as at university colleges, to be consumed at the Audit Dinners. These dinners were given by the landlords of property on the occasion when their tenants called to pay their rents at audit time. Both Oxford and Cambridge university colleges all brewed Audit Ale in addition to their regular daily small beer. When brewing ceased at the colleges, they continued the practice of Audit Ales by receiving bottled beers from several large brewery companies. This custom was only discontinued in the 1970s.

The Church House at Matching, Essex, which once provided Church ales to the isolated community.

Not only was Yorkshire's Stingo renowned as a strong beer, so was Welsh Ale. Welsh Ale traces its ancestry back to Saxon times, although it was not only brewed in the principality. It was a style of its own, a strong brew laced with cinnamon, cloves and ginger – all expensive spices in their day. In the year 901, the Bishop of Winchester, Denewulf, when leasing property from King Edward, had to pay 12 sesters of 'sweet Welsh ale' as part of his annual rent. It was not uncommon to make the sweetness by adding honey, and of course this style was prevalent before the introduction of the hop. From Henry VIII's time, the authorities insisted that beer should only be made from malt, hops, yeast and water and so the spiced Welsh Ale went rapidly into decline. Another ale from this early period was Gruit Ale which dates from about 1300. This was made with pale malt, carapils, sweet gale, marsh rosemary and yarrow, no hops, producing a strong ale in the region of 1080 OG.

Harvest Ales and Dinner Ales were both weak or 'small beers', drunk in large quantities. The former was for the workforce of labourers, while the latter was for the more 'refined'. Dinner Ale was more often bottled, whereas the Harvest Ales, produced for the farm workers, were always a draught beer. It was sometimes put in glass bottles when the workers collected it but it was drunk within several hours from collection. The more usual vessel for carrying the beer into the fields was a very small wooden cask. This was coopered, but held only three or four pints.

In the alehouse it was customary for beer to be mulled in the open fire and for this purpose a copper 'boot' or 'slipper' was used. This would be kept hanging on a hook beside the fire for general use. There was also a mulled ale whose recipe was: 'One quart of good ale, one glass of rum or brandy, one tablespoonful of caster sugar, a pinch of ground ginger. The method was to put the ale, sugar, cloves, nutmeg, and ginger into an ale-warmer or stewpan, and bring nearly to boiling point. Then add the brandy or rum, and more sugar and flavouring if necessary, and serve at once.' This recipe is taken from Mrs Beeton's *Household Management* of 1927, so from this it is clear that the warming of beer was still a common practice at that time. From the same source is the recipe for Hop Beer. The ingredients were 5 oz of hops, 8 gallons of water, 2½ lb of brown sugar and 3 or 4 tablespoonfuls of yeast. The method was to boil the hops and water together for 45 minutes, add the sugar and when dissolved strain into a bowl or tub. As soon as it is lukewarm, add the yeast and let it work for 48 hours, then skim well, and strain into bottles or a small cask. Cork securely and let it remain for a few days before drinking it.

Several ingredients were used from medieval times to the seventeenth century, for medicinal beers. Meadowsweet flowers were used in the Middle Ages and also coltsfoot, which made a medicinal beer called Cleats. Horehound Beer was made using horehound, and this was also used as a hop substitute. Cowslips, a readily available plant, made Cowslip Ale in the eighteenth century when the flowers were placed in a cask of beer for two weeks prior to bottling. Hyssop Ale was popular in the seventeenth century and another commonly found plant was horseradish, the root of which was used to make Scurvy Grass Ale. In Scotland the abundant heather made Heather Ale which has been reintroduced again after a very long time by one of the new micro-breweries. Dandelions have been used for at least 300 years to make Botanic Beer. Elderberries and its flowers have also been used, particularly in Porter.

Cumberland will be remembered for its ale known as Morocco, brewed at Levens Hall. Tradition has it that the brewing recipe was brought to this country by the returning crusaders. Everyone dining at the hall for the first time was required to drink a glass of the

ale, with the toast to the health of the Lady of Levens. The recipe was a secret, but it was believed that ox-blood or some form of meat was an ingredient of this strong brew. In the district of South Devon, stretching from Kingsbridge up to Tavistock, on the edge of Dartmoor, a strange and curious liquor known as White Ale was made. Again the full recipe was a secret held by only a few families, but its origins were ancient and the ale was subject to a local tax. White Ale was believed to have been made with malt, hops and a small quantity of flour, spices and a mysterious compound known as 'grout'. This grout evidently contained milk, gin and eggs. A more recent brewing of White Ale used a simplified recipe, with flour and eggs being added to the malt beer. A Dr Paul Karkeek, medical officer for Torquay, was quoted in 1877 as saying that, 'the beverage would soon be numbered among the things which had been'. He said that the appearance of White Ale was like that of tea, it was thick and there was a knack in drinking it so as to avoid leaving considerable sediment in the glass. The ale was likened to the old English Ale, in which it was necessary to tap the cask within four days of brewing. A curious fact is that at one time a tithe on White Ale was paid to the Rector of Dodbrooke. In about 1840 the local innkeepers combined together to resist this payment and the rector evidently no longer enforced his claim for the tithe payment.

Brewing vessels from the medieval times were made of two materials, timber and copper. Mash-tuns, fermenting vessels, storage vats, cooling trays and transportable casks were all made of timber. The most suitable timber was the native oak which was becoming in short supply in Queen Elizabeth's reign, due to heavy demands from shipbuilding and other growing industries. An alternative supply came from the Baltic regions and the port of Memel gave its name to oak from that area, which gradually replaced the British oak. When oak is cut correctly it is impervious to liquids, and so was an excellent medium to make vats and casks of all sizes. There were numerous shapes of brewing vats but the most commonplace was wider at the base than the open top. For shallow cooling trays sometimes softwoods were used in monasteries and estates, and these were later often lined with lead. A medieval example of this type exists at Laycock Priory, Wiltshire, dating from the sixteenth century. Cooling trays were to be replaced mainly during the Victorian era with copper, or the lead linings replaced with copper.

'Coppers', the now generic term used for the vessel in which liquor was heated to boiling point, was naturally made from this material. These were made in several sections of thick copper riveted together. Depending on the size, the sides would be made up of either two or three sections with a separate section for the base. The copper was built into brickwork or occasionally stone, with metal bars supporting the base. Some installations had a gap of a few inches all around the sides which allowed the heat from the fire below to pass around the entire heating surface. A turned over heavy lip also helped support the container which, when full, weighed a considerable amount. The furnace below held the fire area with metal bars, usually cast iron, and at the base was an ash pit. During the Victorian period many small brewers replaced previous

Medieval brewers rousing the mash-tun.

A Victorian mechanical mash-tun driven by belts and cog wheels.

coppers with cast iron. These were cast in one complete unit. Not all of these, however, incorporated an emptying tap or cock. In most coppers, particularly those made in the last hundred years, incorporated a heavy brass valve. Earlier taps were made of wood, and these have been used in stoneware bottles up until the 1930s.

Cast iron came into more general use, even in a few very small home-brewhouses such as at the Golden Lion, Southwick, Hampshire. Here mechanical treadles, powered by a series of bevel gears, wheels and belts, were installed for the mash-tun. With a small steam-powered horizontal engine, it became possible to mechanize even the smallest of breweries. Via various sizes of bevelled gears, drive-shafts, wheels and canvas belts, power was brought to all activities previously done by hand. Water could be pumped up from wells, sacks of malt and hops could be taken via a lucarne to the top storage floor, malt mills could be driven to grind the malt into a grist and the strenuous mashing of the grist and water in the mash-tun was able to be done mechanically. With these great Victorian advances, many small brewers boldly proclaimed that they were 'steam breweries'. Cast iron had arrived to make life easier for the brewer! Many of these bevel gears and drive-shafting installations would be made by local iron foundries and engineers. Boilers and horizontal engines were a more specialized installation, although most large regional towns had firms capable of this type of construction. There were brewery plant specialist firms and there were several in Burton-on-Trent. Likewise there were specialist firms for boring artesian wells, such as E. Timmins & Sons, of Runcorn, established in 1827, and Isler & Son. E. Potterton & Son of Villa Street, Birmingham, were brewers' engineers who not only made boilers but also brewing vessels. G.J. Worssam & Son of City Road, London, specialized in malt mills and mechanical bottling machines. One of the most renowned brewers' engineers was Robert Morton & Co. Ltd of Burton-on-Trent, who could manufacture and erect complete breweries. There were many others, all readily available to the small brewer, but most, however, used local firms. In the nineteenth century every town with a population of over several thousand people was able to support several coopers, wheelwrights, saddle and harness makers, plumbers, and in some cases, an iron foundry. An example of this was the city of Winchester which had a population in 1821 of 5,165 inhabitants and where these traders would be required by the home-brewer. There were three coopers, two wheelwrights, four saddlers and harness makers (including an ancestor of the author, a

Robert Peaty, at 123 High Street), three plumbers, five braziers and tin-plate workers. There was also the Hyde iron foundry in the late nineteenth century. On average there was one cooper for every 1,100 of the populace.

In country districts local agricultural engineers were able to carry out intricate work. At Coggeshall in Essex, in the 1930s, James Potter & Son carried out full inspections and repairs to the several small local brewery firms' equipment. From renewing a mercury tube to the boiler thermometer of E. Gardners & Sons Brewery, for £1 5s 0d in 1935, to cleaning out the boiler for the annual inspection by the insurance company inspector, nothing was too much for the local tradesmen. The chance for a local workman to carry out a job at the brewhouse would be too good to pass by; who could resist the opportunity to have a few quaffs of free ale as a reward?

An invoice sent to the Old Cross Brewery, Hertford, in August 1831, by Pontifax & Sons & Wood, well illustrates the costs of setting up a small common brewery of the time:

Plan of Brewery	£5-5-0
Copper with cock (10cwt)	69-9-6
Securing the bottom of the cock	10-0
Ironwork fix bricks and Welsh Lumps (coal)	28-0-0
One Wort Iron panned for cock	5-0
A set of Pumps for Liquor & Wort	32-0-0
A Hollow Key 3 way Cock for bottom Pump, 25ft of copper pipe to go to well and 20ft of copper pipe	12-0-0
Horse Wheel for 15ft Track with Carriages draught arms, Yoke with bevil house wheel & 2 bevil nuts to work into bevil house	32-0-0
A mashing machine for a 7ft tun with 10ft horizontal shaft & top wheels – labour of fixing Horizontal Shaft to Pump, pair of Clutch Boxes	9-0-0
Pair of small Bolts with Cart framing top hopper & screen in the same & a pair of spur wheels wood and iron	50-0-0
	£238-9-6

The Coopers' Company was in existence in London in 1440, but for a craft guild to have full control over its members, it was necessary for each guild to have a royal charter. Henry VII granted the coopers their charter in 1501 and it became thirty-sixth out of eighty-nine guilds. Their coat of arms has a red and black quartered background with three gold 'hoops', a gold chevron with two coopers' adzes. The Brewers' Guild, correctly known as the 'Warden and Commonalty of the Mistery of Brewers of the City of London', was fourteenth

Sixteenth century coopers at work.

in the order of ranking. They received their charter in 1292. The Brewers' Guild coat of arms is three bunches of two crossed stooks of barley, with a chevron in which there are three 'tuns', supported by ears of barley on the left and hops twining round poles on the right. The motto is 'In God is all our Trust'.

An Act of Parliament passed by Henry VIII in 1531–2 defined cask sizes for beer. This was the hogshead at 54 gallons, the barrel at 36 gallons, the kilderkin at 18 gallons and the firkin at 9 gallons. The smallest measure was a pin, at 4½ gallons. For ale the sizes were 32, 16 and 8 gallons. To indicate the contents of these casks, records show that when the monks brewed at Sherborne Abbey, Dorset (and many other abbeys and priories) they marked the heads of casks with signs of the cross. One X meant that the ale was very weak and suitable for children and young persons (small beer), two Xs was ale suitable for women, and three Xs was for men (strong beer). Over many centuries the strength of brews increased, with four Xs being required. H&G Simmonds, common brewers of Reading, even bottled a strong ale with five Xs on the label!

In addition to the branding on the heads of the casks with the beer quality, branding irons came into regular use by coopers during the nineteenth century. Each cask was given a number and the owning brewery's name. Also the bung hole at the 'belly' of each cask received a metal bush, made of cast brass, on which the owner's name and town appeared. The largest coopering firm in England in 1810 was John Chippendale of London and Bristol (the latter port because of the high imports of wine and sherry). This firm also made brewing vats. The prices of casks in the mid-eighteenth century were butts at 16s each, hogsheads at 7s and barrels at 6s each.

It was essential that as soon as a wooden cask had been emptied of its contents, it was corked and pegged. This was to prevent the ingress of any insects and to keep the timber moist. Failure to seal the cask would mean that it could dry out, also it would become a 'stinker' due to the sediment left in the bottom of the cask, consisting of hops and yeast and the remains of the wood bung. Should a cask be detected as a 'stinker' by the brewery 'smeller', who sniffed each cask after cleaning, then it would be returned to the cooper to be broken down and shaved clean. Should spare casks be idle in quiet times, they were washed and stacked in the yard, having received a small quantity of bisulphate of lime. To prevent drying out, casks would be sprayed with water in hot summer months although this was not often necessary, due to the peak time when casks were used.

Fuel for the copper furnace would have been gathered locally from the hedgerows and woods. Cut into suitable lengths, referred to as 'faggots' or 'billets', this method of heating water had been in use for centuries. Only with the coming of the railways in the 1840s did this allow for cheap coal to reach everywhere. Each local railway station had its goods yard, where one or two coal merchants supplied the needs of industry and the households. Many coal merchants, such as Thomas Moy Ltd who had seven depots in London and forty-nine in East Anglia, were able to supply any quantity of the required grade of fuel. Steam coal, for boilers, cost £1 12s 6d per ton in 1934, and was delivered to the most remote of country brewhouses.

Besides the wooden casks previously mentioned for transporting beer, the other commonly used container was the stoneware jar. Stoneware jars came in several sizes, the largest holding 2 gallons down to the smallest holding half a pint. The London firm of Doulton of Lambeth were by far the most prolific manufacturer of these jars. They were glazed inside and out with a single heavy-duty handle on the shoulder. The sloping top and 'bell-mouth' were in a ginger-brown glaze, while the remaining body of the straight sided jar was a pale stone colour. It was normal for the ownership details to be either transferred on or done in deep-cut lettering. Occasionally an applied cartouche with simple decorations was applied to the shoulder. More elaborate transfers, including company logos and coats of arms, were used by large brewery companies. For the small retail brewer or publican brewer, he would have his name and initials followed by the name of the pub or brewery, and underneath that, of the town or village. The narrow mouth was sealed with a cork and at the base there was usually a hole in which a small brass or wood tap could be inserted. These 2-gallon stoneware jars were ideal for the family trade, with the smaller sizes being used by farmworkers. A few types of stoneware jar were made with a metal carrying handle strapped around the neck. Stoneware jars remained in use up until the 1950s, as well as being impervious, they were easily cleaned and reused, being of very stout construction. Many examples may still be found in antique shops and continue to reveal often previously unknown home-brew pubs. Many were encased in a protective cane sheath. Their share in the container market started to decline, having to face the competition from the introduction of glass in the 1850s. However, for the majority of retail and publican brewers, this was not a problem, as stoneware jars could hold larger quantities of draught beer, and few embarked on the glass bottling of their beers.

Beer, when first bottled in the seventeenth century, was in bottles similar to the wine bottles of the day. They had long necks which used wired-on corks as a closure. By the 1820s a squat-shaped form was in use, these being handmade in three sections from a mould. The beer was the same as the draught beer and is known as bottle conditioned, which meant that it continued to ferment in the bottle and improved with age. Heavy glass taxes prevented its more general use, until this was repealed in 1845, when it became more economical to bottle beer. From the earlier three-moulded glass bottle, developments reduced this to two moulds with applied 'blob' necks for the cork closure. The method of fixing the corks into the bottle neck was done by hand. A leather gaiter called the 'boot' was strapped to the top of the thigh, in which the bottle was placed and leather strap was used to hammer home the cork; this contraption was called the 'boot and flogger'.

A leather 'boot and flogger' used to cork seal bottles.

The colour of the glass at this time was primarily dark green and dark brown, this was to prevent exposure of the beer to sunlight which, over a period of time, has a detrimental effect on its quality. By 1875 the still familiar swing stopper came into use, where a ceramic 'plug' with a rubber washer on a wire frame held the contents in. Also at this time the internal screw-thread stopper was in use, with either a milled edge or flat pinched projection for screwing the lid up tight.

Moulded bottles up to this time had embossed lettering and often the brewer's logo device, all excellent forms of advertising. Beer labels first came into use in about 1862 at the time of one of the many beer competitions held in Europe. Both Bass and Allsopps, the two premier Burton brewers, were early exponents of the labelling of their bottled beer. Guinness in a bottle was advertised as such in the early 1880s to be closely followed by Whitbread's, although Guinness almost certainly had been in the forefront in the 1860s.

In 1892, an American, William Painter, introduced the Crown Cork to this country. This is the flat crimped metal closure in use today, and revolutionized the packaging of beer. Bottle sizes have varied over the years, with quart bottles used in the 1930s for the off-sales trade. Imperial pints were the general size in use for a long period leading up to the 1950s, when the general shape now in use was adopted. One or two micro-breweries have reintroduced the use of the imperial pint sized bottle including the Chiltern Brewery's Three Hundreds Old Ale, also bottling by Holden's Brewery, West Midlands, and the now defunct Heritage Brewery Museum, Burton-on-Trent, for their range of beers.

To speed up the bottling process in the 1880s, the firm of Farrow & Jackson, of London and Paris, introduced a syphonic bottle-filling machine. This was a cast-iron frame with a side handle giving an adjustable height. A copper trough received beer from the cask. An elongated shallow 'S'-shaped copper tube, with a lead weight over the trough, had the open spout end which was put into the neck of the empty bottle. The bottle, being below the level of the trough of beer, allowed the syphonic action to fill either four or six bottles at a time. The establishment of this firm in Paris indicates that the syphon bottle filler was also used for wine. During the late nineteenth century, carbonization, pasteurization and filtration came into general practice. This process made the beer clear and sparkling, stable and inert and therefore gave bottled beer a longer shelf life. This comparatively expensive form of bottling was outside the scope of most smaller brewers, who confined themselves to bottle-conditioned bottling. Many smaller brewers ceased bottling in the late 1920s and 1930s.

As will have been noted, the 1960s was a very productive decade in which many special bottlings took place. Most of these were by the larger common brewers, but of special interest were the bottled beers with religious connections. Pulloxhill Church Ale was produced by both Whitbread and Thomas Wethered of Marlow for the Chequers Inn, Pulloxhill, probably to raise funds for the church repairs, organized by the landlord of the pub. Eldridge Pope & Co. Ltd of Dorchester, Dorset, brewed and bottled Sherborne Abbey Ale in a nip-sized bottle. In both these cases, the close affinity between the church and inn as centres of the community have worked closely together, just as many have done so for hundreds of years.

No greater compliment can be made other than by imitation, and during the 1960s many medium and smaller regional brewers produced 'home-brewed' bottled beer. Among these were Arnold & Hancock of Wiveliscombe; Arkells of Swindon; Felinfoel Brewery, Llanelli; Gray & Son, Chelmsford; Home Brewery, Daybrook; Wadworth's of Devizes; Brains, Cardiff; T. Hoskins, Leicester, and many now defunct regional brewers. Mr Stanley James King, of J.K. King, brewers of Coggeshall, Essex, wrote in January 1885 the following notes on bottling ale: 'Great care should be taken to have the bottles perfectly clean. After cleansing, by means of a bottle-washer, or if done by hand, shotting them, rinse them repeatedly afterwards with clear water. Let them drain dry. Use the best corks, as a poor quality will soon permit the escape of gas, and the ale is flat, insipid and worthless. Drive the cork in as soon as the bottle is filled, and do not let the filled bottle stand open. Three-quarters or more of the length of the cork (about 1¼ inch is the best size) should enter the neck of the bottle. Soften the corks in hot water or steam them previous to driving. Leave half an inch clear space between the cork and the ale; and the hose or siphon should be arranged so as to prevent frothing by leading the liquid to the side of the bottle and not perpendicular allowing the ale to stick to the bottom. Frothing of the ale should be avoided, as it causes loss of gas. Ale is best bottled between 5 and 9 months old. The writer has kept ale bottled at six months old for ten years, and then found it mild and in great perfection, and weighing five pounds, or one-such of its original gravity. The bottles were kept in an upright position the great part of the time. It was bottled at 6 pounds gravity. In general, ale should become attenuated to one-fifth of its original gravity before bottling. It's seldom then that any reduction of gravity will occur after the ale is bottled. Those who prefer ale of a sweet flavour can bottle it sooner, and at a heavier gravity. The bottles should be kept standing upright in the cellar, and not lying on the sides, as is sometimes noticed in bottled storage cellars. When opened, be careful not to disturb the sediment at the bottom of the bottle [yeast]; and the consumer should be informed of this important fact. Ale should be bottled at least three months before it is drunk. When opened it should be highly charged with gas, but not violently so, less it cause a disturbance of the sediment at the bottom of the bottle. The remnant of ale in a cask is not so well adapted for bottling if it has become at all flat. The real secret, if any there be, of an excellent bottled ale depends, next to using none but a well brewed article, on a proper ripening which is effected only by lapsed time and intelligent handling.' As an addendum, possibly gleaned from another source, Mr King wrote: 'One of the most essential points in reference to the bottling of beer turns upon the absolute dryness of the bottle itself; and we are informed on the best authority that it takes 10 or 14 days for bottles to become absolutely dry, even when kept in an atmosphere of about 75°. If this precaution be not taken, the deposit of bottled beer shows a strange tendency to adhere to the sides of the bottle in place of gravitating to the bottom, so that it is perfectly impossible to draw off the contents bright. Moisture again facilitates the formation of mould, so that bottle drying constitutes an essential feature of the "bottler's preliminary process".'

Most of the information is valid today except that now very few home-brewers use corks. Bottles today are supplied plastic shrink-wrapped, sterile and dry. How much easier this part of the job has become.

Inn Brewing Limited, of Chalfont St Giles, Bucks, provided a full range of equipment for home-brew installation in 1984. A full mash system, including a malt mill at an additional cost of £4,600, cost £10,000 for a 4-barrel per week plant with a brew length of 2 barrels. A 10-barrel per week plant with 2 gyles of 5 barrels each cost £15,500. These two prices were based on a typical wort concentrate plant. The same firm also gave the following produce costing to yield 5 barrels of beer at an OG of 1040.5.

Wort Concentrate	£61.43
Hops	£5.80
Liquor Treatment	£1.32
Yeast	£2.50
Finings	£4.69
Energy	£12.88
Water	£0.36
Duty	£253.28
Cleaning Materials	£0.58
Shives and Keystones	£2.10
	£344.99

No labour and depreciation charges were included. By comparison the wholesale cost of a barrel of standard Bitter was £105. The production cost per barrel of home-brew was £69, giving a saving of £36. Based on this calculation, a weekly trade of 7½ barrels (390 barrels per annum) gave an improved profit margin of £14,000 a year, and double that figure for a plant producing 15 barrels a week (780 barrels per annum). Incentive enough to go into commercial home-brewing.

S. Briggs & Co. Ltd of Burton-on-Trent claim to be one of this country's oldest engineering businesses, having absorbed several competitors in the town during the past 250 years. The most notable of these companies to be absorbed was Thornewill & Warham who could trace their founding to 1732, when Thomas Thornewill was an edge toolmaker. Steady growth over the years in supplying tools, pumps and engines to the many breweries in Burton led to a partnership with J.R. Warham in 1849. At this time the business was described as an engineers, ironfounders and iron merchants. In the early 1860s the firm had supplied sixteen steam railway locomotives to breweries for their private railway systems. In 1929 S. Briggs purchased the company, as it complimented the engineering that Samuel Briggs had learnt from 1865 as an apprentice to Thomas C.

Bindley in the High Street. Briggs married Bindley's daughter and became a partner in the Burton Copper Works, supplying copper and brass equipment to the Burton breweries. During the period 1880–1900 the firm expanded considerably, both in the variety and volume of the work undertaken for large and small breweries. In 1900 S. Briggs & Co. had latterly been the brewery premises of the Burton and Lincoln Brewery Co., who had gone into liquidation the previous year. In 1863 a John Dickenson had a brewery erected; he entered into partnership with brewer William Nicholls of Burton. Dickinson & Co., one of the smaller breweries of Burton, were unable to repay their mortgage and so by 1872, Edwin Dawson, a brewer from Leeds, had acquired the premises. Dawson sold the business in 1890–1 to the Burton and Lincoln Brewery Co., who were in financial difficulties by 1896, and so merged with Albion Brewery Ltd.

Modern brewing copper in a Firkin Brewery home-brew pub in Hertford.

In 1912, S. Briggs & Co. purchased the firm Buxton & Thornley, an engineering firm established in about 1860, who were noted for making steam-pumps, turning machines and a wide range of brewery equipment. In March 1988 Briggs acquired the fabrication and project management business of Robert Morton D.G. in Burton-upon-Trent. This company was a direct competitor to the then new stainless-steel fabrication and construction business, from the design and building of brewhouses and brewery process plant. This joint company is now the UK leader in quality stainless-steel fabrication and construction for the process industries. Briggs of Burton PLC, located at the Trent Works, Derby Street, is the site of Robert Morton & Co. Ltd, who in July 1960 drew plans for a quarter brewing plant for a development brewery. This was subsequently built in a two-storey white-painted brick building with a first floor projecting girder arm above double doors. The wort copper was of 5-barrel capacity, as was the wort receiver. The hop-back between had a capacity of 4 ½ barrels and the single fermenting vessel contained 4 barrels. The mash-tun held 2 barrels and above this, the grist case held 4 bushels of malt. The entire experimental plant was housed on the top floor, with racking being carried out by gravity feed on the ground floor. This has now been dismantled for a number of years but had it remained, the company would no doubt have benefited from the resurgence of the micro-breweries in the 1970s and 1980s. At least the company was very forward thinking when the development brewery was built in the early 1960s.

Today the renaissance of the micro-brewers has also brought back many bottle-conditioned beers. Even some of the smallest have introduced one or two in addition to their excellent cask-conditioned draught beers. The revival of the small brewer is on the ascendancy and long may it be so. The clock is coming round full circle, taking us back to the early days when brewing started on a small scale. The micro-brewers provide a superb range of beers with local tastes in mind and for the imbiber of what was once a rarity, the home-brewed beer, fortune now smiles upon him. 'To quaff an English ale is to drink in this country's history, its products of the soil, its very heart. It enriches the very well being of the soul; what more could one ask of a humble pint of beer?'

'He that buys good ale, buys nothing else': nineteenth-century Doulton ale jug.

GLOSSARY

ABV – Alcohol By Volume.

ALE – Alcoholic liquor made with malt and no hops.

ALVAUM – a trough.

AMERCED – To punish by fine fixed by the court.

ATTENUATE – To make thin or fine.

BARREL – A cask which holds 36 gallons.

BARZISSA – worte.

BERE/BEYRE – Beer. Malt alcoholic liquor with hops.

BOOT & FLOGGER – A leather gaiter tied to the thigh and a hammer to insert a cork for bottling.

BOTTLE CONDITIONED – Beer that is live and has a secondary fermentation in the bottle.

BRASIATRIX – a brewster.

BRASIUM – malt.

BRUYNGE – Brewing.

BURUEHOWSSE/BRUEHOWSE/BRUH OWS – Brewhouse.

BUTRY/BUTREY/BUTTREY/BUTARY – Buttery, a room where beer is stored.

BUSHEL – Equal to 4 pecks or 8 gallons (a bushel was also known as a strike).

BUTT – A cask that held varying quantities, from 108 to 180 gallons.

CALDERIUM – cauldron.

CAPPEL BOOTHES – Portable shop or booth in which beer was sold.

CASK CONDITIONED – Live beer which has a secondary fermentation in the cask.

CAUDLE – A warm drink given to rich people.

CAULDRON – A container of 36 bushels (28.8 gallons).

CESTERNE – Cistern or reservoir for steeping barley, or for water storage.

CIMA, A KYUNELL – wash tub.

COMMON BREWER – One who wholesales beer to publicans and produces more than 1,000 barrels per annum.

COOMBE – Four bushels or half a quarter (coombe) of malt.

COULS/COULLES/COWLES/COWLE RS – A cooling tray of wood, sometimes lined with lead.

CRONN – Half a quarter of malt.

CUVELLA – a small tub.

DRAGIUM – grains.

FATTE – Vat or large open wood container.

FIRKIN/VIRKYN – A cask which holds 9 gallons.

FORNAX – a furnace.

GAWDY DAY – Religious feast day.

GILL – Measure of capacity containing the fourth part of a pint.

GROWTE – Ground malt or grist ready for brewing.

GUILE/GYLE – A single brewing of beer (a batch).

HIKKESTER – Itinerant or travelling beer-seller.

HOGSHEAD – Cask which holds 54 gallons.

JETS – Large ladle for emptying vats. A tap.

JORUM – A large drinking vessel.

KELER/KEELER – A wood coopered vessel with three legs.

KILDERKIN/KIDERKYN – A cask which holds 18 gallons.

KNEDYNGE TROUGH – Kneading trough for mixing bread dough, or a wash tub.

LAST – A last of beer is 12 barrels. Also a measure of malt or grain in the sixteenth century – 12 quarters, but now 10 quarters, that is 80 bushels.

LING – Heather used in bottom of mash-tun to prevent clogging of tap.

LIQUOR – Brewers term for water.

LOAD – Equal to 5 quarters (200 gallons).

MALTODE – Medieval malt tax.

MARK – Currency or coin (originally a German coin).

MASH TUN/TUB – Vessel in which the malt 'grist' is mixed with water to make wort.

MOLA – a quern/handmill.

NOGGIN – Measure equal to a gill; a small drinking vessel.

OG – Original Gravity; indication of alcoholic strength

PECK – A liquid and dry measure equal to 2 gallons.

PIN/PIPKYN – Smallest cask size which holds 4½ gallons.

PIPE – A cask which holds half a tun, or two hogsheads.

PITCHING – Putting hops or yeast into a vat.

POKIS/POCKET – A long hessian sack for hops (weighs 2½ cwt, about 6 ft 6 ins long).

POTTLE – A measure of 4 pints (2 quarts).

PRUERA – heather.

PUNCHEON – A cask containing between 72 to 120 gallons.

QUART – 2 pints.

QUARTER – 8 bushels equal to 64 gallons.

QUERN – Hand mill used for grinding corn or malt.

RACK – To fill a cask with beer.

REPUTED PINT – One twelfth part of a gallon; imperial pint is (⅛) of a gallon

RUNLIT/RUNDLET – A small cask that holds 18 gallons (kilderkin).

SELLER – Cellar for beer storage, not always underground.

SHIVE – Wood 'plug' in cask hole in which the tap is driven. The 'bung-hole' is the hole in the cask through which it is filled then, in cask-conditioned beers, a vent peg is driven.

STALE ALE – Strong ale or beer.

STILLAGE – Low wood trestle or built up brick/stone base on which beer casks are placed in a buttery or cellar.

TABERDAS – Poor boys (as at Oxford University colleges).

TARANTARUM – a sieve.

TILDER – A triangular frame used to tilt a cask on stillage when the level of beer is getting low.

TIPPLE – To drink alcohol regularly without being drunk.

TIPPLER – One who sells beer.

TUN – A container of various sizes used in brewing.

TUNNED – Racked or filled casks of beer.

WILSH – A wickerwork or straw mat to prevent grains being lost via the tap in the mash-tun.

BIBLIOGRAPHY

Allen, B. *Morrells of Oxford*, 1994

Barber, N. *A Century of British Brewers, 1890–1990*, 1994

Barnard, A. *Noted Breweries of Great Britain and Ireland*, 1890

Beeton, Mrs *Household Management*, 1927

Bell, J., Jones, G. and Martin, J. *Oasthouses in Ewhurst Parish*, 1988

Bikerdyke, J. *The Curiosities of Ale and Beer*

Boggis, Revd R.J.E. *A History of St Augustine's Monastery*, 1901

Bowerman, D. *Historic Thames Valley Taverns*, 1976

Brewery History, the journal of the Brewery History Society, various

Brewer's Journal: various

Brewing Review, The Brewer's Society, 1981

Burke's Peerage, 1904

Clarke, A. *Register of the University of Oxford*, Vol. 1, Part 1, 1887

Clerk and Willis, *Architectural History of the University of Cambridge*, 1886

Cobbett, William, *Cottage Economy*, 1821

Cook, A.K. *About Winchester College*, 1917

Coppack, G. *Abbeys and Priories*, 1990

—.*Mount Grace Priory*, English Heritage, 1991

Coysh, A.W. *Historic English Inns*, 1972

Evans, M.L. *Llanerchaeron, A Brief History*

Goodley, G. and Moynihan, P. *Westerham Ales*, 1991

Gwilt, C.F. *Inns and Alehouses of Bridgnorth*

Hedges, A.A.C. *Bottles and Bottle Collecting*, 1975

Holmes, R. *Ely Inns*, 1984

Howells, B. *A Short History of Stackpole*

Jekyll G. *Old English Household Life*, 1925

Jennings, P. *Inns, Ales and Drinking Customs of Old England*, 1987

Kelly's Directories: various

Kemp, R.A. *The Legends and History of Britain's Oldest Inn*, 1994

Keverne, R. *Tales of Old Inns*, 1939

Mashell, H.P. *The Taverns of Old England*, 1927

Megrath, J.R. *Queen's College 1341–1646*, Vol. I

—.*Queen's College 1646–1877*, Vol. II

Meriton, G. *The Praise of York-shire Ale*, 1684

Monckton, H.A. *A Historical Survey of English Ale, Beer and Public Houses*, 1968

Patton, J. *Additives, Adulterants and Contaminants in Beer*, 1989

Peaty, I. *Essex Brewers: The Malting and Hop Industries of the County*, 1992

Pigot & Cos National Commercial Directories, 1830

Richards, J. *A History of Holden's Black Country Brewery*, 1986

——.*The History of Batham's Black Country Brewers*, 1993

Ritchie B. *An Uncommon Brewer. The Story of Whitbread, 1742–1992*, 1992

Robinson, P.W. *The Emergence of the Common Brewer in the Halifax District*, 1980

Ross, B. and Searle, E. *Accounts of the Cellarers of Battle Abbey, 1275–1513*, 1967

Steer, F. *Archives of New College*, Oxford, 1974

——. *Farm and Cottage Inventories, 1635–1749*

The Brewer's Assistant, 1915

The Licensed Victuallers Official Annual, 1940

The Manual of British and Foreign Brewery Companies, 1924

Tusser, T. *His Good Points of Husbandry*, 1557

Victoria County Histories

Warren, W.T. *Winchester Illustrated*, 1905

Willis. *History of the Monastery of Christ Church*, Canterbury

Woodriff, C.E. *Schola Regia Cantueriensis*, 1908

INDEX

Acts of Parliament 10, 11, 12, 40, 129, 134, 153, 155, 201
additives and adulterants 4, 19, 24, 48, 62, 34, 90, 191, 193, 194, 197
Adnams, Southwold 1
ale-conner 26, 29
alewives/brewster 29, 46, 186
Alford Arms, Frithesden 174
Alfred Beer & Co., Canterbury 42
Allied Domecq 2, 176
All Nations, Madeley 136, 137, *137*, 195
All Souls' College, Oxford 45, 48, 55
Alloa Brewery Co. 176
Alnwick Abbey 20, 114
Alnwick Brewery Co. 114
Alswick Hall, Layston 79, *79*
architects 80, 82, 102–4, 107, 117–19, 134, 152, 158, 177, 200
Arkells, Swindon 1, 204
Arnold & Hancocks, Wivelscombe 180, 204
Assize of Bread and Ale 25, 44, 57, 129
Audley End, Essex 118–21, *119*

Balliol College, Oxford 55
barley 10, 26, 73, 74, 83, 101, 104, 131, 187–9, 201
Barnsley Brewery 95, 96, 98
Bass, Ratcliff & Gretton, Burton 2, 40, 49, 51, 55, 68, 138, 194, 203
Batemans, Wainfleet 1
Bath Brewery Co. 158
Battle Abbey, Sussex 28, 122, 124
Beacon Brewery, Oakhill 180
Beacon Hotel, Dudley 182, *184*
beer styles
    Audit Ale 54, 55, *58*, 59, 60, 195
    barley wine 59, 193
    Beer Ale 101
    Botanic Beer 191, 197
    bitter 50, 51, 174, 183, 194
    Brasenose Ale 48
    Bride Ale 195
    Chancellor Ale 50, 51, 53
    Centenary Ale 68
    college ales 51
    Church Ale 195, *196*, 204
    dinner ale 59, 184, 196
    Election Beer 64, 65
    Harvest Ale *9*, 128, 153, 196
    Honey Sop 24
    lager 67, 172
    Lord Anson's Ale 107
    March Beer 112, 113, 192
    Mild 136, 138, 146, 150, 171, 180, 193, 195
    Morocco Ale 197, *197*
    Nut Brown Ale 42, 193
    Old Ale/Beer 49, 55, 150, 157, 171, 193
    ordinary beer 27, 63–5
    Old Tom 106
    Pale Ale (IPA) 59, 168, 180, 193, 194
    Porter 164, 174, 189
    Scotch Ale 192
    Stingo 176, 194, 196
    Stout 13, 51, 59, 144, 153, 189, 193
    Traquair House Ale *101*, 194
    White Ale 197, 198
    Yorkshire Ale 194
Bell Brewhouse, Shoreditch 193
Benskins Brewery, Watford 158
Berden Priory, Essex 37, *39*
Bird-in-Hand, Stone 166
Black Bull, Derby 183
Black Friars Inn, London 124, *124*
Black Sheep Brewery, Masham 180
Blue Anchor, Helston 136, 138, *139*, 194
Boat Inn, Ashleworth Quay 154, *155*, 155
Boot & Flogger 202, *203*
Bowling Green Inn, Ribbleton 166
Branscombe Valley Brewery 183
Brasenose College, Oxford 46–8
Brecon Brewery Ltd 180
brewery engineers 199, 200, 205, 206
Brewery Farm, Polstead 74
Brewers' Society/Brewers' Guild 44, 45, 165, 166, 168, 200
brewing equipment
    hop-back 49, 66, 141

keeler 118, 191

under-back 70, 82, 117, 171, 192

grist mill/grist case 28, 49, 66, 75, 113, 143, 153, 168, 171, 183, 199, 206

Briggs S. & Co., Burton 205, 206

Bristol Brewery Georges Co. Ltd 158

Britannia Inn, Upper Gornal 149 *149*, 150

Burton Bridge Brewery, Burton 173, *173*, 174, *174*, 193

Buckingham College, Cambridge 57

Caius College, Cambridge 59

Calke Abbey, Derbyshire 107–11, *109*

CAMRA ix, 141, 172, 174, 183

Carlisle & District State Management Scheme 3

Carpenters Row, Coalbrookdale 70

cellerer 14, 17, 20, 27, 28, *28*, 29, 39, 40

Charlecote House, Warwickshire 114, 115, *115*

Charles Wells, Bedford 68

Charrington & Co. Ltd, London 2, 145

Chatsworth House, Bakewell 101–3, *103*

Chiltern Brewery 183, 203

Christ Church College, Oxford 55

Christ Church Priory, Canterbury 14, *16*, 18, *18*

Clare College, Cambridge 59

Clarksons Brewery, Barnsley 87, 94

Clinch & Co., Witney ix

coaching inns 126–9, 161

Cobbs Brewery, Margate 180

Combes Brewery, Brockhampton 131–3, *131, 133, 134, 135*

coopers 2, 50, 63, 199, 200, 201, *201*

Corpus Christi College, Cambridge 57, 57, 59

Corpus Christi College, Oxford 47

Cotleigh Brewery, Wivelscombe 180

Courage, Bristol 158, 159, 168, 175, 180

Cricketers Arms, Basford 147, 148, *148*

Crown Inn, Northill *156*, 156, 157

Crown Inn, Walsall 148, 149

Dales Brewery, Cambridge 60, *60*

Daniel Batham, Brierley Hill x, 11

Davenports, Birmingham 176, 179

Defence of the Realm Act (DORA) 3, 11

Dog & Parrot, Newcastle 176

Donnington Brewery, Stow-on-the-Wold 38

drinking vessels

  Black Jack 5, 22, 63, 112

  Costrels 7

  Frog Mugs 10, 55

  Glass 10

  Mazer 10

  Mocca 9, 10

  Mugs 7, 10, 23, 29, 76

  Peg Tankards 9, 55

  Pewter

  Pitchers 6, 188

  Posset Pots 9, *9*

  Puzzle Jugs 8

  Tankards 8, 9, *9*, 10, 28, 107, 125, 153, 188

  Trick Glasses 10

  Whistling Jugs 55

  Yard of Ale 8

East India Company 66

Eldridge Pope Ltd, Dorchester 204

Emmanuel College, Cambridge 59

Engine Row, Coalbrookdale 71

Enville Ales 184

Eton College, Windsor 58, 60, 62–6, *64*

Excise Duty 3, 10, 12, 34, 37, 38, 46, 50, 53, 87, 88, 129, 134, 136, 166, 188

Exeter College, Oxford 47, 55

Farmers Arms, Apperley 174, *175*

Felinfoel Brewery, Llanelli 204

Finings 95

Firkin Brewery 175

Fleece, Inn, Bretforton 8, 10, 153

Flints Brewery, Canterbury 180

Fox Brewery, Bishops Stortford 157, 158

Fox Hunt Brewery, Old Hill 165

Friary, The, Bridgnorth 35

Frog & Parrot Brewhouse, Sheffield 176

Fletchers House, Woodstock 115, 116

Gardner & Son, Coggeshall 200

Garrowby, Yorkshire 83, 84, 88, 94, 96, 99

George & Dragon, Much Wenlock 161–4, *162, 163*

Glenny Brewery, Witney 9, 180

Golden Hill Brewery, Wivelscombe 180

Golden Lion, Southwick 167–9, *167, 168, 169*, 199

Gorrells Farm, Highwood 74, *75, 76*

Grafton Brewery, Cheltenham 132

Gray & Son, Chelmsford 74, 129, 204

Greene King, Bury St Edmunds 60, 77, 157

Guest House 14, 19, 20, 21, 22, 25, 41, 43, 114, 122, 125

Guinness, A. & Son, Dublin 13, 54, 138, 180, 193, 194, 203

Haileybury College, Gt Amwell 66, 67, *67*

Halls Brewery, Oxford 46, 55, 175

Hambledon Ales, Thirsk 183

Hansons Brewery, Dudley 140

Hawkes Brewery, Bishops Stortford 158

Hellewell, Clarence 84, 88–99

Heritage Brewery, Cardiff 176

Hickleton Hall, Yorkshire 83–99, *86, 93, 100*, 107

Highgate Brewery, Walsall 142

Hogs Back Brewery, Tongham 183

Holt, Plant & Deakin Ltd, Langley 175

Home Brewery, Daybrook 1, 204

home-brew kits 11, 131, 132, *134*, 144

Hook Norton Brewery 1

hop oasthouses 159, *160*, 189

horsepower/horse-gins 26, 37, *38, 39*, 49, 113

Hoskins, T. Ltd, Leicester 1, 141, 204

Hospice 122, 125, 126, 160

Ind, Coope & Co., Burton and Romford 2, 40, 111, 128, 173

Ind Coope & Allsopp Ltd 128

Ingatestone Hall, Essex 111–14

Jesus College, Cambridge 57

John Smiths, Tadcaster 87, 98

Joseph Watkins & Co., Dublin 41

Kelham Island Brewery, Sheffield 175

Kimbolton Castle, Huntingdonshire 116–18, *117, 118*

Kings College, Cambridge 57, 60

Laycock Priory, Wiltshire 29–32, *29, 30, 31, 32, 33*, 198

Lansdowne Arms, Calne *127*, 127, 128

Lincoln College, Oxford 47, 55

Linfit Brewery, Linthwaite 180

Little & Son, Slaughterford 130, *130*

Llanaeron House, Llanaeron 80

Lordship, The, Cottered *78*, 79

Magdalen College, Oxford 45, 46, 55

Magdalene College, Cambridge 59

Marston, Thompson & Evershed Ltd, Burton and Winchester 23, 41

Merton College, Oxford 55

Methuen Arms, Corsham 126, 161

Meux Brewery, London 164

Mitchells & Butlers Ltd, Birmingham 2, 49, 54, 68

Moorhouses Brewery, Blackburn 184

Morland Brewery, Abingdon 133

Morrells, Lion Brewery, Oxford 52, *52*, 54–6.

Moulton Chapel Brewery, Spalding 165

Mount Grace Priory, Yorkshire 20, 21, *21*

Nailsworth Brewery, Stroud 132

National Trust 80, 101, 107, 154, 183

Nelson Inn, Armley, Leeds 144, 145, *145*, 146

New College, Oxford 55, 56, 61

Nuffield College, Oxford 55

Old Hornchurch Brewery, Essex 7

Old Swan (Ma Pardoes), Netherton 136, 139–41, *140*

Offilers Brewery, Derby 111, 145

Orange Brewery, Pimlico 174

Oriel College, Oxford 47

Ostrich, Colnbrook 160, 161

Palmer, J.C. & R.H, Bridport, 1, 38

Peterhouse College, Cambridge 57, 60

Phipps & Co, Northampton 157

Plympton Brewery, Devon 175

Portcullis Inn, Badminton *170*, 170–72

Portsmouth United Breweries 168

Prittlewell Priory, Essex 26

Puzzle Hall Inn, Sowerby Bridge 150, *150, 151, 152, 152*, 153

Queens' College, Cambridge 58

Queen's College, Oxford 5, 35, 45, 49, *51, 52, 53*, 55

Radcliffe Infirmary, Oxford 12

recipes 48, 59, 76, 105, 183, 192, 194, 196, 197

Redruth Brewery, Cornwall 138

Rowleys House, Shrewsbury 36, *36*

Ruddle, G. & Co., Oakham 165

St Augustine's Monastery, Canterbury 42, *42*

St Cross Hospital, Winchester 22, *22, 23*, 39, 124

St John's College, Cambridge 58, *58*

St John's College, Oxford 46

Samuel Allsopp & Son, Burton 2, 40, 46, 55, 65, 66, 194, 203

Samuel Price, Uley 179

Samuel Smiths, Tadcaster 83, 107

Sarah Hughes, Dudley *181, 182*, 182, 193

School House Row, Coalbrookdale 70

Scottish & Newcastle Breweries, Newcastle 2, 146

Shepherd Neame, Faversham 2

Shibden Hall, Halifax 81, 82

Shugborough, Milford 103–7, *105*

Showells Brewery Co. Ltd, Oldbury 132

Sidney Sussex College, Cambridge 59

Soames & Co., Spalding 165

Stackpole Court, Pembrokeshire 82, 83, *83*

Stanway House, Winchcombe 176–9, *177, 178*

Staplecross Brewery/Oast, Sussex 159, 160, *160*

Star Inn, Alfriston 122 *,123*

Steward & Patterson, Norwich 165

Taylor Walker, London 176

Tea Kettle Row, Coalbrookdale 71, *71*

Tetleys, Leeds 2, 145, 174

Theakstons, T. & R, Masham 87, 98

Three Tuns, Bishops Castle 8, 136, 141–4, *142, 143*

Traquair House, Innerleithen 100, *101*

Trinity College, Cambridge 58, 59

Trinity College, Oxford 55

Uley Brewery, Gloucestershire 179, *179*, 180

University College, Oxford 44, 47, *47*, 55

Ushers, Trowbridge 159

Vaux, Sunderland 179

Viaduct Inn, Monkton Combe 158, 159, *159*

Wadham College, Oxford 46, 55, 74

Wadworths, Devizes 204

Wards, Sheaf Brewery, Sheffield 153

Watney, Combe & Reid, London 133, 174

Wheatsheaf Inn, Moulton Chapel 165

Whitbread, London 60, 157, 164, 172, 174, 176, 203

Whitworths, Son & Nephew, Wath-on-Dearne 85, 87, 92

William Younger, Edinburgh 42

Winchester Brewery Co. Hants 23, 41

Winchester College 24, 60, *61*, 62, *63*

Winchester Standard Measure 33, 64

Wiltshire Brewery Co., Tisbury 141

Wothington & Co., Burton 2, 55, 138

Wrexham Lager Brewery 67

Wychwood Brewery, Witney ix, 180

Ye Olde Trip to Jerusalem Inn, Nottingham 146, *147*